International Trade Procedures and Management

To Laura, Megan, Fiona, Alex and Bryn

International Trade Procedures and Management

A. G. Walker

Fourth edition

Butterworth-Heinemann Ltd
Linacre House, Jordan Hill, Oxford OX2 8DP

℞ A member of the Reed Elsevier plc group

OXFORD   LONDON   BOSTON
MUNICH   NEW DELHI   SINGAPORE   SYDNEY
TOKYO   TORONTO   WELLINGTON

First published as *Export Practice and Documentation* 1970
Second edition 1977
Reprinted 1978, 1980
Third edition 1987
Fourth edition 1995

British Library Cataloguing in Publication Data
Walker, A. G.
    International Trade Procedures and
    Management – 4Rev.ed
    I. Title
    658.8480941

ISBN 0 7506 2023 4

Typeset by Datix International Limited, Bungay, Suffolk
Printed in Great Britain by Clays Ltd, St Ives plc

Contents

Preface

In offering this new edition it is most gratifying to look back over the years and contemplate the marked growth of professionalism in the practice of international commerce, encouraging me to extend further the management aspects of the subject. Equally, the continued growth and coalescence of trading groups of countries and areas makes possible an increasingly international approach. This is, in a sense, reflected in the new title.

As always, I have in mind this work as a tool-kit for busy professional exporters and because they find themselves increasingly systematizing their reading and studies with a view to preparing for Institute of Export qualifications or NVQs I have, accordingly, provided a selection of self-assessment questions.

Any work such as this must always be a cumulative process of experience and input received from one's colleagues and the institutions with whom one has worked. I would like to mention particularly the Institute of Export, UNCTAD Geneva and the Foreign and Commonwealth Office. In addition, I am constantly indebted to the many delegates I meet on my public training courses who provide much stimulus and encouragement and, indeed, are a constant reminder that in this subject one is always a student. Special mention must be made to Mrs Mary Stewart for her splendid work with the word-processor on the manuscript.

Finally, as always, my dedication to all those throughout the world who through the medium of international trade contribute so much to not only a growing material prosperity but, equally precious, to growing harmony and understanding between nations.

A. G. Walker

1 *International marketing*

There are many definitions of marketing, all of them of importance, but a useful starting point might be the definition:

Marketing is the process of providing

> the right product
> in the right place
> at the right price
> at the right time

And to this we could add: to achieve the appropriate objective (such as profit, growth, etc.), and to meet the corporate target of the seller.

When we apply the above to international marketing it is obvious that although all the principles set out above remain equally valid, they must by their very nature take place against a more complex background.

Products may have to be 'right' for many different countries and in the 'right place' in markets perhaps long distances away against the background of different climates, political and cultural conditions. There will also be a more complex pattern of transportation methods required to move the products into the 'right place' at the right time: therefore patterns of shipment by sea, air, road, roll-on/roll-off, with their attendant costs and complications, will be encountered.

Decisions as to the 'right price' will be influenced by many factors such as transportation costs, foreign exchanges and, sometimes, in the international scene, by overseas governments and institutions.

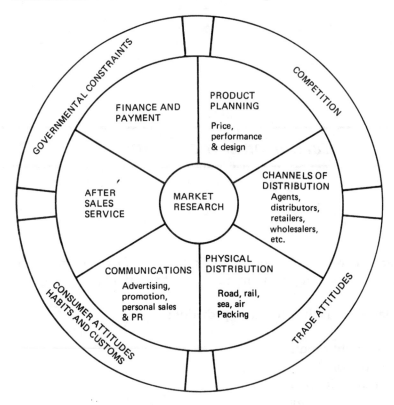

Figure 1.1   International marketing mix

Essentially, the international marketing operation will be one of recognizing a pattern of variable factors and responding to and adjusting these in order to achieve the correct balance. This pattern is normally referred to as the 'international marketing mix' as illustrated in Figure 1.1. The first and most vital point of the marketing mix is to highlight the relative *degree* of importance to the exporter of the various segments. It must be stressed that although all the variables are important, their degree of importance will vary from exporter to exporter and market to market, depending upon the type of industry and product involved.

To an exporter of basic chemicals, bulky and low cost, the segment of physical distribution will be a key area of marketing in order to achieve the most economical transportation, storage and packing costs. Such a company may have little power to influence the price which may be virtually a market price level to which the seller must conform.

On the other hand, an exporter of high-technology scientific instruments may place greater importance on the back-up after-sales segment and product performance and design, whereas price may be less relevant and transport costs perhaps form only a very small fraction of the overall selling price.

An exciting aspect of the marketing mix, particularly internationally, is that these variables also have to be viewed against a sometimes rapidly-changing background of international events.

The periphery of the marketing mix diagram stresses aspects such as government restraints and legislation, changing degrees of competition, and customer and social attitudes.

The starting point for all good overseas marketing should of course, be market *or* marketing research. The distinction between the two (sometimes a little blurred) is that the former envisages more of a quantitative measurement of the likely size and volume of sales, population figures and growth, etc., whereas the latter extends the process into researching other factors such as distribution channel analysis, promotion methods, terms of sale and payment, etc.

Some degree of research must be undertaken, but the degree will itself depend very much upon the size and resources of a company. It can vary from very precise research carried out in a most sophisticated manner by specialized departments, to very much ad hoc work carried out by a harassed export manager.

Essentially, the research is going to consist of:

Basic desk research
- Referring to various published sources of information

Research in the country
- Conducted by visits, forms of survey and analysis into the market/industry itself

A surprising amount of information can be assembled by an exporter utilizing government, banking and trade association sources and studying appropriate trade publications. In the UK for example, the exporter is well supported by such organizations as the British Overseas Trade Board (BOTB) with its many specialized departments and operations. All major international banks regularly publish detailed profiles of individual countries. Chambers of commerce at local level represent a powerful force in focusing attention on particular marketing problems for specific countries. At a more international level the International Chamber of Commerce (ICC) maintains relationships with its membership of over 160 countries.

When 'focusing the microscope' in more detail, methods of surveying markets overseas will be developed and investigation and analytical techniques developed. For example, in the industrial sector much use can be made of correlation techniques; that is, relating the anticipated demand for the exporter's product with other back-up data on, say, industrial projects, statistics of industrial growth and output, etc. In the consumer and consumer durable fields attention must be paid to methods of surveys and motivation research, i.e. what is really influencing the customer to make a purchase; is it price, name, colour, or some other psychological factor?

Attendance at or visits to an industrial exhibition or trade fair can by itself be a very effective step along the road of market research. Figure 1.2 illustrates a framework of market research, and although this looks complex it must again be stressed that if a systematic approach is made then useful research results can be obtained with quite limited resources.

Essentially, therefore, the object of the research has been to discover:

1 Whether there is in fact a market of the appropriate volume and price for our product in its present form.
2 Whether a market potential does exist, provided that some product modification or price adjustment is made.
3 Have we in fact discovered a demand for some quite new product which it is within our resources, experience and capacity to supply?
4 If the marketing mix variables can be adjusted to bring about a successful sales and marketing operation.
5 To what extent there is any domestic or other competition.

Some of the marketing mix variables should now be considered in greater depth.

Product

This should be considered under three main headings:

Product design
Suitable and efficient for its purpose

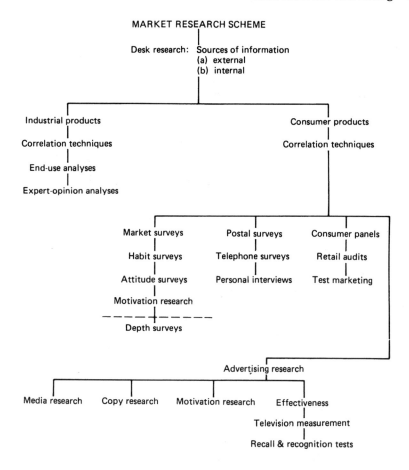

MARKET RESEARCH SCHEME

Desk research: Sources of information
(a) external
(b) internal

Industrial products

Correlation techniques

End-use analyses

Expert-opinion analyses

Consumer products

Correlation techniques

Market surveys

Habit surveys

Attitude surveys

Motivation research

Depth surveys

Postal surveys

Telephone surveys

Personal interviews

Consumer panels

Retail audits

Test marketing

Advertising research

Media research   Copy research   Motivation research   Effectiveness

Television measurement

Recall & recognition tests

Figure 1.2   Market research scheme

Necessary safety factors and reliability
Conforms with any regulations in the overseas market
Necessity of attractive appearance

Production adaptation
Degree of change, if necessary, to meet customer/market's preference
Change of operation, e.g. from hand- to power-operated (or vice versa)
Size or measurement change – to metric, for example
Suitability for different regulations – health, safety and environmental regulations vary from country to country
Packaging of product in different sizes or volumes.

Product presentation
To catch customer's attention
To provide a brand 'image'
To identify the company that made the product
To identify the product and quantity.

With regard to product design and adaptation in international marketing it will be vital to be aware of any particular specifications and standards that may be laid down by particular organizations. These may well be legally required and therefore mandatory to the design of the product. Over the years there has been a progressive move towards various degrees of harmonization but the starting point will usually be the considerations of a particular country's own set of standards.

In the UK a prime source of standards and codes is the British Standards Institution (BSI). It will be necessary, however, to view this matter internationally and therefore in international trade, reference will constantly need to be made to other sets of standards. In France, for example, there is the Association Francaise de Normalisation (AFNOR), in Germany DIN Specifications (Deutsches Institut fur Normung) are frequently encountered.

It should be appreciated that the various national standards authorities will often recognize and co-operate with other industrial bodies and associations. The Verband Deutscher Elektrotechniker, or VDE (Association of German Electrical Engineers), plays a large part, and in the USA, in addition to the American Standards Institute, there are currently more than 400 organizations actively involved in the preparation of standards and codes.

There is both a growing degree of international standards and at the same time an emergence of more nationally-adopted practices. We might find, for example, that one country, say Algeria, will tend to adopt French standards whereas in Australia and New Zealand there is a move away from British standards to writing their own to meet their *own* requirements. Iran is a country where there have been moves towards adopting 'home-grown' specifications.

A powerful tool in the hands of UK exporters is to be found in the institution Technical Help for Exporters (THE) based at Milton Keynes. This body offers a wide range of services which help to identify and relate various international requirements and standard specifications.

Appreciation of possible technical specification requirements should therefore play a large part in the design or adaptation of a particular product for a specific market. It should also be borne in mind that the interpretation and application of standards can sometimes be employed as a 'non-tariff barrier' and therefore may represent one of the many obstacles to be overcome when penetrating an overseas market.

With the growing together of groups of countries for trading, social and political purposes such as the EU Single Market, it will naturally follow that international standards institutions will be created. An example is the CEN (Comité European de Normalisation), European Committee for Standardisation.

It should not be overlooked that apart from actual technical standards, requirements may also apply to such items as pre-packaging, net weights and labelling of foodstuffs. Just to give an example, certain French requirements published in *Journal Officiel* applied to:

Pasta and pasta products
Coffee, chicory and coffee substitutes
Ingredient labelling
Manufacture date and batch markings
Quantity labelling and exempt products
Milk: net volume for retail sale

The above will give some idea of the detail into which a manufacturer may proceed when considering the product's suitability for a specific overseas market.

The relative degree of importance of product planning will vary enormously from product to product, e.g. consumer products or industrial products. It must be remembered that there is no hard-and-fast rule; an industrial power tool could succeed or fail in the market according to whether its design, colour and shape are either better than or not so attractive as a competitor's, even though the mechanical functions of both are identical.

With product presentation, even a name can be vital. This is particularly important in overseas marketing when there is often the problem of translation into a different language. There are many recorded cases where a name has lacked appeal or even proved to be downright offensive. It is interesting to bear in mind the difficult decisions that sometimes have to be made in this field. On the one hand the projection of a specifically-named product globally means a greater international image and draws strength from overall promotion. On the other hand, it may be necessary to

Figure 1.3   Supply and demand curves – standard economic model. The supply/demand function will influence sales volume and selling price ratios.

formulate, for the same product, a series of names suitable for different countries.

Pricing

Pricing is easily understood and manipulated whereas quality, customer reaction, visual appeal, etc., are more difficult to assess.

Flexibility in pricing is regarded as important in the economic theory of a free-enterprise state system.

Economists tend to give less weight to non-price variables than to price as tools in stimulating/matching demand.

The phenomenon described as 'negative price-elasticity of demand' could, in many cases, be labelled 'positive promotion-budget elasticity of demand'.

A higher degree of competition in marketing occurs in non-price areas.

Circumstances in which pricing is important (or more so)

1 New product pricing.
2 Cost changes.
3 Increasing demand → inflation.
4 Stagnating/declining demand → deflation.
5 Competitors' changes in marketing mix.
6 Changes in interrelated product prices.
7 Submitting bids for important (large) orders.

Assumptions associated with the model (Figure 1.3):

1 The curves are generally used in connection with either of two implied objectives: profit maximization or revenue maximization – both generally short run.
2 Information received is likely to be biased towards current market structures – the only customers specifically considered are actual and potential ones on the present basis. The opportunity to change this drastically is not implied.
3 It assumes that prices are independent of cost levels of other marketing variables.
4 Assumes that the demand curve is accurate and invariable in the short term.

Some marketing objectives with pricing implications

– in additional to maximization of profit and revenue!

Market penetration

Used when

1 Market is either growing or susceptible to growth stimulation.
2 Market is relatively highly positive price elastic.
3 Production and distribution economies of scale exist.
4 Low price discourages actual and potential competitors.

Market skimming

Used when

1 Some market segments have relatively inelastic demand.
2 Diseconomies of scale are not excessive.
3 There is little danger of encouraging rivals to 'cream off' the same market. This fear would be counteracted by patent, high technology, long lead-time, high promotion costs, etc.

Early cash recovery

Used when

1 Rapid positive cash flow is the overriding need.
2 The future appears uncertain – the market may be declining or random-variable.

Although pricing is rarely carried out purely on either a cost basis or a demand basis, it is nevertheless useful to look at these two basic models:

Cost-oriented pricing

1 *'Mark-up' pricing*
A percentage is added to cost, and this varies from product to product.

2 *'Cost-plus' pricing*
A percentage is added to cost, constant throughout the range of products

3 *'Target' pricing*
An estimate of sales volumes used to derive price – it being accepted that price influences turnover.
Profit, costs, revenue, and turnover are also simultaneously targeted and are incorporated into budget.

Generally:

Pros: 1 Easy and accurate to apply.
      2 Socially equitable, provided that the percentage is not too high.
      3 Tends to avoid price wars.

Cons: 1 May fail to extract high profits.
      2 Reduce competitive ability vis-à-vis price cutters.
      3 During periods of inflation it will lead to either declining profits or frequent price readjustment.

Demand-oriented pricing

Price discrimination – an item is sold at two or more prices:

1 *On a customer basis,*
– depends upon (a) Volume taken
                (b) Bargaining power/ability
                (c) Economic strength
                (d) Relative importance
                (e) Lack of communication between customers

2 *On a version basis,*
The provision, for example, of 'extras' or luxury features which are charged to a greater extent than their cost would imply. Also, of course, simplified versions can be offered.

3 *On a place basis*
   - theatre seats
   - regional and geographical price differences
   - different shopping areas in the same town
   - different outlets

4 *On a time basis*
   - so as to even out usage fluctuations
   - so as to extract more cash from an inelastic situation

Competition-oriented pricing

1 Going-rate pricing – either charge the same rate as competitors or, by some process of assessment, price according to the relative merits and/or marketing effort of your competitors.
2 Bidding.

Channels of distribution

Chapter 2 deals with many of the administrative aspects of the employment of agents, etc., and the impact upon the operation of export transactions. At this juncture it is necessary to consider the question of channel selection as a part of marketing strategy. Broadly speaking we can distinguish three main sectors of channel utilization, namely:

Outside the market
The use by an exporter, in the company's *own country*, of specialized export merchants, buying houses or confirming houses. In practice, therefore, a manufacturer could sell its products overseas but be based domestically.

Selling into the market
At this stage the alternatives multiply into the choices of agents, distributors or setting up the exporter's own company in the overseas market.

Operating within the market
Depending upon the type of product there will be the question of the channels of selling within the country itself in the possible employment of a wholesaler/retailer chain (particularly for consumer products) and the use of stockists and authorized dealers. Joint ventures, assembly arrangements, and even licensing agreements, can come into this category.

Much of course, will depend upon the nature of the actual end-user who could literally be the man or woman in the street or, at the other end of the scale, a state purchasing organization or large corporation. Some exporters will be selling to a small number of industrial companies but some could find themselves selling to a very large number of individual companies.

It should also be borne in mind that the channel selection may also have a bearing upon another marketing mix segment, namely 'after-sales service'. Clearly, the use of stockist and authorized dealers will play a large part in the maintenance of spare-part availability and repair services so very essential for a sustained and growing export marketing effort. It has been said in the past that UK exporters tended to neglect this aspect of export marketing. It is obvious that for many types of products the ultimate user must have confidence in a back-up service and it is often suggested that laying down the firm foundation of a back-up after-sales service should really come first in the overall export offensive.

Figures 1.4(a) and 1.4(b) illustrate some of the patterns of channels of distribution in more detail. It should be stressed, however, that the use of channels should not lead the exporter to abdicate from the responsibility of being involved with the effective buyer. In *Figure 1.4(a)*, for example, the seller could easily regard the importer/distributor as being the 'cut-off point', but in practice should really also be carrying out research into the consumer 'end point'.

Marketing communications

Under this heading of the 'mix' the concept of actually being in touch one way or another with the actual purchaser should be considered in the widest context. Here, the actual promotion of the product is taking place together with the selling element. Very rarely can a product be expected to sell itself, although there will be varying degrees of effort needed depending upon various background circumstances. Even in hard times there will be fortunate exporters who may find themselves in a seller's market. At the other end of the scale the majority of manufacturers are more likely to operate in highly competitive conditions where the selling and promotion efforts have to be at their peak. Even if a seller's market was in fact available, times change; therefore, there is never any real justification for complacency.

Basically the promotional effort can be seen to encompass the following elements:

Figure 1.4(a) Basic marketing channels

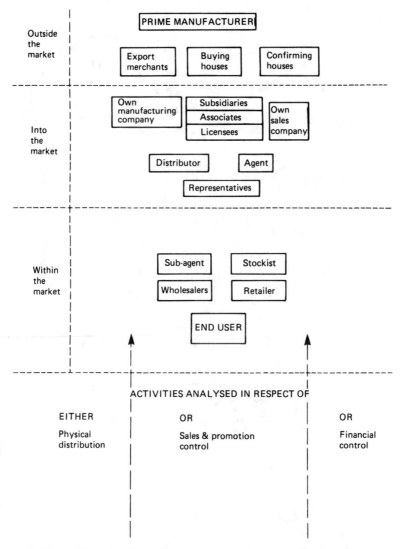

Figure 1.4(b) Channels of distribution

1 Making a potential buyer aware of the product's existence.
2 Placing the product in a favourable light compared with any competition which might exist.
3 Creating a desire to purchase on behalf of the buyer.
4 Obtaining an actual order and finalizing all the various sales contract terms.
5 Ensuring a continuous relationship with the market to ensure further business.

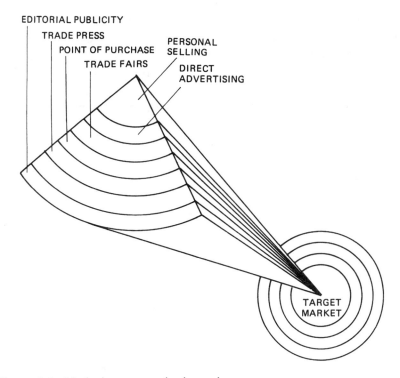

Figure 1.5   Marketing communications mix

The overseas sales and promotional operations will make use of a variety of methods to achieve the selected objectives. Figure 1.5 illustrates a spectrum of such means that are available and may be used in various combinations. It must be borne in mind that the employment of the various approaches and indeed their very viability will depend heavily upon the nature of the product and the market itself. There will be quite a difference between the marketing of say, heavy capital equipment and high-volume consumer products. Similarly, the selling into a market of a centrally-planned economy country where state industrial programmes and state buying organizations are the order of the day will present many different problems compared with operating in a highly-developed market economy such as in the USA or Germany.

Nevertheless, the differences should not be exaggerated and the underlying principles of an export promotion effort remain valid for a wide range of different international marketing operations.

It is probably true to say that the most direct form of communication and promotion will always be the actual personal selling effort expended by a sales executive or sales force in one way or another.

It has already been seen that the actual employment of overseas channels could possibly involve, say, the employment of an agent who may be charged with, amongst other things, the responsibility of carrying out direct selling effort on behalf of the exporting company.

On the other hand, another approach for the exporting company might be to employ a national residing in the target market country. This could be compared with the exporter sending the company's own personnel on selling missions overseas.

Naturally the various choices will depend heavily upon many variables such as volume of business, relative costs and the basic personnel resources available to the exporting company.

As an aid to considering the various permutations the following aspects should be considered in the formula:

$S + P + L$
Where S = Selling/negotiating skill
    P = Product knowledge
    L = Linguistic ability

The above selling mix should assist in relating to the various proportions of skill required for different types of product and market conditions.

Selling/negotiating skill

Here we consider the importance in a particular product–market relationship of the ability to discuss with a potential buyer the proposed sale and to succeed in actually obtaining a concrete order. In sales training parlance we really have in mind the ability to 'close' a sale. In selling a simple basic raw material, for example, where, by and large, market prices and conditions prevailing and are well-known to the potential buyer, much may depend upon the sales executive's personality, determination and ability to succeed in ensuring that the buyer actually places the order accordingly.

Alternatively, complex negotiations with, say, a state trading purchasing organization, might call for a high degree of background knowledge of personalities, political conditions and bureaucratic procedures to ensure a smooth series of negotiations and ultimate success in obtaining the contract.

These skills will not only call for a considerable degree of training but will also tend to put a premium on actual experience in the field. Success will depend a lot upon the executive becoming well-known, respected and accepted in the appropriate circles. The need for personal contacts, knowledge of sources of information and other background details will be vital.

Product knowledge

A knowledge of the product as such is of course essential to all export sales personnel whether they are selling a simple range of textile goods or a multi-million pound aerospace project. The question is, how easy or otherwise is it to acquire this knowledge and how vital is it as a part of a sales presentation? Selling paper sacks, for example, might mean that it is fairly easy to obtain product knowledge quickly and that given basic quality, sales discussions might not place as much emphasis on the technical nature of the sack as opposed to price or delivery position. Automobile engine filters may not be too difficult in themselves but their application might call for a high degree of 'product application' knowledge, i.e. what particular versions of a car utilize which particular filter. Any misunderstanding in the latter aspect could be very serious.

At the other end of the scale it might be that very precise technical knowledge is required to present a product to a potential buyer/user necessitating considerable technical or scientific qualifications. In some cases the sales and negotiating processes may involve technical aspects so complex that a 'team approach' has to be adopted to include specialists in the product itself and personnel more skilled in selling and negotiating.

It will be seen therefore that there are varying degrees of relativity in the need for knowledge of the product itself and/or knowledge of the application and use of that product. This product factor, therefore, plays a vital part in the assessment of the marketing mix in particular.

Linguistic ability

There can be little argument as to the desirability of being able to sell overseas in the language of the market itself. Clearly, however, the average exporting company is generally going to sell to a large number of overseas markets and a considerable number of languages could be involved. Unless a company possesses a large and specialized field sales force, compromises will generally have to be made.

There are, of course, bound to be certain languages which can be regarded as 'keys' in the sense that for historical and political reasons they have come to be in widespread use outside their originating countries. We can, perhaps, identify French as providing a key to many African and Middle East countries. German can be a very widely useful language for dealing with, say, the Eastern European markets. Spanish is of inestimable value for certain South American countries. English is naturally likely to be in wide use because of the Commonwealth and North American connections.

From the export executive's point of view, therefore, there will be the desire, naturally, to speak the overseas language, or at least to be able to cope by using a mutual key language. There will be the need, however, to identify the markets where this may be either relatively easy or in some cases downright impossible, and the feeling may be that any business conducted must be in the overseas language. If this language is highly specialized then it may lead to reliance upon either the indigenous overseas agent or the employment by the company of an overseas national.

Naturally the ideal situation would always be where an export sales executive combines all the three above-mentioned factors perfectly. This will not however be a state of affairs easily achieved and therefore the marketing effort will generally have to cope with various combinations and compromises. It is felt that the above-mentioned features should be seriously considered when planning a sales effort of any sort. There can be very little doubt that if export markets are to be taken seriously then there must be a considerable investment in sales personnel because to succeed there must at some time be a marked degree of face-to-face contact in the promotional operation.

Even if the exporter is in fact operating through various channels such as agents or distributors, etc., there will always exist the need for the manufacturer to exert some sort of initiative in the personal selling effort.

The above will also assist the exporter in systematically awarding degrees of priority of selling initiative to a growing pattern of export markets.

Before leaving the personal selling aspect it should be borne in mind that on top of all the factors indicated export personnel need natural resourcefulness, self-reliance and an ability to operate in different climates and surroundings and, in most cases, to exercise their own initiative particularly where communications with the parent company may be difficult.

Within the marketing communications mix, of course, the personal selling aspect will take place against a background of other promotional factors. On page 14 five factors of the promotional effort were mentioned. The export sales executive can in a sense span all these aspects in sales calls, but naturally they will be backed by recourse to media and other promotional tools.

Media

Selling/negotiating skill, product knowledge and linguistic ability could be supported by the employment of advertising through technical journals and other forms of trade press. National or regional newspapers could carry the message. If a television network is available then this would be a powerful instrument, particularly in the form of consumer goods or services. Naturally these promotional tools are likely to be expensive and they must normally be carried out on a reasonable scale to make them effective. The suitability of such means will naturally vary between the type of product, i.e. consumer, consumer-durable or industrial goods, and indeed how large a budget is available for this type of advertising. Careful planning can sometimes achieve a reasonable promotional effort at modest expense. In selling say, computer software with new or improved applications, much can be achieved on a modest budget by linking selected adverts with editorial publicity. Correct timing can be a vital attribute in this type of situation.

Sales literature

This is obviously going to be of importance in international sales and will almost always represent an essential form of marketing communication. The sequence will usually be as follows:

- Fairly simple basic leaflets or booklets with sufficient text/communications to awaken interest.
- More detailed catalogues with sufficient detail to provide information to enable a potential buyer to make decisions.
- Back-up literature to accompany the products to cover operations, utilization or installation.
- Literature to cover point-of-sale outlets, etc.

Designing good sales literature is an art in itself and of course in international trade such matters as translation of the text, use of names, and even colour, can be of vital importance. Today, if one studies sales literature it is surprising to find incorrectly-translated text emanating even from exporting countries such as Japan and Italy which otherwise exhibit high standards of promotional material.

Again, decisions will have to be made as to whether specific languages can be catered for, although this could be difficult in the case of very specialized languages. In most cases the use simultaneously of a number of key languages can be employed to enable a wider range of countries to be catered for and yet still allow a fairly standardized form of literature to be produced.

A certain amount of literature distribution can be achieved by the use of 'mail shots' despatched directly to addresses obtained from such sources as the *Kompass Registers* or accumulated data obtained from government sources using their various overseas embassies and consulates. In the UK the BOTB and various sources of export intelligence can provide a considerable amount of valuable data.

Naturally the viability of such methods will vary enormously with the type of product/market situation. It may be simple if a particular overseas market consists of a relatively limited number of industrial users for, say, material handling equipment compared with sales of high-volume consumer goods needing the penetration of sophisticated dealer/wholesaler/retailer outlets requiring point of sale merchandising material.

Unless this type of promotional material is of a very high standard it is probably wiser not to employ it at all since such material can, by inference, reflect an impression of the quality image of the exporter's products and standing as a worthwhile supplier.

It may even be possible at times with products of particular classes to combine a certain amount of market research with the promotion itself. Literature combining questionnaires can be quite effective as a means of actively involving a potential customer and indeed alerting their interest.

Trade fairs, exhibitions and missions

Another category of marketing communication of importance to the exporter will be some form of collective involvement in an overseas market. An extremely effective activity is participation in a trade fair or specialized form of exhibition where stand space can be hired and products physically exhibited to stir the interest of potential buyers. Here, under one roof, it is possible to rub shoulders with large numbers of potentially interested companies or individuals (and even competitors). Valuable contacts can be established and much useful market research data including addresses, can be accumulated as a result of the many conversations that can take place during even a week or fortnight.

There are many specialized companies who can help with the administrative planning and shell construction, etc., and translation services are normally readily available if required. Care must be taken to observe all the regulations and use the appropriate paperwork, such as carnets, to satisfy the various customs requirements as products will have to be shipped abroad to the host country and perhaps returned when the fair or exhibition is over.

Generally speaking, information is normally easily available from government or trade association sources as to forthcoming calendars for various exhibitions covering many specialized needs. In many countries some form of government financial and promotional assistance is available. Indeed, under this heading there may also be the possibility of support for outward and inward missions for both exporters and importers. Under this scheme a number of companies can together organize a group visit to certain designated target market areas overseas. This may sometimes operate on a geographical basis, i.e. a number of different types of companies from a local area perhaps operating in conjunction with a local chamber of commerce. Other approaches may be on a more industrial basis, i.e. companies sharing similar types of, say, industrial customers.

International exhibitions can focus in considerable depth in different product categories. In the field of fashion, for example, there could be the Paris Exhibition, the Carrousel de la Mode, of which the Premiere Classe would be very suitable for very upmarket accessories. In the UK for example, such bodies as the BKCEC (British Knitting and Clothing Export Council) can play a very large part in supporting the potential fashion exporters.

It will be seen, therefore, that for most exporters there can be a wide range of choices relating to active *communication* with their potential markets, and the point to stress is that even on a modest scale with quite a limited budget, much can be achieved by positive planning with a thorough grasp of the various approaches that do exist.

An essential component part of planning the various forms of promotion is for the exporter to be selective and discriminating with regard to market selection. It is no use just considering the whole world as the object of export marketing in blanket terms.

Key market selection should be the theme by which a company examines, selects and operates a short list of markets appearing to have the best potential, and *concentrates* resources on these key areas. Spreading the promotional effort too widely and thinly could mean that no real success is achieved anywhere. Some of the great export success stories attributed to such countries as Japan, USA and Germany can usually find their roots in a careful assessment and concentration in depth on selected key markets.

Physical distribution

The art of ensuring correct packing, handling, storage and transportation of the goods overseas, plus correct accompanying paperwork, is now firmly established as a vital discipline by itself, and later chapters will deal with various aspects of this operation in more detail.

After-sales service

In order to sustain an on-going success in export marketing the provision of a reliable back-up service is of vital importance in almost every category of product. This means that suppliers must maintain repair and spare part facilities and also be able to give technical and sales services to their customers or through the appropriate distribution channels. We have seen that this concept will, in most cases, be linked with the channels of distribution employed.

The finest quality product and the most competitive price may easily count for very little if the consumer lacks confidence in having complaints or queries, spare parts or repairs, attended to promptly and efficiently. In the case of automobiles, as a classic example, a vital component part of the marketing mix in the buyer's mind will be reliability plus after-sales attention. Many users of products can accept the fact that things can go wrong and that breakdowns can occur with even the best model, but their final judgement is usually based on the speed and efficiency with which problems can be solved. As mentioned earlier, in some cases the creation of a suitable after-sales operation may actually *precede* the promotional effort of launching a product into an overseas market. It is useless regarding this as an afterthought and relying upon the outcome of events.

Finance and payment

Again, aspects of payment terms and export finance will be covered in other chapters in more administrative detail, but suffice at this juncture to say that the overall corporate marketing objective must envisage the receipt of money for goods supplied with the least possible delay and maximum reliability. An element of profitability for one's export effort is required in all cases, even where in the case of planned economy countries other objectives may be paramount.

To the export manager of today, the question of granting credit terms, access to lines of credit, or the knowledge of various development fund sources such as the European Development Fund, is a vital tool in the marketing approach. In some cases there may be little difficulty in locating customers only too willing and anxious to purchase the exporter's product but the main problem lies in obtaining the necessary funds. In these cases the skill of the export marketer might well depend on the ability to stage-manage available sources of money and therefore play a part in helping buyers to be able to pay for the goods within reasonable periods of time.

In looking back over this chapter, the wisdom of the Institute of Export in placing increasing emphasis upon the Total Export Concept (TEC) can be readily appreciated. Good market research, correct product planning and development, plus efficient packing and transportation, leading to satisfactory receipt by the buyer of the goods and rewarded by correct profitable payment all lead to a successful and continuous export trade.

Functions of the export department

This book is concerned mainly with the handling of international trade procedures. It will therefore be necessary to consider the export office in the light of these requirements.

A manufacturing organization will often be chosen as an example, although this does not imply any limitation of the analysis – it can be applied equally to purely commercial or service firms.

It is customary to regard an industrial organization as having three basic functions, namely: finance, production and sales. Although this is an over-simplification, it does offer a suitable starting-point. We have seen in the previous chapter the importance of the marketing concept, meaning that all the diverse activities of the firm are directed towards the objective of meeting the customer's needs and should therefore be regarded as an integrated exercise of business activity.

Accurate administration is essential to enable goods to move safely overseas, whether by air or road/rail; to enable the customer to receive quick and trouble-free delivery; and to enable the exporter to obtain full and satisfactory payment for the transaction.

An indication of the importance of some aspects of the need for documentary accuracy can be gained from various bank and Simplification of International Trade Procedures Board (SITPRO) surveys. These estimate that the delay and expense due to inaccurate documents presented to banks against letters of credit alone cost UK exporters an annual total of anything between £50m and £80m. This would not allow for extra warehousing charges, etc., which may be incurred in the importing country through late or inaccurate documentation.

The export office acts as a link between the finance, production and sales operations. It will support the sales function in providing data on methods of payment, building up the cost elements to provide an accurate quotation and advising upon and arranging the methods of packing and transportation. The export administration manager will work closely with the works and production managers in order to harmonize the production and delivery schedules as far as booking shipping space and transportation, etc. are concerned. With regard to the financial aspects, the export office will co-operate with the accounts department in varying degrees with respect to letters of credit, bills of exchange, credit status checks and final invoicing.

The precise shape and responsibilities of the export department will vary considerably. Some principal determinants are size of company, nature and spread of markets, types of selling organization, complexity of product and, quite often, the stage of evolution reached by the company itself. All too frequently, unfortunately, the export side of a business is the result of haphazard growth, but there is now a trend towards a much closer study of export organization and the induction and training of appropriate personnel.

Bearing in mind the various determining factors that will underlie the organization of the export activities of a company, one can identify certain basic functions (Figure 2.1). There is first of all the export sales element under the direction of an export sales director or manager. The task of this department will be to handle the selling activities necessary for the various overseas markets. This executive will often concentrate mainly on controlling the sales force, corresponding with customers, preparing quotations and price lists, receiving orders and sending out suitable acknowledgements. Sometimes an organization will tend to divide these activities into two main areas, giving rise to an export sales manager and an export office manager.

A basic task facing any manager is that of maintaining efficient communications. In no sphere of commerce is this more important than in the field of export. Although the world is shrinking year by year as transport and communication systems improve, it is nevertheless not always economical or practical to use the telephone/fax for many overseas markets and carefully constructed correspondence is essential. In many cases, letters have to be addressed to

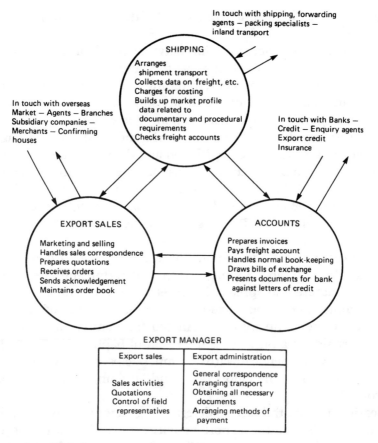

In touch with shipping, forwarding
agents — packing specialists —
inland transport

SHIPPING

Arranges
  shipment transport
Collects data on freight, etc.
Charges for costing
Builds up market profile
  data related to
  documentary and procedural
  requirements
Checks freight accounts

In touch with overseas
Market — Agents — Branches
Subsidiary companies —
Merchants — Confirming
houses

In touch with Banks —
Credit — Enquiry agents
Export credit
Insurance

EXPORT SALES

Marketing and selling
Handles sales correspondence
Prepares quotations
Receives orders
Sends acknowledgement
Maintains order book

ACCOUNTS

Prepares invoices
Pays freight account
Handles normal book-keeping
Draws bills of exchange
Presents documents for bank
  against letters of credit

EXPORT MANAGER

Export sales	Export administration
Sales activities Quotations Control of field representatives	General correspondence Arranging transport Obtaining all necessary documents Arranging methods of payment

Figure 2.1   Basic functions of a self-contained export department

overseas buyers who use a different language and employ different units of measurements. The ability to correspond in a foreign language is daily becoming more and more necessary for any export department which prides itself on its professionalism. Needless to say, the use of a foreign language must be of a high standard; otherwise more harm than good could be done, particularly if technical and commercial terms with very precise meanings are used. For example, interpretations of the word 'agent' can vary enormously.

Equally, it should be borne in mind that many overseas countries use more than one language, sometimes concentrated in different geographical areas. The use of French for certain Canadian markets, or Flemish in Belgium, are examples, and Switzerland, of course, uses French, German and Italian. Also a language itself may vary, as in the case of Spanish as spoken in Colombia differing somewhat from the Spanish of Argentina.

The employment of units of measurement or currencies in correspondence, quotations and orders must be precise, and any possibility of misunderstanding, such as with the American short ton of 2000 lb or English long ton of 2240 lb, must be avoided. Naturally with the adoption of the metric system and wide international usage there is much more standardization. Nevertheless, some variations may still be encountered in the use of units of measurement by some very specialized industries. Similarly, with currencies, the use of the dollar for example, must make clear reference to the particular nationality of that currency, e.g. US, Canadian, Australian, Singaporean dollars, etc.

Within the export organization in general will function the shipping and transport sections. These are of paramount importance in international trade because of the range and complexity of transport facilities available to carry the exporter's goods to an overseas market. It is becoming more and more apparent that a scientific approach to physical distribution is now a vital part of marketing. Nowadays, total physical distribution costs, i.e. packing, insurance, warehousing and transportation, can amount on average to between 15 and 40 per cent of the selling price. The shipping manager of today, therefore, has many complex decisions to make when choosing methods of transportation and comparing their overall costs. Air freight might mean a higher freight cost but it reduces the time period during which money is tied up in stocks. Packing costs can often be reduced by utilizing different means of transport. So important has this concept of physical distribution become over the years that this subject will be covered in more detail in Chapter 5.

One of the key activities of the shipping department will be the negotiation of freight and carriage charges. The export sales department, when calculating the selling price, will need accurate freight rates, costs of insurance premiums, packing costs and various other incidental charges. Many of these are constantly fluctuating and a professional shipping manager has to work very hard to keep completely up-to-date and obtain the best rates consistent with good and reliable service. A miscalculation which over-estimates carriage charges could mean that the sales department might lose a potential order at the quotation stage. Similarly, a mistake in the other direction could seriously reduce or even at times eliminate the profit margin.

Any commercial organization must, of necessity, see the objective of all its activities as a satisfactory profit margin. Marketing strategy may at times dictate that overseas business carries a lower profit margin or even sometimes be operated at cost in order to break into a difficult market. In the long term, however, overseas business can only be carried on satisfactorily with a reasonable profit margin and a satisfactory settlement of overseas payment. Consequently, only when the proceeds of an export sale have been safely received can the transaction be considered successful. Thus, the invoicing function and accounting activities have to be dovetailed with the export sales and transport activities.

Types of export organization

It is extraordinary that there appears to be a lack of uniformity in export organization and that two companies of similar size, selling almost identical products to similar markets, will organize themselves quite differently. Some will establish a completely separate and independent export department which will look after all the costing, transportation, invoicing and payment for every export transaction. Other organizations may distribute the export activities throughout the various departments. For example, the export order will be split up into its various component parts, i.e. invoicing, transportation and payment, and the invoicing department of the company will handle the export invoice alongside its activities for invoicing home market orders. Similarly, the transport department will handle shipment and air freight, together with road transport operations for the home market.

Again, different approaches are to be found in the division of the parts of the export order itself. There are many systems in use, varying in degree between the two extremes which, for the sake of simplicity, will be referred to as the 'horizontal' and 'vertical' (Figure 2.2):

1 *Horizontal:*   Here the approach is to parcel out whole orders to individuals or departments so that an export order is treated as an organic whole. The specialization here will usually be geographical. Personnel will handle the total order and look after the processing from receipt to final invoicing, but will be allocated specific market areas. For example, groups of personnel will handle, say, South America, or Europe, both areas

Vertical organization

1 Correspondence
2 Credit status enquiries
3 Order processing
4 Preparing packing specification details
5 Negotiating freight rates, booking shipping space
6 Preparing bills of lading/air waybills, etc.,
7 Checking freight accounts
8 Invoicing
9 Preparing bills of exchange
10 Handling letters of credit
11 Sending statements
12 Checking overdue accounts
13 Filing
14 Recording

Horizontal organization

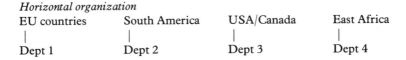

EU countries	South America	USA/Canada	East Africa
Dept 1	Dept 2	Dept 3	Dept 4

While each of the four departments would handle an export order as an organic whole, they would specialize in different geographical areas as shown for examples.

Figure 2.2 Two principal types of export-order organization

which may be sub-divided; for instance, Europe into EEA or the EU.

2 *Vertical:* The company divides the order itself into the various parts of the spectrum, i.e. receipt of order, acknowledgement, processing despatch, correspondence and final invoicing. A department, or perhaps even an individual, will look after one particular segment and will consequently become a specialist in, say, order acknowledgements or booking shipping space, and looking after consular documentation or invoicing. Under such a system, personnel will become accustomed to handling in depth small parts of the order process.

Between these two extremes there will, of course, be many permutations, conditioned by market and product categories and the historical development of the organization.

It is always presumptuous to be dogmatic about the superiority of one method over any others, as such factors as economy, availability of staff and existing personnel patterns will determine the issue.

There is also no doubt that the growing use of computer systems and internal documentation structures call for much more specialization. There seems to be little doubt, however, that, wherever possible, the creation of a separate export department should be the ultimate objective and will increase efficiency in the long run. The morale of export personnel must also be considered. Operation of the 'vertical' system, for example, will certainly promote simplified documentation and lend itself to increasing computerization but, on the other hand, may turn much of the order processing into a large number of fairly irksome tasks where no-one experiences the pride of handling an export order in its entirety. Consequently, there may be a lack of job identification. In this case, however, it may be akin to automation where much of the repetitive work will be removed from human hands, and a complex computerized system will be controlled and operated by a small number of highly-skilled 'documentary technologists'.

The export order

When considering the structure and operations of any export organization, it might be profitable at this stage to take an analytical look at the export order itself, that is, from documentary and procedural points of view. Basically, an export order can be divided into four main parts, namely transport, methods of payment, risk element and regulations.

Transport

This will be either by sea, or air, or combinations of road/rail, or perhaps post. The appropriate documents will therefore be bills of lading, air waybills, consignment notes or postal receipts.

Methods of payment

Four main methods are employed: cash with order, open account, documentary bills and documentary credits. These procedures will necessitate bills of exchange, invoices and various types of letters of credit, as well as calling for credit status enquiries. There will of course be a number of possible permutations under these four main headings.

Risk element

By this is meant the covering of special risks in international business, e.g. marine insurance, export credits guarantee cover, foreign exchange variations, insurance policies, certificates and cover notes.

Regulations

This is perhaps the most difficult aspect from the exporter's point of view, as there are so many varieties of documents encountered in this field. The heading can be sub-divided into two. First of all, the regulations encountered internally, i.e. in the exporter's own country. This might mean encountering such documents as export licences, forms and various types of customs entry declarations. Externally, the documentary requirements will vary from country to country. Some countries may require consular invoices, others special invoices or certificates of origin agreements. Other countries may require special wording and markings on packing or bills of lading. When considering this particular aspect of the order, the exporter will always check the background regulations of a market whilst negotiating an order with the customer. Some countries' regulations may specify for example that all shipments must be made against freight payable in their own country. This could lead to, say, bills of lading being marked 'freight forward' and, of course, would influence the type of price quoted in the sales contract.

The four headings above are not absolutely self-contained and there will, of course, be a good deal of interaction. The 'regulations' heading will often condition the 'methods of payment'. Similarly, a letter of credit will determine the type of documentation required, e.g. by insisting upon certain types of bills of lading. The usefulness of such a method of analysis is to provide a framework of reference against which can be judged the formation and structure of an export department and the allocation of the various tasks to the personnel involved in these activities.

Channels of export selling

Any approach to export procedure must of necessity primarily take into account the methods an organization employs to conduct its export business, which will be called the 'channel of selling'. An exporter may use any one or a combination of the following:

1 Export houses
2 Agents
3 Distributors

4 Own selling organization
5 Branch offices
6 Subsidiary companies

It is not intended to consider the above in all the technical, marketing and legal detail that will be found in the specialized textbooks on these subjects, but rather to identify them and to see how they shape and influence documentary responsibilities and procedures. The main points are set out below and in Table 2.1.

Export houses

1 *Export merchants*

The export merchant acts as a principal. The classic contribution is to locate an overseas demand and to satisfy this by finding a suitable source of supply in the UK. The merchant will usually have extensive experience in shipping, insurance and arranging exports, will often place the order and look after packing and shipping. This will enable a UK manufacturer to treat the business almost on the same basis as a home order. The merchant will make payment and subsequently take the overseas credit risk. It is often the merchant who first introduces a manufacturer's products to the overseas market. Such skill and expertise may often make it more convenient for the UK company to continue this relationship. Much will depend on the nature of the product, the size and growth rate of the manufacturer and the exploitation of the merchant's image and identity.

2 *Confirming houses*

This type of organization has historically grown up along the lines of acting as agent for the overseas buyer. Whilst at one time they tended to decline, they are once more very much in evidence. Nowadays, they are perhaps more active in the provision of credit for the overseas buyer. Orders from confirming houses are usually placed with the manufacturer on an *indent* basis. If the indent is closed, it means that the buyer has specified a particular manufacturer. On the other hand, an open indent enables the confirming house to seek sources of supply and to evaluate them on the basis of competitive price, quality and availability. Again, confirming houses will often be assembling orders from a number of companies and may

Table 2.1
Channels of exporting

Exporters	*Export merchants*	*Overseas customers*
Get business which they may not have realized exists	Use specialized marketing knowledge	Manufacturer's products are brought to their attention, but they may not be able to bring enough influence to bear on manufacturer
Save trouble – reduce many transactions to almost home orders	Bring products to customer's attention	
Can save specialized staff	Act as principal	
May not establish identity and image	Take credit risk	
Difficulty perhaps of keeping abreast of market needs and linking product/design with market growth		
May fail to detect a declining market and finish up over-producing		
Sales forecasting difficult		

Exporters	*Confirming houses*	*Overseas customers*
Often a source of business because credit being supplied through confirming house		A powerful and often traditional link, particularly with Commonwealth and developing countries
Confirming houses often offer specialized shipping and packing facilities, which can simplify the transaction		
Most of the same advantages and disadvantages as with export merchants, except that it is often easier to make and maintain contact with ultimate customer and there is greater possibility of establishing image		Can often obtain credit facilities

Note: Crown Agents for the overseas governments and administrations in many ways provide the same effective link for the exporter as confirming houses.

Table 2.1 *Continued*

Exporters	Overseas agents	Overseas customers
Can look to agent to hold stocks (a), or underwrite certain bad debts (b) Care necessary when drawing up agency agreements to ensure energetic promotion by agent Must take a large part in the export transaction, i.e. despatching, invoicing, administration, etc.	Examples: (a) Consignment (b) Del credere (c) Exclusive (d) Commission Intimate knowledge of market, language, etc.	Can deal with somebody in their own country After-sales service

Exporters	Distributors	Overseas customers
Can look to distributor to take title to goods Deal with only one entity Expect distributor to be very involved in marketing policy and operations	A degree of exclusivity Greater control over sales, etc., operation. Closer identity with manufacturer Greater possibility of exercising policy initiation	Usually, more points of contact Greater degree of back-up in their own country Bring contacts more closely to resemble dealing in own domestic market

Exporters	Overseas customers
Full force of company's own promotion put into the market Intimate knowledge and feedback of market information Complete company image and identity Exporters take whole responsibility of export transaction (they can of course avail themselves of ancillary services) and need knowledge of overseas regulations, duties, shipping, etc. Need fully-sophisticated export department salesforce and administration	If market is sophisticated, large and complex, this type of customer will expect to be approached direct

Table 2.1 *Continued*

Exporters	Branch offices	Overseas customers
Can look to branch to clear many awkward problems on site	More durable and effective extension to exporter's activities	Obtains more personal contact by dealing with branch office
	Can simplify debt collection and credit control, and provide information obtained on the spot re taxes, duties, regulations, etc.	
Extra cost – sometimes legal difficulties such as percentage of nationals to be employed, etc.	Gives company domestic appearance	

Exporters	Subsidiary companies	Overseas customers
Possible tax concessions	Perhaps associated with overseas factory	Main basic overall gain should be lower price and superior after-sales service etc.
Avoidance of tariff barriers	Vulnerable to overseas politics	
Avoidance of import quotas	Assembly KD (knocked down) CKD (completely knocked down)	
More comprehensive representation and promotion		
Large capital outlay generally required with perhaps slow return		
Legal problems – controlling interest may have to be vested in nationals		

Note: As a variation of some of the above channels, companies may export through associating with a group of similar companies in order to join forces and share promotion costs; they may also combine in the shape of export groups of particular industries. Basically, however, most of the points set out above apply in principle just the same.

group them together for packing, shipping and transport in order to achieve economies in space and freight rates.

The above two categories represent the most important type of operation to the exporter/manufacturer so far as export houses are concerned. Organizations such as these are represented by the British Export Houses Association, who can provide considerable assistance to manufacturers seeking help in their overseas market. It must also be made clear that 1 and 2 above refer to *functions* and that these functions can often be represented in different combinations. For example, normally, a merchant operates legally as principal but, in some cases, might conduct a transaction more in the capacity of an agent. Similarly, a confirming house in some cases will place orders and confirm them in its own name. The basis of remuneration will vary. The manufacturer must be prepared at times to look after packing and shipment, even when handling business through institutions such as these. The most important thing is that flexibility in outlook can be maintained and it is possible to identify the actual function of the particular transaction. The combined efforts of the export houses make a powerful contribution to the UK's overseas earnings.

Agents and distributors

Use of the services of these operators is, of course, very widespread amongst exporters. It must be borne in mind that the employment of these terms is by no means clear-cut, and confusion can arise owing to different forms of interpretation. If in doubt, legal advice should be sought. From the strictly legal outlook, there is a clear distinction between agent and distributor inasmuch that the former is only really taking orders on behalf of the principal, i.e. the exporter. This would mean that in many cases the credit risk of non-payment by customers will be the responsibility of the seller. However, this may be qualified in the case of del credere agents who assume a degree of credit risk involvement in exchange for a higher commission.

The distributors are really taking orders *on their own account*, having already taken title to the goods, and subject only to the limitations in their agreement with the principal.

The actual size and nature of the *territory* covered does not necessarily vary with the nature of the appointment. However, there is a general tendency for distributors to have larger territories, within which they may even themselves employ agents, etc.

It will be seen, therefore, that the essential difference is a contractual one concerning the ownership and financial responsibility for goods and services. An example of the blending of these can be seen by the consideration of the consignment agent. Here, stocks can be held by the agent and therefore good follow-on and after-sales services is provided. However, in contrast to the distributor the goods are being held on behalf of the exporter and not being paid for until subsequent sale.

When using agents or distributors, exporters will normally expect to be responsible for handling the transaction completely as far as documentation is concerned. The agent/distributor, however, can often help by advising upon customs formalities, duties and taxes. Great care is necessary when drawing up agreements and the questions of responsibilities and basis of remuneration should be covered fully. It is also very important to be familiar with the laws relating to agencies in the overseas territory, as these can vary from country to country.

Sales by UK exporter direct to overseas market

This, of course, entails more involvement with the overseas market, as exporters will need sufficient skill and knowledge to plan and execute the whole transaction and consignment. They will, therefore, handle all the documentation and procedures.

Branch offices

An expansion of the manufacturer's overseas marketing may call for the opening of a branch office. The aim will usually be to use this mainly as an administrative and selling foothold, but such an office can be of great assistance in dealing with documentary problems, e.g. with overseas customs, clearance and import duties. By studying freight rates and inland transportation costs, the branch office can assist the exporter in finalizing costing and quotations. It can also play a useful part in collection and transmission of proceeds.

Subsidiary companies

These play a large part in modern exporting. Nowadays, the exporter often finds that it is essential to extend the company overseas and this process is frequently associated with assembly, shipping on a knocked-down basis and manufacture abroad under licence. This process has been greatly accelerated by the desire of companies to set up subsidiaries in some countries to avoid tariff barriers. This pattern often enables large-scale shipments and consignments to be carried out and reduces the burden of the individual shipment/consignment routine. The problem of payments is on many occasions reduced to the equivalent of inter-departmental book-keeping transactions, consistent with exchange control regulations.

Ancillary services

Other factors that exert an influence upon the procedural pattern are those that may result from the employment of various ancillary services which are at times available to the exporter. Any practitioner will therefore need to have some knowledge of the various types of organization which will assist with the export transaction. At the outset, a distinction should be drawn between the services that will be used *directly* and those that will be of *indirect* assistance. The types of aid can also be classified, i.e. whether they are 'advice' or 'guidance' or 'practical, functional' help. Having identified these functions, it will be possible to relate them to particular institutions. For example, a bank could give an exporter some general background information and marketing intelligence for a particular country, and thereby act in an advisory capacity. Alternatively, the bank might function directly at the exporter's bidding by arranging a specific payment transaction, or carrying out a precise financial investigation into the credit-worthiness of the customer.

Equally, shipping and forwarding agents will work directly for the exporter by arranging particular shipments and making customs entries. They might also function in an indirect manner by obtaining for the exporter some freight rates or advising on a particular shipping route. The specialized services of the British Overseas Trade Board through the DTI provide a very wide range of advisory services and to an increasing extent carry out functional activities for the UK exporter.

During the course of this work, the reader will be referred from time to time to various organizations which come within the category of ancillary services. The main types of institution involved are listed in Table 2.2.

There exists, therefore, a whole range of institutions and services which skilled practitioners will know how best to employ to assist them with their transactions. However, the professional exporter will never wish to abdicate responsibilities; although, for example,

Table 2.2
Types of institutions offering ancillary services to the exporter

Organization	Service performed
Shipping and forwarding agents, ship owners/air freight agents	Arrange shipment/air/road/rail transport. Enter goods at loading customs. Might pay freight. Can arrange insurance. Provide information about sailings, routes, frequency, freight rates; can sometimes provide services in country of destination and, in the case particularly of air forwarders, can carry these services right up to a COD basis.
Packing specialists	For highly-specialized products, i.e. aircraft, machinery, extra-heavy, bulky or unwieldy loads. Such companies generally incorporate in their services the collection of goods from the manufacturer, packing and subsequent delivery to docks or airport.
Clearing banks	Provide information on markets, regulations, currency, credit, status checks. Arrange payment methods, transfer of money. Deal in foreign exchange, lend or advance money. Discount or advance against bills.
Merchant bankers, discount and acceptance houses	Provide acceptance credit facilities; discount and accept bank bills, long-term loans. Participate in international transactions and loans. Provide financial consultancy.
Various customs authorities such as the US Bureau of Customs and the UK HM Customs and Excise via Head Offices, etc. and various branches and offices at docks and airports – in many cases a highly personal contact with individual officers necessary for detailed problems.	Functional in the sense of the need for the exporter/importer to make customs entries; obtain drawback in certain cases and conform to customs regulations regarding exchange control, export licensing.
UK Department of Trade and Industry, Head Office, London; various regional offices. Several departments, e.g. export licensing branch, export services and promotions division.	Provides a wealth of information on markets, overseas regulations, payment restrictions; details of overseas customs duties; taxes. Participates in schemes for improving and simplifying documentation.

Table 2.2 *Continued*

Organization	Service performed
Lloyd's of London, insurance companies, brokers	Main interest to exporter is to cover marine and other forms of insurance for overseas shipments. Insurance policies and certificates, information related to types of cover, nature of risks and costs of premiums may be obtained from this section. Lloyd's also play a large part in assessing and categorizing ships and through such publications as *Lloyd's Loading List* and various supplements provide a wealth of information on international transport movements.
Various types of export credit insurance and factoring organizations such as COFACE, HERMES, ECGD, NCM Indemnity, Alex Lawrie, etc.	Provides various types of risk cover not normally available from the commercial insurance houses. Exporter will negotiate type of trade policy applicable to his business and arrange limits of individual cover. There will be a constant interchange of information and monthly returns.
ICC, local Chamber of Commerce, Arab British Chambers of Commerce, etc.	Sources of information and publications. It is also from some of these offices that the exporter normally obtains certificates of origin and has invoices verified and countersigned. Membership of a chamber is often a great advantage to the exporter.
Overseas embassies and consulates	Provide information on current regulations and requirements of the particular country. Exporter obtains, where necessary, consular invoices, invoice legalization, etc.
Professional bodies: Institute of Export (with a world-wide range of associations), Institute of Freight Forwarders, Institute of Physical Distribution, Institute of Marketing	Maintain libraries and other sources of information and data on export education. Active in the whole field of export practice. Offer examinations and Institute professional membership.
Export organizations and associations for various trades and industries	Can be very useful, as such associations often provide in-depth information about individual products or industries.
Simplification of International Trade Procedures Board (SITPRO)	Main objective is to guide and assist the rationalization of international trade procedures and documentation. Provides many booklets, reports and checklists.

a shipping and forwarding agent may prepare customs entries and arrange shipment, it is still necessary to have a knowledge of the mechanics of the procedures involved. In the first place this will be necessary to enable an exporter to pass clear and concise instructions; in the second instance, to take appropriate and swift action if anything should go amiss with the transaction.

3   *Export sales quotations*

Export sales terminology

When exporters and importers negotiate orders, decisions have to be made as to the use of a particular delivery clause such as FOB or CIF, etc. This is a vital element in the export transaction and determines the procedural and documentary responsibilities of the export department. The sales clause is, of course, important in all commercial transactions. In overseas trade, with its complex overseas transportation and specialized insurance and payment requirements (Figure 3.1), a thorough understanding of export sales terminology is vital for efficient management.

For example, a chemical manufacturer quotes a customer as follows:

> 200 × 100 kilo cartons of Carbon Black Mk 11-A @ 60p per kilo
> ex-works

From the seller's and buyer's points of view this implies the following:

1 That the price per kilo covers the cost of the carbon packed in cartons as it stands at the seller's works or warehouse.
2 That the buyer will have to arrange collection of the goods and bear all costs of transferring them to an appropriate destination. These costs will be additional to the 60p per kilo.
3 That the seller need only supply the packing mentioned in the quotation which will enable the buyer to carry out a satisfac-

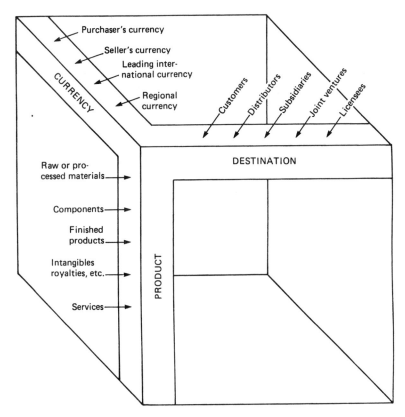

Figure 3.1 Export quotation matrix

tory collection. Should any additional protective packing for transit be required, it would be for the account of the buyer. This point may need careful clarification as with some products specialized export packing may be very expensive.

Two points emerge:

1 The manufacturer has a minimum costing problem, virtually nothing more than assessing the cost of the finished product, allowing a profit margin and adding a cost for packing.

2 From the viewpoint of the buyer, the 60p per kilo price leaves a whole range of unknown expenses. The total ex-works price can be calculated, amounting to £12 000 per 200 cartons. In addition to this, however, will be collection and transport charges, and, if the goods are being bought by an overseas buyer, then packing, freight, insurance, import duties and

taxes and final transportation costs will all have to be added to the primary ex-works quotation. Only then will the importer be able to see what his final price will be, thus enabling him to calculate his own mark-up, or see how much the charges will affect the cost of production, depending on whether he is importing the material for resale or for use in manufacturing a finished product.

It will be seen that the ex-works quotation might mean very little to a potential overseas customer and at this stage it would be profitable to examine another type of quotation representing the other extreme, namely delivered 'duty paid'. In this case, the quotation might read as follows:

200 × 100 kilo cartons of Carbon Black Mk 11-A @ 75p per kilo delivered duty paid
(a total of £15 000 for the whole consignment as compared with £12 000 ex-works)

This time, the position has been virtually reversed. The buyer can look at a quotation and know that the sum of £15 000 represents the whole amount which will have to be paid for the 200 cartons. The 'delivered' price includes all the charges involved right up to delivery at the appropriate address. The quoted price can be compared at a glance with other possible competitive prices, and the buyer need not fear the many variations in charges which there might be in packing, transport and tax, etc.

It will follow that the exporter is now involved in a complex sequence of costing items, and the export department will need to have all the necessary expertise to identify and calculate the various expenses involved. A simplified breakdown of the delivered 'duty paid' price structure could appear as follows:

	£
200 × 100 kilo cartons Carbon Black @ 50p per kilo ex-works total	12 000.00
Extra packing/strapping for shipment	600.00
Loading onto lorry and transport to docks	150.00
Wharfage/porterage, dock dues, loading on to ship	150.00
Sea freight charge	1 200.00
Landing charges plus duty/taxes, etc.	600.00
Loading onto lorries, handling and delivery to final destination	225.00

Marine insurance premium plus warehouse-to-warehouse clause	75.00

Total £15 000.00

Total £15 000.00 delivered duty/tax-paid to Paris

The above two types of quotation can best be summed up in the following manner:

	Exporter	*Importer*
Ex-works	Easy to calculate, involves a minimum of responsibilities.	Leaves many unknown factors. Not conducive to placing an order on this basis. May find it difficult to compare with other quotations.
Delivered duty-paid	Places considerable responsibility on export department. Calls for many calculations. Numerous variable factors – changes in freight rates, etc., may reduce profit margin once quotation has been accepted. However, there is an advantage, inasmuch that the exporter can exercise a greater degree of control over the complete process of the transaction.	Able to see at a glance – the full cost of product. Knows that any unexpected changes in freight or duty, etc. charges will have to be borne by exporter.

It should be borne in mind that the above type of price structure is based very much on a conventional type of sea shipment, hence the itemization of the various cost elements. It will be seen in later chapters that the modern developments of transportation such as containers, through road transport and combined transport operations have revolutionized shipping practice. This has had a considerable impact upon quotations and pricing and costing. For example, in many cases a container operator, etc. will be able to give an exporter a 'through delivered freight rate' and to telescope together the various freight elements.

In between the two extremes of ex-works and delivered duty-paid the international trader will encounter a spectrum of intermediate clauses. These may be summarized at this point very broadly as ranging from:

EXW
FCA
FOB
CFR
CIF
Ex-ship
DDU
DDP

Subject to more detailed clarification below, these delivery clauses define the sharing of the costs and responsibilities between buyer and seller. For example an FOB quote would envisage the seller providing the product/packing, delivering the goods to a port or perhaps container depot and arranging for the goods/container to be loaded on board a ship. The seller would obviously have to meet all the relevant charges up to this point. The buyer would have to actually make the necessary shipping arrangements, pay freight and insurance charges up to the appropriate final destination. With a CFR quote the seller would have to increase the price to cover the actual freight cost up to the nominated destination point and assume the responsibility of booking and arranging the shipment plus the procuring of the appropriate shipping document such as the bill of lading. Moving further forward to the more classic CIF quotation, the seller would now arrange and pay for insurance and obtain, in addition, the necessary insurance certificate.

It is important to bear in mind that as these various expressions are being used internationally, variations in interpretation may always arise. Different legal systems, industries and traditions could lead to misunderstandings and disputes. The quotes will always need to be clarified geographically, e.g. FOB Felixstowe or more generally FOB UK Port. A German importer will naturally need to differentiate between being quoted CIF North German Port or CIF Hamburg. Any possible differences should, if necessary, be qualified in the quote such as 'export packing excluded' or 'CIF plus landing charges'.

Because of this possible 'collision' between different interpretations, the International Chamber of Commerce has carried out valuable work in the field of standardization of international trading terminology and practice. Wherever possible therefore, it is desirable to relate the terms to this more widely understood international reference point. The precision of the quote could be greatly increased therefore by the use of such an expression as 'DDP

Chicago' (*Incoterms 1990*), this being the current operational publication of the ICC.

The types of ICC terms are set out below.

Types of quotation (Incoterms)

The main types of export sales quotation can now be examined.

EXW (Ex-Works – might be ex-warehouse, ex-mill, ex-factory, etc.)

Care must be taken to show clearly a geographical place name such as 'ex works, Liverpool' It may be, for example, that a manufacturer selling to an export merchant in Kent, and quoting from his London office, may be using a storage warehouse in Birmingham. In the absence of any specific location being mentioned in the quotation, the merchant might assume that the goods are ex-works, London, and a big haulage charge discrepancy could result. Similarly, it may be necessary, to avoid misunderstanding, to clarify the position pertaining to packing. Although 'ex-works' implies only primary packing, it might well be preferable, if selling to a buyer who is going to export the goods, to indicate that export packing is extra. To comply with an ex-works contract, the manufacturer must have the goods available at the correct place, provide suitable primary packing and notify the customer when available for collection.

FCA (Free Carrier)

Handing over of goods normally cleared for export into the charge of a nominated carrier, e.g. road haulier, 'RO/RO' or airline 'FCA Airport'.

FAS (Free Alongside Ship + departure port, e.g. FAS London; sometimes FAS + name of vessel)

The responsibility in this case extends to transporting the goods to the docks and normally to a dock or wharf designated by the buyer. The seller should ensure that the buyer is notified accordingly and should also obtain, if required, appropriate dock receipt or wharfinger's receipt. In this quotation, care should be taken with regard to the geography of the particular port. The FAS quotation might on occasions mean transporting the goods by lighter and laying them physically alongside the vessel.

FOB (Free On Board + departure port, e.g. FOB Liverpool)

A widely-used type of quotation in export trading. In this instance, the exporter is responsible for all risks, responsibilities and expenses involved in having the consignment of goods placed over the ship's rail. At this point it is essential that the buyer be advised that the goods are in an FOB position so that steps can be taken to effect insurance and make all necessary arrangements to receive the consignment when it arrives at the destination port.

CFR (Cost and Freight + destination port, e.g. CFR Lagos)

This will involve most of the obligations as set out under CIF. Obviously the exception will be that the exporter does not arrange insurance and therefore will not include the premium in the price and not have to be responsible for procuring the insurance certificate/policy. This type of clause may be mandatory in some overseas markets. For example, currently in Nigeria the sales terms are normally CFR.

CIF (Cost, Insurance, Freight + destination port, e.g. CIF Calcutta)

This is perhaps still the classic export sales clause used in international trade and around it have crystallized all the traditional methods and procedures pertaining to bills of lading, tendering of documents, transferring of ownership and methods of payment. The responsibilities of the CIF seller involve the supplying of goods suitably packed, delivering them to the docks, arranging shipping space, obtaining a bill of lading, arranging the correct type of marine insurance applicable to the goods and finally handing over to the buyer a bill of lading, insurance policy, invoice of the appropriate type and other peripheral documents that may be necessary to enable the buyer to take sale delivery at the port of destination, e.g. a certificate of origin.

CPT (Carriage-Paid to a named destination point e.g. CPT Dusseldorf Airport)

This is rather similar to CFR but is normally employed today with air and road transportation.

CIP (Carriage- and Insurance-Paid to a named destination)

This is similar to CPT but with the insurance obligation.

DAF (Delivered at Frontier to a named place)

The seller places goods at the frontier but before the customs border of the adjoining country. Normally insurance is the obligation of the buyer.

DES (Delivered Ex-Ship to a named port of destination)

The seller fulfils the obligation when goods have been made physically available to the buyer uncleared for import at the named port. This clause can have some complex legal obligations but very briefly the difference between this and say, CIF, is that with a DES contract the actual goods have to arrive, whereas in some circumstances a CIF contract can be fulfilled with the passing over of shipping documents.

DEQ (Delivered Ex-Quay/Duty-Paid to a named port of destination)

In this case the seller would be expected to bear the responsibility of the unloading, clearance at importation, payment of taxes/duties and therefore makes the goods available for the buyer to take delivery.

DDU (Delivered Duty-Unpaid to a named place of destination)

The seller's obligation to make the goods available at the named place in the country of importation less any taxes of duties but normally including certain import customs formalities.

DDP (Delivered Duty-Paid to a named place of destination)

This logically represents the other end of the spectrum from EXW and envisages the seller making the goods available to the buyer import cleared and tax/duties-paid. As with DDU there can sometimes be confusion on such costs as VAT and import clearance charges and, if in any doubt, these points should be clarified by qualification of the quote, such as, Delivered Duty-Paid VAT/ unpaid place of destination. It should be noted that neither DDU or DDP specifically obligate the seller to take care of insurance, so again this point should be made clear in the contract terms.

Detailed reference should of course be made to the official handbook of the ICC, *Incoterms 1990* where the rights and obligations of both buyer and seller are set out in depth. It will also be evident that the terms must adapt to rapidly changing patterns of international trade particularly where the various types and modes of transport are concerned. The ICC have increasingly drawn attention to both importers and exporters of the need to utilize certain clauses for particular types of transportation.

Set out below is a list of the groupings of the various terms as applied to the relevant modes of transport.

Mode of transport and the appropriate incoterm 1990

Any mode of transport including multimodal	**EXW**	Ex-Works (. . . named place)
	FCA	Free Carrier (. . . named place)
	CPT	Carriage-Paid To (. . . named place of destination)
	CIP	Carriage and Insurance-Paid To (. . . named place of destination)
	DAF	Delivered at Frontier (. . . named place)
	DDU	Delivered Duty-Unpaid (. . . named place of destination)
	DDP	Delivered Duty-Paid (. . . named place of destination)
Air transport	**FCA**	Free Carrier (. . . named place)
Rail transport	**FCA**	Free Carrier (. . . named place)
Sea and inland waterway transport	**FAS**	Free Alongside Ship (. . . named port of shipment)
	FOB	Free On Board (. . . named port of shipment)
	CFR	Cost and Freight (. . . named port of destination)
	CIF	Cost, Insurance and Freight (. . . named port of destination)
	DES	Delivered Ex-Ship (. . . named port of destination)
	DEQ	Delivered Ex-Quay (. . . named port of destination)

A degree of flexibility of outlook must also be maintained, and although the modern tendency is to use Incoterms wherever possible, it must be borne in mind that other systems may be encountered, such as the American Standard Trading Terms and the German Combiterms, particularly adapted to international groupage traffic. Common expressions such as franco domicile and door-to-door often used closely related to DDU and DDP are still employed. If in any doubt, the professional will never hesitate to qualify any particular point if there appears any possibility of misunderstanding.

Once the customer has been quoted with a particular sales clause and an order has been received, then basically the price has to remain firm. Care must be exercised if it is wished to retain some flexibility with regard to price alterations, in the event of any unexpected increased cost such as in freight rates or insurance premiums. An exporter might wish to insert a clause into the contract to cover a freight increase and consequently may state in the conditions of sales, for example, 'The price CIF Calcutta is calculated on the basis of a freight rate of $4.60 per cubic metre, any variations in this rate for buyer's account'. It may be that an exporter's price is subject to variations in the price of basic raw materials such as steel or hydrocarbon oils. It is often quite customary in such cases for appropriate clauses to be inserted into a contract during the negotiation stage.

There will be a marketing element involved in the decision pertaining to the insertion of any variation clauses. Obviously, it is safer for an exporter to retain as much right as possible to alter a price or condition of an order. If, for example, freight costs represent a high proportion of the selling price and the rates are very unstable, or if the contract is one spanning a lengthy period of time, then such clauses may be imperative. Equally, however, the customer will always prefer precise and definite prices and conditions.

Implications of different types of quotation

It will be seen therefore that, dependent upon the type of export sales clause employed, the exporter will become involved in varying degrees with no less than three contracts, namely:

1 the normal contract of sale
2 contract of affreightment
3 contract of insurance

For example, in an EXW sale the exporter has only the sales contract to consider. With CFR there would be additionally a contract of carriage. A CIF seller would engage in all three contractual relationships.

Normally, the CIF contract will be discharged when the seller hands over the appropriate set of documents to the buyer, thus enabling the latter to arrange customs clearance and payment of duty, and to obtain the goods from the shipping company. It is important to distinguish the right of the buyer to reject documents when tendered, as opposed to the right to reject the goods.

Practical marketing aspects of quotations

When considering the question of type and structure of the quotation, the exporter should bear in mind the following points:

1 The competitive and sophisticated markets, e.g. USA, Germany, France and Canada represent areas where precise and comprehensive quotations are essential. Often it will be desirable to advance the quotation to the DDP stage.
2 The background of exporter's business should be borne in mind, e.g. the stability of raw material prices and the predictability of freight rates or insurance premiums, etc.
3 The duration of the contract. With orders extending over a period of some years, it might be very difficult to quote firm prices.
4 The type of market. How stable is it economically and politically? What are the business ethics of the customer?
5 The extent of profit margins. If they are slender, they will be very sensitive to slight changes in, for example, freight and insurance, charges, etc.

Equally it is important to consider the importer's views. It may well be that they have extensive international commitments, and advantageous connections in the fields of shipping, transportation and insurance. Consequently they may prefer to arrange shipping and insurance and therefore require an FOB or even an EXW quotation.

Another vital factor is the regulations that apply to a particular market area. It is always possible that a country may wish to develop and expand its shipping and insurance facilities. Consequently, importers in these countries may be obliged by law to place orders on an FOB or CFR basis only. This is also affected by a nation's ability to find necessary foreign currency to pay for shipping and insurance services.

Equally, it is important for the professional exporter to keep informed with regard to the way overseas markets assess duty payments or grant currency allocations or import licences. It may well be the case, for example, that a particular country grants an import licence or provides foreign currency on an FOB basis. In this case the exporter should ensure that when submitting a quotation, it shows clearly the various component parts of the price structure. The quotation could be on a CIF basis but care should be taken to show also the FOB cost so that the customer's authorities can make the necessary calculations.

A typical illustration of such a breakdown might be considered as follows:

1 Mk II heavy-duty compressor 200/250 V, 50 Hz, a.c., complete with extension cable @ ex-works Birmingham	£2250.00
Cost of export packing-loading on a lorry and delivery to docks and other incidental charges	£125.00
FOB London	£2375.00
Cost of ocean freight, etc., charges	£ 310.00
CFR Calcutta	£2685.00
Cost of marine insurance and charges	£ 30.00
CIF Calcutta	£2715.00

Such a quotation would ensure that both the potential customer and the authorities would be able to identify the main component parts of the price structure. So long as the main elements are identified, there is often no need for excessive detailed information.

Subsequent chapters will examine in more detail the various aspects of charges encountered in an export transaction, particularly in respect of freight and insurance costings, but it is useful at this stage to refer to the invoice shown in Figure 3.2, which illustrates certain detailed items. This particular invoice is an example of one which might be received from a shipping and forwarding agent who has handled a shipment on behalf of an exporter, to whom this invoice would be sent, with the appropriate shipping documents which in this case would be the necessary number of copies of the bill of lading, together with an insurance certificate. In this particular instance the sum of £531.00 would in fact represent the amount that an exporter would have to add to the ex-works (plus export packing) price to convert it into a CIF figure. As was explained in Chapter 2, the export department of a company might well itself carry out many of these tasks, such as insurance, and arranging shipment.

Having identified the *cost* and *performance* obligations involved in some of the main export clauses, it is important to bear in mind that in a large number of cases the sale is handled on a 'mixed-contract' basis. This is, in effect, a useful compromise in which the exporter for example quotes an FOB price and enters into that type of contract but undertakes to arrange all, say, shipping and insurance for the customer and invoice at cost. It could be said that the normal operation of an FCA Airport sale is, in effect, quite often

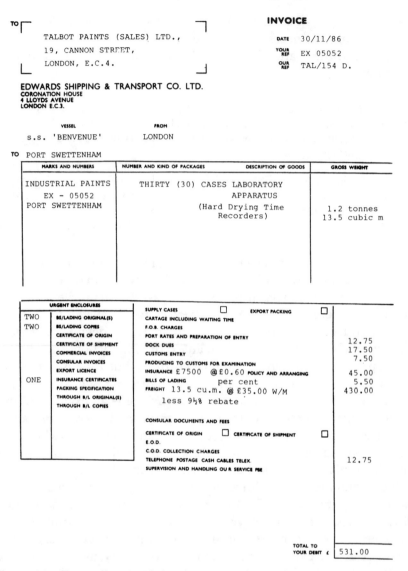

Figure 3.2 Forwarding agent's invoice

on a mixed-contract basis, as the exporter will sometimes arrange and pay for the freight and then debit the charges additionally to the customer. This method could also apply to the other terms such as EXW.

Legal aspects of quotations

To view the problem in perspective, it might be useful to consider very briefly the background to a normal contract of sale. Such a contract contains the component parts of 'offer', 'acceptance', 'performance'. and 'consideration'. Such contracts may well be concluded verbally, by implication, as well as by a formal contract or quotation. In any form of commercial correspondence pertaining to buying and selling, there are bound to be time-lags; this is very noticeable in overseas trading. Basically, therefore, the first task of the export manager will be to consider just how far to commit the company, and for how long, once a quotation is submitted to a potential buyer.

Generally speaking, the ideal situation is for a quotation to be considered as an 'invitation to make an offer'. Consequently, should an order result from the quotation, the seller is in a position to consider the order as an 'offer' and is therefore free either to accept or reject. This is, of course, all very well, but in commerce, particularly with overseas markets, it is natural that the customer requires some degree of stability. For example, in quite a number of countries the overseas buyer, upon receipt of a quotation from the exporter, has then to apply for an import licence or currency permit before proceeding. It would be extremely frustrating if, having obtained the necessary permit, it was then found that the price had been raised. The exporter will 'accept' the order when an appropriate acknowledgement letter or form is sent to the buyer.

When evolving an appropriate strategy for quotation procedure, therefore, the exporter will have to take into account the length of time involved between quotation and order and the number of variable factors involved in a price structure such as materials, labour and physical distribution costs. Equally important is to distinguish between the general type of quotation and the more specific. Usually the more general type will be represented by the price list and catalogue. Here it is normal procedure to incorporate a clause indicating that the company reserves the right to change the price or specification, etc. of the product in question. Usually such lists give basic ex-works or perhaps FOB quotations. More detailed quotations are given upon request.

On the other hand, if the enquiry and resulting quotation cover a very specific situation, it would be good policy to indicate that the price and conditions would remain firm for a prescribed period in order to enable the potential buyer to make the necessary preliminary arrangements, e.g. obtaining an import licence. In situations such as these, it is often customary to submit a quotation the shape of a 'pro forma' invoice. This document may be required by an importer's authority for any appropriate licence or permit. This type of invoice, as distinct from the normal commercial or trading invoice, does not pass through the ledger system. Consequently, if an order does not materialize, there is no need for a credit note to be issued. When an order does result from a pro forma, then a 'definite' commercial invoice is subsequently sent to the customer.

Particular care has to be taken when submitting 'tenders'. Here the potential buyer, often a government department or a very large organization, puts out tenders which really represent an invitation to the seller to put forward for acceptance a form of quotation. Normally, such transactions should involve the most careful scrutiny of the conditions surrounding such potential orders, as the obligations and requirements are generally very precise and most exacting. Sometimes manufacturers may be called upon to provide 'Tender Guarantees', which may mean paying a sum of money if their tender is accepted, and yet they cannot fulfil the tender obligations.

Bearing in mind the complex pattern of costs and responsibilities in the overseas transactions, it will be seen that it is of crucial importance for the export department to ensure that routine procedures involved in quoting potential customers and processing subsequent orders are clear-cut and free from ambiguities. Normally a company is in touch with a circle of potential buyers through the medium of:

1 Circularizing price lists and catalogues.
2 Responding to individual enquiries by means of quotations and pro forma invoices.
3 Submitting tenders.

The export managers will have the responsibility of ensuring that the methods employed by their departments will provide maximum satisfaction for overseas buyers, at the same time making sure that the company is not taking upon itself any unnecessary risks of price variations which might make inroads upon profit margins. Equally, should any problems arise, there will be no possibility of misunderstanding with regard to the price or performance obligations.

Conditions of sale

All that has been considered so far pertains to the quotation and order stages. The next step will be when the exporter, having received an order, responds by sending an appropriate acknowledgement. This acknowledgement will in fact represent the seller's official acceptance of the order, and it is most essential that the 'conditions of sale' as envisaged when the quotation was made, are clearly understood by both parties. Details must be checked carefully against the order as, very often, the buyer will include certain 'conditions of purchase' and if any of these are not in line with the seller's wishes then this point must be clarified before the contract proceeds further.

Naturally, the exporter will seek legal advice when initially drawing up terms and conditions of contract which will be printed on the quotation and order forms. Such conditions will have to be drafted to meet the particular requirements of product category and markets. A typical set of conditions which cater for the main points at issue could well be as follows:

1 Our aim is to provide you with good service and a first-class job in accordance with this quotation.
2 Unless otherwise stated in the quotation or varied by written agreement, the terms of payment on which this quotation is based are as follows:

   FOB shipments. Payments in cash against delivery of goods to nominated vessel.
   CIF Shipments. Payment terms to be agreed. The price is based on a London Banker's Confirmed Irrevocable Letter of Credit, or Documents against Payment under Documentary Bills of Exchange. Any variations in the method of payment may render an amendment of price necessary.

3 Dimensions, descriptions and weights supplied by the company for the purpose of shipping or transport requirements are approximate only and shall not form part of the contract.
4 The purchaser will be responsible for obtaining import licences, currency permits or any other necessary documents of this nature, for complying with all regulations governing the admission of any goods into the country of destination, and for payment of all customs duties, port dues and other changes arising therefrom.

5 Delivery dates are given in good faith, but are subject to the movement of transport and may be amended by us due to strikes, lock-outs and other causes beyond our control.

6 The quotation is based on the present cost of materials, transport and labour. If any of these costs decrease or increase our price may be amended accordingly.

7 Our liability under this quotation for any damage or loss is limited to making good any defects in our contract work which may arise directly from any failure of our design, material or workmanship and of which we have received notice in writing within six calendar months of the practical completion of our contract work.

8 The contract shall be interpreted in accordance with English Law including Statute Law.

It must be emphasized that the above would not suit every type of business and would, of course, depend upon the framework of the particular export sales clause that was being used. Nevertheless, the items set out indicate the main points of emphasis.

The exporter may very well find that there is available some standard model contract form that has been drawn up by a particular trade association. The United Nations Economic Commission for Europe has sponsored model contracts for various categories of products including cereals, citrus fruit, potatoes and steel products.

4   *Licensing and export control*

International customs controls

International trade involves the complex flow of goods and services between many countries who in most cases will all possess organized customs services to monitor and control this flow. Various authorities will be encountered such as the UK HM Customs and Excise, US Bureau of Customs, South African Customs, etc. This will be necessary to implement tariff and trading agreements between individual or groups of countries (such as the EU, LAFTA, etc). There will be the need at times, to levy duty or tax and to administer possible quotas or other trading agreements, such as GATT. Owing to the gradual formation of trading groups there has been a move towards greater standardization of procedures. The controls will impinge upon international operations in two main ways:

1 The observance of certain types of procedure and documentation to satisfy the exporter's own country's customs requirements.
2 The necessity of being aware of possible import licensing or currency exchange controls or other tariff requirements in the countries to which the goods are being exported.

In this chapter the main examples will be the permutation of procedures and ensuing documentation that may be encountered by the exporter when sending goods out of the UK.

Before arranging a contract and the subsequent overseas

transaction, it will be the exporter's responsibility to ensure that full attention is paid to any official requirements that may affect the transaction. In Chapter 2, when an analysis was made of the export order, it was seen that the fourth heading covered regulations encountered in various countries. It will be appreciated that it is necessary to view these activities as two sides of a coin and that importers will be considering the formalities, requirements and possible tax or duty payments when goods arrive for them from overseas suppliers.

At the present time there is the minimum number of obstacles placed in the exporter's path. On the contrary, every emphasis is placed upon assisting and encouraging the export of goods and extension of overseas markets.

Nevertheless, there are bound to be some occasions when a particular restriction might be encountered due to the nature of the product, the market to which the goods are being consigned or some financial aspect such as remission of duty or VAT. In practice, such problems are likely to be encountered under the following headings:

1 *Export licensing* – making it necessary for application to be made for types of export licences and for the necessary documentary procedure to be carried out when shipping the consignment from the UK.
2 *Customs entries* – certain formalities are necessary and will call for the completion of customs entry forms and for these to be produced to HM Customs and Excise at port or airport, known as Entry Processing Units (EPU), or to provide certain declaration forms for parcel or postal despatch.

The type of customs entry and form and procedure will vary according to whether the goods are, in fact, subject to export licence or perhaps some other specialized factor such as agricultural products linked with the Common Agricultural Policy (CAP) of the EU. There will, however, be one common factor in all types of entry and that will be *classificatory*. This will mean provision of certain input of statistical data concerning the type of goods exported, the FOB value and certain other transport, information, etc. From this, HM Customs will be able to build up the balance of trade and ultimately the balance of payment figures so essential for monitoring the economy.

Types of export licence

Logically, the first category that will be dealt with when considering a potential export order will be the question of *export licensing*. The UK authorities will naturally wish to avoid, wherever possible, placing any restrictions upon the exporter, but circumstances may make some control inevitable. In the field of international trade a number of basic factors will influence the attitude of a government when considering export licensing operations.

Sometimes, and this is of paramount importance to exporters, there is the possibility that their products may have some military or strategic character and therefore be subject to export control. Most countries are now becoming increasingly sensitive to the export of cultural and historical objects which, together with antiques, often need export licences. Another reason may be the sudden appearance of a political problem leading to one country imposing economic sanction against another. In circumstances such as these it may well be the case that all exports to a particular country may overnight become subject to control and consequently require licence application.

With the above factors in mind, therefore, it will always be the task of exporters to aquaint themselves with the current prevailing requirements, so that they can fulfil the necessary procedures relevant to products and markets. The appropriate source material will emanate from the Department of Trade and Industry, Export Licensing Branch, in the shape of the current Export of Goods (Control) Order. Subsequent modifications or amendments should be watched carefully in such publications as Croner's and other similar export reference books.

Basically, the Order in question will set out a schedule which lists a range of items arranged into groups.

Examples of some of the groups are:

Group 1
Military, security and para-military goods and arms ammunition and related material.

Group 2
Atomic energy minerals and materials and nuclear facilities, equipment, appliances and software.

Group 3
Industrial goods (naturally this group is only concerned with

certain types of highly specialized equipment, items and materials).

By studying the current Export of Goods (Control) Order, the exporter will be able to see whether products fall within any of the various groups and therefore whether or not an export licence is required. This will very often depend upon the country to which the goods are being exported.

The term 'open general export licence' (OGEL) is encountered in the Export Control Order and, applied to a particular commodity category, means that at the particular time there is no need to apply for a 'specific licence'. The OGEL may, of course, be limited in application to certain countries.

The exporter should, therefore, be in a position to check the various sources of reference pertaining to export licensing and, if appropriate, to take steps to apply for an appropriate licence. In most cases an application form, shown in Figure 4.1, will be needed.

It is necessary for the value of the goods to be shown as FOB and, most important, precise units of quantity and measurements as per the current export list should be given. Applications should always show a reference number to be used in all subsequent correspondence. The status of the signatory should be given and they should represent the party directly interested in the transaction as consignor. Signatures by forwarding agents or other similar persons are not acceptable. No export licences are transferable and obviously no unauthorized amendments are allowed. Any changes in destination must receive the consent of the Export Licensing Branch, Department of Trade and Industry.

In addition to the above-mentioned OGEL and specific licence the exporter may encounter a type known as 'general' or 'bulk'. Whereas the specific licence normally refers to goods shipped in one consignment, the general covers goods despatched over a certain specified period.

There may arise the need for a 'transhipment licence' if a UK company wished to import goods which, if they were produced in the UK, would need an export licence. If the intention was merely to bring them into a British port for the purpose of transhipment to an overseas destination, then a transhipment licence might be required. The application form needs rather more detailed information, such as proposed method of payment and purpose for which goods are required. The value is required CIF UK port.

Department of Trade & Industry
Export Licensing Branch

Import, Export & Customs Powers (Defence) Act 1939

Export Licence

Form A Part 2

Official reference

Consignor's reference

Continuation sheets numbered
form part of this licence

Total value of licence including continuation sheets

Revalidation (if any)

● Name of consignor & full address for the return of the licence

▶ For the purpose of any Export of Goods (Control) Order made under the Import, Export and Customs Powers (Defence) Act 1939 the Secretary of State licenses the consignor above to export from the United Kingdom and the Isle of Man to the consignee and the country of ultimate destination opposite within a period of 12 months from the date of this licence, the following goods.

▶ **Important**
If more space is needed, please continue on a separate official continuation sheet.

● Consignee's Name

● Address

● Country of ultimate destination

Item number (official use only)	Full description of goods for the purpose of identification	Quantity: State in units used in Customs & Excise tariff	Value FOB £
		Total value FOB £	

Signed on behalf of the Department of Trade & Industry

Date

Figure 4.1 Application form for an export licence

Transport arrangements, either for exports direct from a UK port or for transhipment, should not be made until the appropriate licence has been obtained. Penalties for offences against export licence regulations are heavy, including forfeiture of goods. Neither must it be overlooked that the existence of an export licence does not by itself relieve the exporter of the responsibility of ensuring that the customer has complied with all regulations and obtained any appropriate import licences or currency permits. The export licence is concerned strictly with actually shipping the consignment from the UK and not with entry of goods into the destination country.

Strategic goods

Running closely parallel to export licensing, is the control exercised over 'strategic' goods. This is operated through the Strategic Goods Control Order. This Order provides one schedule which covers the categories of goods and another which lists countries subject to the embargo. Strategic goods imported into the UK, for example from the USA, may be brought under official control, and sometimes the UK importer/exporter may encounter import certificates or 'waiver licences'. The exporter involved in transactions with these types of product must also be careful to ascertain whether any transit authorization or delivery verification certificates may be needed if the goods are crossing the frontiers of different countries.

Types of licences

Summing up therefore, it can be seen that after checking the above points, if it is considered that the products do appear to fall under some form of control, then the broad categories of licences are as follows:

1 Specific Licences:	Authorizes the export of goods of specific quantities and types to specified destinations. Licences for large amounts are known as 'Bulk Licences'.
2 Open General Export Licences (OGEL)	Authorizes exportation of specified goods to some or all destinations by any exporter.
3 Contract Licences (CL)	Used for material and equipment supplied under large contracts.

| 4 Open Individual Export Licences (OIEL) | Authorizes exporter for unlimited quantities of specified goods to specified destination. |

Special adaptations of the above can take into account such situations as exporting to exhibitions or demonstrations as well as repairs. Specialized advice may be needed particularly when the exporter comes across borderline cases such as say, machine tools which may or may not have strategic applications, as well as normal industrial. An essential piece of knowledge will be an understanding of the tariff classification codes, aspects of which will be considered a little later in this chapter. Although the above may seem a little forbidding it must be borne in mind that the larger proportion of exported and imported items are not subject to any form of control but it is naturally always important to be aware of the possibility.

Customs entries

Before proceeding with the more specific procedures and documents, it will be appreciated from the above that generally speaking the various customs authorities are interested in:

1 Export formalities
   These will be concerned with collecting various types of trade statistics, i.e. type of product, value, transport details and the existence of any form of control such as licensing plus the possible administration of any particular 'regime' such as drawback of duty, CAP, bonded or customs warehouse movements, etc.

2 Transit
   Depending upon the type of transport and the geography of the situation, goods may move across and out of countries in order to reach the ultimate destination. A RO/RO movement may entail leaving the UK, a ferry crossing, moving through France and Germany say, in order to reach the destination country of Austria. In a case such as this, depending upon certain factors, the customs authorities in the intermediate countries will have an interest in monitoring these shipments in order to ensure that there is no transgression of any controls, duties or taxes, etc.

3 Import formalities

Upon a consignment of goods arriving, the customs authorities again will be interested in collecting statistics, administering any controls, and, most important, often collecting duty or tax payments. This latter point explains why import formalities are often more stringent than at export.

It should be borne in mind that the gradual growth of trading areas and the coalescing of countries such as the EU within a single market lead to considerable simplification or even the disappearance of the need for the above type of customs formalities. This is examined in greater detail in Chapter 7 International trading areas: documents and procedures.

Having considered some of the factors involved in the need for customs control, we are now in a position to identify some of the documents and procedures involved. Remember, when we mention export 'customs entry', we are in this context thinking of the exporter preparing some form of document and lodging it with HM Customs and Excise in a particular fashion.

For customs purposes, the term 'exporter' includes the shipper of the goods. If an exporter is normally utilizing the services of a shipping and forwarding agent, it is quite permissible to appoint the agent to conduct customs business on their behalf. In such a case, an authorization is lodged with the customs authorities with an appropriate specimen signature.

It should be borne in mind at this stage that the permutation of customs entries can be quite complex and it is essential to build up a working familiarity with the appropriate regulations and background information. In the UK, HM Customs produce a massive corpus of three volumes of *The Integrated Tariff of the United Kingdom* which details a range of general information, customs freight procedures as well as the actual tariff classification system itself which gives what are known as the 'commodity codes' of the various range of products under chapter numbers. This information is supplemented by a range of Customs Notices, for example Notice No. 60 INTRASTAT – A General Guide.

Most customs authorities throughout the world will devise various methods of administering different systems, and again with the growing, gradual harmonization of international trade there will be a move towards different countries adopting similar approaches. In order to consider this more specifically, let us examine aspects of UK practice.

The first task is to identify the various types of customs entry, how they relate to different circumstances and what differences arise with regard to the appropriate forms and procedures. Customs entries can be divided broadly into two categories, namely 'pre-entry' and 'post-entry'.

Pre-entry

With pre-entry, the particular entry form, together with any other necessary documentation, is made available at the entry processing unit at the particular point of exportation in time for it to be passed and presented to the Officer of Customs and Excise for clearance before shipment.

Some examples where pre-entry procedures would be mandatory are:

1 Goods subject to specific export licences.
2 Shipment drawn from bonded customs warehouses.
3 Goods on which relief from import duty has been claimed.
4 CAP goods (Common Agricultural Policy), only applicable to EU countries.

Post-entry

The other method, or entry, which can better be distinguished by referring to it as 'post-entry', allows for the lodging of the customs entry at any time within fourteen days after the clearance of the carrying vessel or aircraft. This is a very simple type of entry and falls into the category described as 'classificatory'. The sole purpose is to provide HM Customs with details and value of the consignment plus certain statistical information. Naturally it will be necessary for the various authorities to devise documentary systems to administer the above-mentioned requirements. First of all, if an exporter/shipper wishes to take advantage of the simpler post-entry system which is described as the SCP or Simplified Customs Procedure, then it will be necessary for the party which is accepting the responsibility of making the entry to apply to Customs for a CRN or Customs Registered Number. This is a permanent number and will be used on certain documentation such as shipping notes, etc. to indicate to the authorities the responsible party, be it exporter or forwarder/carrier.

In addition to the CRN which will be a five-digit number, another nine-digit number will be added. This latter number will be an appropriate number which can actually identify a particular

Figure 4.2   Export Consignment Identifier (ECI)

consignment. This could be say, an air waybill, invoice number or other numbers such as a shipping company's booking reference. The overall number will be known as the ECI (Export Consignment Identifier). The number therefore will appear like that shown in Figure 4.2.

It will be seen that there are situations where, although pre-entry is not mandatory, it may be employed because, in certain circumstances the shipper/exporter may find it more convenient.

It will be appreciated that the allocated CRN will remain constant, identifying the party *responsible* for the entry. Exporters themselves might apply to HM Customs for allocation of a number or, as in many cases, they may operate under the umbrella of their forwarding agent's number, whichever is applicable. Whichever technique is being employed the important point is that when goods go forward for shipment they should either be covered by an appropriate pre-entry or reference to the ECI should be made on the appropriate covering documents (post-entry). Again, it must be stressed that these possibilities of post entry will not apply to those operations where pre-entry is mandatory, i.e. export licensing, etc.

Commodity codes and tariff classification

At this stage it is now necessary to examine some of the important data, namely the customs tariff normally referred to by UK Customs collectively as the commodity code and also a range of customs procedure codes (CPCs) which are used to identify not the product but the particular 'regime' or procedure under which the goods are exported or imported.

Basically tariff classification systems have evolved over the years in order to fulfil two main requirements, namely:

1   To provide a statistical classification tool to enable the identification and measurement of the import and export of an increasingly wide and complex range of products and materials.
2   To relate particular categories or products and materials to

possible import duty or tax rates, or to other forms of control such as export/import licences, 'end-use', quotas, countervailing or anti-dumping duties, etc.

On many types of export/import customs form, and in many cases invoices, there will often be the requirement for the insertion of various tariff numbers. As these activities are viewed against the background of international trade it will also be obvious that there has always been the need to try to make classification systems and numbers as international as possible so that a wide range of countries could employ the same systems. Consequently the history of international trade abounds with activities in this direction.

The initial most widely used number was the Brussels Tariff Nomenclature and for many years the BTN number was a very familiar term to international traders and indeed it is still encountered in literature and usage. Much work on tariff development was carried out by an international body, the Customs Co-operation Council, which developed a more refined CCCN number (Customs Co-operation Council Nomenclature).

Since the initial work of the CCC in 1950 leading up to the adoption of the CCCN by a large number of countries, there has naturally been a growing need for further classification development and refinement. Work therefore began in 1973 on a new system which emerged as the Harmonized Commodity Description and Coding System, known as HS, supplanting the existing CCCN system on 1 January 1988. This was embraced also by countries such as the USA, China and Canada, and therefore represented amongst other things a major step forward in the field of internationally accepted classification systems.

It is estimated that over 80 per cent of countries are using the HS system but naturally care must be taken to remember that some are still employing the CCCN version. A glance at two examples from Croner's illustrates the point.

Arab Republic of Egypt: Tariff is currently based on the CCCN
Czech Republic: Tariff based on the Harmonized System (HS)

Obviously individual countries have absorbed the HS into their own systems in various ways.

Looked at from a member state of the EU we can see:

Figure 4.3

Digits 1–6	HS code
7–8	CCT/NIMEXE code – Combined Nomenclature (CN), INTRASTAT
9	National statistical subdivision for member states i.e. UK★
10–11	To identify certain aspects such as quotas, licensing or other community measures on imports from third countries and possibly some intra-EC trade regarding end-use, etc. TARIC
12 and above	Might be utilized by individual countries for say, specialized excise or VAT identification.

It can be seen therefore that exporters/importers might find themselves referring to:

CN No.	8 digits
Short code	9 digits
Long code	11 digits
Additional codes	possible extra numeric or alphanumeric characters.

This can be illustrated by Figure 4.3:

Figure 4.4 illustrates a typical extract from the UK tariff publication showing a broad Chapter Heading No. 84 which embraces machinery in general and the particular page illustrated pinpoints a specific type, namely weighing machinery. The column showing 1. kg 2. Number relates to the units required by customs which might vary with different commodities. In this case, the customs declarations would show the number of machines and the weight in kilos. Other requirements might be metric tonnes, packages, pairs or just a single unit.

As mentioned above, in addition to the various commodity code/ tariff numbers, a CPC may be encountered in order for the customs authorities to identify a particular 'regime.' There are a great many possibilities here but a few examples can be mentioned:

★As from 1 January 1996 an EC Regulation revises the code structure, effectively making the 9th digit part of TARIC.

84 23 Weighing (machinery excluding balances of a sensitivity of 5 cg or better), including weight operated counting or checking machines; weighing machine weights of all kinds:				
Personal weighing machines, including baby scales:				
Household scales	842310 10 0 00	1. kg 2. Number	4.4%	CC, EFTA, GSP, S Misc.P-Free
Other	842310 90 0 00	1. kg 2. Number	4.4%	CC, EFTA, GSP, S Misc.P-Free

Figure 4.4

1 a straightforward export sale
2 import purchase
3 goods from a bonded warehouse
4 CAP commodities
5 temporary dispatch
6 goods under IPR drawback or suspension
7 entry from free zone

The numbers themselves are available from HM Customs publications and should be checked as they can be changed or modified from time to time. Usually they will be a six-digit number, namely:

100001 Permanent despatch/export for national goods not subject to any customs/excise control
400000 Basic import entry

It will be seen that the numbers will cover both exports and imports and will of course be needed for various customs documentation.

Customs relief

An important customs procedure is that known as 'Inward Processing Relief' (IPR) which, in effect, means that in certain circumstances manufacturers may claim remission or reimbursement from

Figure 4.5   Basic outline of Inward Processing Relief (IPR)

any import duty they may pay on, say, raw materials or components which they import from overseas and utilize in the production of items which they subsequently export. Figure 4.5 shows a basic outline of this operation. Apart from certain special procedures involved at the time of importation the exporter will normally 'pre-enter' shipments.

Outward Processing Relief (OPR) is a procedure whereby goods are being sent out of the country for process and return. Upon return it will be necessary for the procedure to be identified so that any import duty is based only on the added value.

Bonded or customs warehouse

A bonded warehouse is one which is licensed to accept imported goods for storage before payment of customs duty, revenue duty or VAT. This can be of considerable benefit to importers and exporters covering goods which are perhaps not required immediately for home use or where there is a chance of re-exportation.

One of the most important aspects of customs warehousing is that of excise duty and of course applicable to items such as tobacco and alcohol. Many companies in this field are now registered excise dealers, REDS. A development of single market operations within the EU has been the use of the Administrative Accompanying Document (AAD) shown in Figure 4.6, to move goods between excise warehouses.

EUROPEAN COMMUNITY
PRODUCTS SUBJECT TO EXCISE DUTY　　　　　　　**ADMINISTRATIVE ACCOMPANYING DOCUMENT**

1

1 Consignor　　　　　　VAT reg. no.	2 Consignor's excise no.　　　　3 Reference no.
	4 Consignee's excise no.　　　　5 Invoice no.
	6 Invoice date
7 Consignee　　　　　　VAT reg. no.	8 Competent authority at dispatch
7a Place of delivery	
	10 Guarantee
9 Transporter	
	12 Country of dispatch　　　13 Country of destination
11 Other transport details	14 Tax representative
1 15 Place of dispatch　　16 Date of dispatch	17 Journey time

Copy for the consignor

18a Marks and numbers. No. and kind of packages. Description of goods.		19a Commodity code (CN code)
		20a Quantity　　　21a Gross weight (kg)
		22a Net weight (kg)
18b Marks and numbers. No. and kind of packages. Description of goods.		19b Commodity code (CN code)
		20b Quantity　　　21b Gross weight (kg)
		22b Net weight (kg)
18c Marks and numbers. No. and kind of packages. Description of goods.		19c Commodity code (CN code)
		20c Quantity　　　21c Gross weight (kg)
		22c Net weight (kg)

23 Certificates (certain wines and spirits, small breweries and distilleries)

A Record of control	24　　Boxes 1-22 certified correct
	Signatory's company and telephone no.
	Name of signatory
	Place and date
	Signature

Form No. 500　　Published and sold by FORMECON SERVICES LTD. Gateway Crewe CW1 1YN　Tel: 0270 500800 Fax: 0270 500505

J479/001

Figure 4.6 Administrative Accompanying Document

Customs documentation

It is now possible after considering the above factors to examine in outline the documentation encountered with customs entries. Since 1988 the basic document has been the SAD (Single Administrative Document) shown in Figure 4.7. When considering this document constant care must be exercised between operations within the single market of the EU and those with external markets.

Essentially the SAD was designed as a multi-page (8 sheet) document with numbered boxes which could be used in various permutations depending upon its usage because various pages with appropriate data entries in the various boxes could enable the document to be used as:

1 Pages 1–3 Combinations of these used for the **export entry**.
2 Pages 4–5 For **transit** across the EC. Note that with the advent of the single market this only applies in certain specialized cases such as say, moving a consignment across the community into an EFTA country such as Switzerland.
3 Pages 6–8 Combinations used for the **import entry**.

From what has been said so far in this chapter, it can be seen that the various boxes can cope with the data and information needed. A few examples are as follows:

Boxes 18, 19, 21	Type and nationality of carrier
Box 33	The commodity code classification
Box 37	Identifying the 'regime' by the CPC No.
Box 44	Possible licence numbers if applicable
Box 46	Statistical value (normally FOB)
Box 47	For use when operated as an import entry for duty and tax calculations
Box 48	When importer operates a deferred payment scheme and employs a TURN (trader's unique reference number)

Mention should be made of Box 1 as this was designed to contrast exports/imports outside the Community when the designation EX is employed as opposed to within the Community when the concept of free circulation is indicated by T2, etc. Free Circulation is dealt with more carefully in Chapter 7.

Summing up therefore, on the use of the SAD, if we look at the position from a UK trader's point of view we find:

EUROPEAN COMMUNITY

1 DECLARATION   A OFFICE OF DISPATCH/EXPORT

Copy for the country of dispatch/export

1

2 Consignor/*Exporter*   No

3 Forms   4 Loading lists

5 Items   6 Total packages   7 Reference number

8 Consignee   No

9 Person responsible for financial settlement   No

10 *Country first destin*   11 *Trading country*   13 *CAP*

14 Declarant/Representative   No

15 Country of dispatch/*export*   15 C disp./*exp.* Code   17 Country destin Code
a| b| a| b|

16 Country of origin   17 Country of destination

18 Identity and nationality of means of transport at departure   19 Ctr   20 Delivery terms

21 Identity and nationality of active means of transport crossing the border   22 Currency and total amount invoiced   23 Exchange rate   24 Nature of transaction

25 Mode of transport at the border   26 Inland mode of transport   27 Place of loading   28 Financial and banking data

1

29 Office of exit   30 Location of goods

31 Packages and description of goods   Marks and numbers — Container No(s) — Number and kind

32 Item No   33 Commodity Code

34 Country origin Code   35 Gross mass (kg)
a| b|

37 PROCEDURE   38 Net mass (kg)   39 *Quota*

40 Summary declaration/Previous document

41 Supplementary units

44 Additional information/ Documents produced/ Certificates and authorisations

A I Code

46 Statistical value

47 Calculation of taxes   Type   Tax base   Rate   Amount   MP

48 Deferred payment   49 Identification of warehouse

B ACCOUNTING DETAILS

Total:

50 Principal   No   Signature

C OFFICE OF DEPARTURE

51 Intended offices of transit (and country)   represented by   Place and date:

52 Guarantee not valid for   Code   53 Office of destination (and country)

D CONTROL BY OFFICE OF DEPARTURE   Stamp   54 Place and date

Result

Seals affixed Number: Signature and name of declarant/representative

identity:

Time limit (date)   8 days

Signature

C88 (1-8)   Printed in the UK for HMSO 03/92 D.8324875 C2500 Sets. 53031 (JULY 1991)

Figure 4.7   Single Administrative Document

Exporting to non-EU markets – use of SAD as export entry.
Importing from non-EU supply points – SAD as import
entry. Supplying or acquiring goods within the EU Single
Market normally no need for SAD. The alternative procedures
and documents will be discussed in Chapter 7.

Developments in customs' procedure

When considering HM Customs' procedures, the exporter must
bear in mind that considerable development is taking place in the
streamlining and simplifying of customs entry and documentation.
In many cases the SAD type of entry lodgement can be replaced by
computer statistical scheduling, information on magnetic tape and
other forms of data transfer (EDI).

One of the most significant changes which is gradually being
phased into operation is that of Local Export Control (LEC). The
facility will become increasingly available for approved exporters,
groupage operators and forwarders. In essence it will mean that
export clearance can take place at the trader's premises, based
mainly on controls exercised by a Customs and Excise Office
which will normally be dealing with customs matters in the locality
of the exporter's premises. This will be known as the 'control
office.'

Normally, approved traders will be those exporting goods in
Full Container Loads (FCLs), pallets and other similar unitization.
Some of the main conditions for approval by HM Customs for
LEC will be:

1 Suitable facilities at the exporter's premises;
2 The maintenance of a high standard of entry preparation,
   record keeping and documentation;
3 Sufficient volume of export activity.

This can be of immense benefit, particularly to a larger exporter,
because it means virtually that all the necessary procedural paperwork can be handled on the premises, and the goods go forward to
airports, seaports, container depots, etc., normally covered by documentation indicating the LEC registration numbers. On their arrival there they can expect to be loaded and despatched with
minimum delay.

Similar procedures are operated with imports under the heading
of Local Import Control (LIC).

Many companies, particularly the larger ones, operating combinations of LEC/LIC can really streamline their international trade. Other examples of customs developments will be considered in a later chapter.

When considering customs procedures in general, the exporter must bear in mind that there are many variations, special provisions and developments to be encountered. Reference should always be made to their various notices and other publications, and if in any doubt, the appropriate customs officers should be consulted.

5

Physical distribution and packing

The efficient and economic ways of international trading today demand that we understand fully the various methods of moving goods. There is no need these days to emphasize the word 'economic' since we must find the appropriate mode of freighting our products if the distribution element in our costings is indeed to be the right one; that is to say, is our price the most competitive and advantageous possible? The nature of our products, the time factor and routes, with service frequency, restrict our choice, but these considerations must never limit the search for, and constant appraisal of, what makes good sense for us.

It is very important to realize the vital place physical distribution has in international trading management. In recent years it has become obvious that we could not continue looking at each transport method separately, and now we integrate these methods into a *total distribution concept*, involving sea, road, rail, air and inland waterway – not forgetting the postal services. For each movement more than one method may be used.

Just as marketing and sales are complementary, so distribution and marketing are close partners in our efforts to move goods onto the market. No one function can exist and operate properly without co-ordination and cohesion with its peers in the organization. Demands of modern marketing, speed of traffic movement and the ever-increasing tempo of communications urge us to make sure we do have the correct answers to our distribution problems. Physical distribution is satisfying demand; marketing is creating demand.

The pillars are materials handling, warehousing and storage, packaging and unitization, and transport. Good planning is the basic requirement, and this covers forecasting, space utilization, inventory control, avoiding damage during handling/transit/storage, protective packaging, security, documentation and order processing. A constant aim must be the reduction of the lead-time (start to finish of order). A useful instrument is a flow chart such as Figure 5.1 to show chain links, strengths and weaknesses. It should be borne in mind that the spread of the 'just-in-time' management concept places even greater stress on lead-time planning.

International transport methods

1 *Sea:* many variations available from small coaster/Rhine vessel, through to large container ship, including LASH (Lighter Aboard Ship) and BACAT (Barge Aboard Catamaran), conventional cargo liners, roll-on/roll-off ferries
2 *Inland waterways:* variety of craft available: dumb barge, powered barge, shallow-draught coaster
3 *Road:* most vehicles carrying goods abroad subject to TIR (Transport International Routiers) regulations, and include rigid vehicles, semi-trailer and road trains. CMR rules apply (see below)
4 *Rail:* wagons hired from British Rail, private wagons or used in joint groupage arrangements through agents – CIM rules apply (see below)
5 *Air:* scheduled or charter flights available. Regulating body is the International Air Transport Association (IATA)
6 *Post*

International agreements

1 The convention on the carriage of goods by sea – Hague Rules
2 The convention on the international carriage of goods by road – Convention de Merchandises par Route (CMR)
3 The convention on the international carriage of goods by rail – Convention Internationale Concernant le Transport des Marchandises par Chemin de Fer (CIM)
4 The convention on the carriage of goods by air – Warsaw Rules

Some of these conventions and agreements will be referred to in more detail in Chapter 6 as to their impact upon documents and procedures such as bills of lading, consignment notes, waybills and carnets.

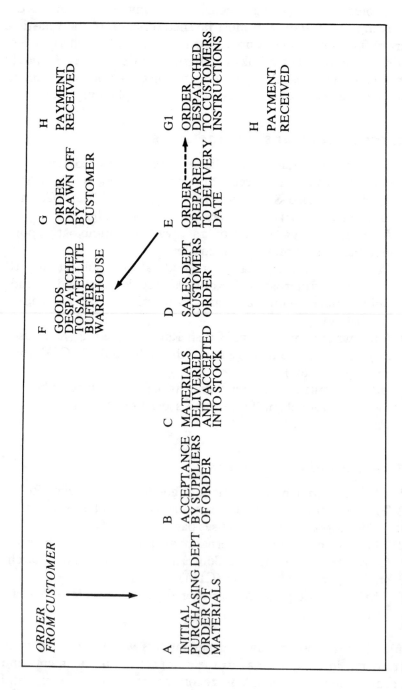

Figure 5.1 Physical distribution flow chart

Costing

Constant monitoring and assessment are carried out by differential cost analysis, e.g. order sizes, transport methods, packaging uses; and these days computer comparisons of differential costs give us answers quickly and help to identify most economic patterns. Fundamentally, costs include:

- in-factory movements and storage
- factory to depot of transit
- depot work: materials handling, storage and overheads
- depot to carriers
- inventory control
- selection of goods to meet order
- packaging
- documentation
- insurance
- securing payment from overseas customer, through bank or other agencies
- transportation charges – dock/rail/airport delivery – freight, port charges
- duties
- foreign distribution charges, e.g. DDP/franco domicile, terms of sale/Incoterms
- interest on transit capital

Costs fall into one of two categories:

- *Direct costs*, or variables, relate directly to particular goods or projects, such as, raw materials, assembly, production wages, direct energy/power costs for running machines.
- *Indirect costs*, or fixed overheads, embrace rents, rates, lighting, heating, repairs/maintenance; each product or project must contribute towards fixed costs such as purchasing, factory office, inspection, progress chasing, quality control, accounts, personnel, advertising, sales and research and development.

Direct costs + indirect costs + profit mark-up = price ex-works

Materials handling

This is the fastest-changing and developing part of distribution and it is essential to keep up with new techniques and means of handling goods, if costs are to be controlled effectively.

From small pallet truck through to heavy-lift trucks there is a wide variety of equipment available to speed the work of goods handling, whether it is of raw materials entering the production unit or manufactured articles leaving to meet an order.

For every type of operation there is an appropriate machine, and to cope with the demand of users for specialist handling more and more varied aids are being introduced.

A simple way of thinking of materials handling is to consider a large factory layout – there are fork-lift trucks, mobile cranes to load vehicles arriving at and leaving the facility, overhead conveyor systems and goods holding areas.

Warehousing and storage

In any distribution system (see Figure 5.1), there are warehouses at many points which are essential to the free flow of goods to the market. Some are used as assembly points, perhaps near a port or an airport, others are at the factory site, whilst others again serve as buffer stock reserve stores, particularly in times of economic stringency and uncertain international financial conditions. To build and equip a modern, efficient warehouse requires the outlay of a substantial capital sum, so very careful planning is needed to fix the correct position and to identify the uses – will it be automated or labour controlled?

It will be seen, therefore, the PDM (Physical Distribution Management) takes its full and proper place in the marketing mix. The choices made, and patterns selected will in turn shape the procedures and documentation necessary to support the appropriate distribution and transport mode.

Consulting the simple flow chart, Figure 5.1, the all-important lead-time of any order can be traced. First, an order from the customer is processed at D. Materials, however, need to be allocated – A, B and C. The necessary planning therefore is: initial purchasing departments' order to suppliers, acceptance into stock, thence to production and despatch.

It is likely that finished goods will move to satellite buffer warehouses regionally and nationally convenient to customers; a good example is trading within the EC, where member states' companies organize such operations – among others, foodstuffs and auto components and spares.

The length of time taken from acceptance of the customer's order to final delivery *and* payment is a measure of the overall efficiency of a physical distribution system.

Packaging and unitization

The three main purposes of packaging are protection, containment and identification. The right balance is required between too costly material and the false economy of using inferior material, but we are bound by considerations of the nature of our goods, fragility, dangerous state, contamination, dampness, ease of pilferage and perishability. Other restraints are the duration of transit, type of transport mode and government regulations.

If for no other reason than economy, the past decade has forced urgent adaptation of freight methods which bulk smaller consignments with others to make convenient unit loads, perhaps by use of a pallet or a shipping container, or specialist product pack, i.e. groupage and consolidation.

Although, of course, the whole concept of unitization in the shape of standard ISO (International Standards Organization) 20 ft and 40 ft container, plus palletization, has revolutionized the whole process of packing there are still many basic packing and packaging problems associated both with unitized and conventional load movement of goods internationally. These factors will have a bearing on both the marketing and transit aspects of the operation.

Packing units

First of all, there are certain basic elements of packing which will face any manufacturer wishing to send products to a buyer, whether in the home or overseas market. The broad concept of packaging and packing can be split into two fundamental parts, namely:

1 *Retail unit pack*. This is closely allied to the selling and marketing function and is itself a highly-specialized study. It embraces many aspects such as the psychological, functional, point-of-sale, display, etc. The choice of the correct type of packaging can be a considerable influence for consumer acceptance. The costs can be correspondingly high, particularly on such products as cosmetics and jewellery. In this respect,

therefore, the unit pack has a marked bearing upon cost–price relationship and consequently upon profit margins.

2 *Transit pack*. Here the concern is with providing a suitable pack to enable the goods to move from the manufacturer's works to the ultimate customer. A customer is interested in receiving goods in perfect condition and is *not* interested merely in collecting insurance claims. Therefore, packing will have to be provided which will hold and protect adequately. At the same time the choice must represent a compromise between maximum protection, relative cost of packing and the impact of the packing itself upon the form of transportation being utilized.

When we apply these two aspects of the packing concept more particularly to exporting, it will be seen that the special problems encountered overseas with the retail unit pack might be:

1 In most cases, a wide range of markets in a number of countries has to be catered for, and might call for a number of different retail packs.
2 On the other hand, decisions have to be made as to whether an international image is to be created or whether single or multiple brand images are to be exploited.
3 There is almost certain to be a range of different legal requirements regarding weights, sizes and labelling.
4 Various overseas consumer protection bodies are constantly reviewing and influencing unit pack requirements.
5 Different markets may have very different preferences regarding shape and colour of packs. Various religious or social customs may entail prohibitions of the use of certain colours or wording.
6 The impact of environmental policies such as the German laws on the recycling of packaging materials and growing international standards is becoming a major factor in packing policy.

There is considerable scope for creative marketing in the sphere of designing unit packs for specific markets.

The transit pack is the one with which this book is mainly concerned. The special overseas problems become more acute because of the distances involved, the different types of climatic conditions and the varieties of handling that the goods will receive.

Let the classic concept of an overseas transaction be considered as follows:

1	2	3	4	5	6
Works packing/ loading	Docks/ airport handling/ stowing	Sea journey/ flight/ ferry/ road	Docks/ airport handling/ unloading, customs inspection	Inland journey, various methods of transport	Customer's warehouse receiving/ unloading, opening

Every one of the six stages will to some extent influence the exporter in the choice of type of packing. The following criteria can be distinguished:

1 Actual method of transportation.
2 Characteristics of the product.
3 Climatic conditions likely to be encountered during journey.
4 Any specific requirements of customers with regard to the type of package that will be acceptable.
5 Any specific regulations or legislation pertaining to the packing encountered, either in the exporting country or country of destination.

Choosing the method of transportation is always likely to be one of the first considerations. First of all, it must be realized that carriers, such as ship-owners for example, will themselves call for certain standards of packing. The Carriage of Goods by Sea Act 1971 excludes the carrier from any responsibility for damage due to insufficiency of packing. Freight rates will often be based upon specified packing for particular commodity characteristics.

Air transportation, by its very nature, does not call for heavy packing. Nevertheless, the latter must be sufficient to protect the goods and to enable them to be handled satisfactorily. The nature of the method employed will also indicate how much handling and unloading will be encountered. Will there be transhipment problems or breaks in the journey which will call for warehousing and storage? What type of inland transport will be encountered in the importing country? It could be extremely primitive such as mule transport and therefore we might envisage a journey that commences with the latest type of twentieth century jet air-freighter and finishes on a 2000 BC ox-train. Higher freight costs can

Figure 5.2   Economical packing needs forethought

sometimes be offset by the use of cheaper packing, as in the case of light, cardboard metal-tape-bound cartons by air transport, whereas heavy wooden cases or crates might be necessary by ship; the nature of the whole journey must be borne in mind. It will be readily appreciated how vast an impact the new types of container and road transport systems will have on packing; the number of stages represented in our table will be radically reduced.

The characteristics of the product itself will also influence packing specification and design. The size and shape, the degree of fragility, the number of units being packed together, and the possibility of shifting and movement will all have to be borne in mind.

If freight is being charged on cubic capacity over a large number of units, there could be a considerable amount of wasted freight space. Sometimes this wasted freight space can present problems. Consider the case of a product such as an electric fire which is mounted on legs (Figure 5.2). In many cases the problems can be overcome by the packing influencing the product's design as, for example, the electric fires being designed with detachable legs which can be reassembled at the point of destination.

Another method in the case of our product example might be for the exporter to pack the wasted space area with other allied products, e.g. spare electric elements. When mixed units are being included in the same pack, care must be taken to ensure that the different units are not rated at different freight categories. Equally, of course, hazardous goods must not be included with products being shipped as general cargo. This might well happen where perhaps mixed chemicals are shipped together but have different flash points or other dangerous characteristics.

Very often a compromise or calculated risk will have to be taken. Let us suppose the shipment is a consignment of electric light bulbs. These are very fragile and to be on the safe side would probably require cardboard cartons within sound wooden crates. Such products, however, are keenly competitive and such packing might amount to about 30 per cent on retail price. The strategy, based upon experience over a period of time, might be to use only carton packing, to accept a percentage breakage and to devise a system whereby the receiving customers, such as retailers, are advised to check immediately upon receipt and return broken bulbs for replacement. This action might, in the long run, be more economical than continually using heavy and expensive packing for every consignment.

International trade means that in a number of consignments goods may pass through several sets of climatic conditions before reaching their destination; therefore the packing might be designed accordingly. There is always the possibility of the exposure of goods to a corrosive atmosphere (e.g. by being opened by customs examination on a quayside.) The popular use of plastic wrapping material can sometimes exacerbate the condition known as 'sweating' unless suitable openings or air holes are provided. Internal wrapping such as waxed paper, etc., can often play a very useful part in catering for climatic conditions.

The possible *tactical uses* of the packing must not be overlooked. In some cases, whatever the exporter's thoughts are on packing, the customer may have fixed ideas on what type of packing is required. Sometimes, as with wooden cases in countries where timber is short, the cases may have a re-sale value which is of considerable importance. Equally, the packing itself may be required for storage of goods.

Another factor which will influence packing design and materials is the risk of pilferage. How easy is it going to be for the contents to be observed and, if desirable, to be broken open? The pilferage factor will, of course, in many cases go hand-in-hand with the method of transportation, the length of journey and how often the goods are handled and warehoused before reaching their final destination.

Regulations pertaining to packing can be considerable and they generally fall into two classes, i.e. the outside packing from the point of view of safety, and the contents of internal packing material. The former case is exemplified by the Merchant Shipping Dangerous Goods Rules and the *Blue Book* which sets out recommendations covering packing, marking and stowage of certain classes of dangerous products such as poisonous substances, corrosives and those having low flash points, etc.

```
                                              A.N. Exporter Ltd
                                   Declaration by Exporter for wood packing

  To: The Customs Authorities

      ...................................

      ...................................


  I, .................................................. of ........................................................ , hereby
  declare that all timber used for packing the goods listed below has been inspected by me
  and was to the best of my knowledge free from bark and from visible signs of insect and
  fungal attack when the goods were shipped to New Zealand.

                                                          ............................

                                                          ............................
                                                          (Signed and
                                                          dated)


  Class of goods              Shipping marks               Port of discharge

                                                           No. of cases
```

Figure 5.3   Specimen declaration by exporter for wood packing

The other class, which mainly relates to internal packing, often springs from health and allied requirements, particularly in predominantly agricultural or livestock breeding countries. Many countries prohibit the use of straw as packing material. In these cases, alternatives such as wood wool should be employed. South Africa, in addition to similar restrictions, goes further and requires that statements be provided certifying that any timber used in packing is free of certain diseases. New Zealand also comes in this category and Figure 5.3 is a specimen of the type of certificate an exporter would be expected to provide for the destination port.

Categories of export packing

Sometimes countries permit the use of materials such as straw, hay or moss for packing, provided that it is certified disinfected.

Canada, which is one such country, also prohibits the use of second-hand bags or sacks.

The choice of packing material is nowadays very extensive and, as always, that exporter will be balancing cost against protection and customer requirements. The following is a list of some of the more usual categories encountered in export packing:

1 *Retail unit packs:* cardboard cartons, cellophane bags, plastic containers, polystyrene mouldings, tin cans, bottles, etc.
2 *Internal packing materials:* wood wool, wood shavings, straw, chaff, waxed paper, sheets of cellophane film, multi-wall paper bags, plastics or paper linings.
3 *Outer transit packs:* hessian sacks, special multi-wall paper bags, steel drums and cans, wooden crates, trusses, wooden cases, sometimes battened, or wire-bound. Plywood cases – occasionally metal-edged. Barrels, fibreboard packing cases and plastic or polystyrene containers which can be very strong and yet light and easily handled.

It should not be forgotten that ship-owners and air-freight operators are by the very nature of their business extremely experienced in the characteristics of packing and can often be a rich source of information for the exporter as they can give the benefit of their experience of shipping different commodities in various types of containers.

Below is a brief classification of some of the relevant types of packing for exportable goods.

1 *Bulky raw materials (carbon black, cement, fertilizers, etc.):* plywood drums, multi-wall bags/sacks.
2 *Machinery and capital goods:* wooden cases sometimes crated, sometimes on flats covered with polythene sheeting as when despatched by air. Care must be taken to see that the items cannot move about inside the crates or cases. Shrink wrapping often employed.
3 *Furniture:* wooden cases, fibreboard cartons, crates, protective polythene and paper wrapping; often shipping on a 'knocked down' (KD) basis. 'Completely knocked down' (CKD) is where the whole article is disassembled in order to save freight space and sometimes assembly costs.
4 *Kitchen and sanitary equipment:* can often be nested, using straw extensively, and then packed in wire-bound crates.

Figure 5.4   Shipping marks

5 *Liquids:* casks, metal drums, carboys (particularly for acids) suitably encased in straw wrapping.
6 *Instruments (electrical apparatus, radios, etc):* cases or cartons, great care being taken with the internal packing.

Marking practice

Of equal importance is the marking of the packages themselves. This is vital in order to make possible speedy identification of the consignment and also to comply with any regulations in force with regard to hazardous or dangerous cargo. Overseas territories also sometimes enforce certain regulations pertaining to marking of export cases. Equally, the marks should include wording or symbols that will enable the personnel handling the cargo to exercise any special care that may be required.

Identification of the consignment

Basically, the golden rule is to keep case marking as simple as possible. A simple example might well be as shown in Figure 5.4. In such a case, U.F.P. might well indicate the initials of the importing company, 397 the customer's order number, 1/6 UP indicating that this particular case is case No. 1 of a consignment of 6 cases. The second case would be 2/6, the third 3/6 and so on throughout the consignment. The port of destination, Copenhagen, should of course figure prominently in the set of markings. Such markings would enable the ship owners and dockers, etc., to sort out the consignment and to link up the cases with the bill of lading, thus enabling the customer or the agent to effect prompt collection. The Carriage of Goods by Sea Act 1924/1971 relieves the carrier from responsibility for delay, loss or damage due to 'insufficiency or inadequacy of marks'.

Of course, it is not always possible to keep the marking simple. On occasions, an importer may call for a number of additional project or serial numbers. This can be of great importance, particularly

Figure 5.5 Poisonous substance label

when shipping components for large capital projects, as the indicator numbers may well have to serve as a form of guidance to assembly engineers. Certain centralized economies, might call for fairly detailed serial number markings which link up with the various official buying organizations.

Hazardous or dangerous cargo

Mention has already been made of the *Blue Book*, which advises that, in certain cases, the nature of the hazardous cargo should be indicated by stencilling or labelling as shown, for example, in *Figure 5.5*.

Sea

In addition to the UK Department of Trade and Industry's *Blue Book*, reference should be made internationally to the IMDG (International Maritime Dangerous Goods) Code Book. This will enable the exporter to identify the various code classifications and to link up with the possible use of the appropriate United Nations Number which is in fact a commodity reference number.

Air

The IATA *Dangerous Goods Regulations* cover a comprehensive list of packing, marking and handling requirements and employ a 'dangerous goods' classification along the lines of the *Blue Book/*

IMDG. Shippers by air, therefore, are legally responsible for complying with the appropriate requirements and the ICAO (International Civil Aviation Organisation) *Technical Instructions for the Safe Carriage of Dangerous Goods*.

Road/rail

The European Agreement for the International Carriage of Goods by Road (ADR), which came into force in July 1969, prescribes regulations for the packing, marking and loading of goods into road transport vehicles which themselves must conform to stipulated standards. Annex 1 (RID) to the International Carriage of Goods by Rail (CIM) covers the regulations for dangerous goods by this mode of transportation.

It will be borne in mind, therefore, that in order to comply with the above, in addition to the actual packing and marking there will be the need for certain data and classification numbers to be inserted in the appropriate documentation such as shipping notes (see Chapter 6), consignment notes and air waybills, etc.

An important point to remember is that even apparently quite innocent products can often exhibit hazardous or dangerous effects, e.g. aerosols, instruments containing mercury batteries, certain protective greases and even magnetic items which could seriously interfere with, say, an aircraft's instrumentation and controls.

A factor to bear in mind is that quite apart from any potential danger aspects, goods may have to be marked with special stowage requirements such as 'Below deck shipment' or 'Stow away from boilers.'

Overseas regulations

When shipping to any overseas territory, care should be taken to find whether or not there are any requirements pertaining to marking. Germany has no general regulations for marking cases but packaged foodstuffs must bear an indication of the country of origin. India requires the gross weight to be stencilled on two sides of each pack or piece. In South Africa, the SA Transport Services accepts goods only if name and address of consignee, destination and port of entry appear on packing cases. Cases weighing over 1360 kg must have the actual weight clearly indicated as part of the shipping mark.

Marks giving handling guidance

Where fragile goods are being transported, it is sound practice to indicate this by marking the cases 'Fragile' or for bags of raw

Figure 5.6 'Fragile' marking

material to bear the notice 'Use no hooks', or where appropriate for other materials, 'Keep dry'. It is important to bear in mind that the goods may be handled at a port where literacy might be of a low level, and therefore, symbols such as a broken wine glass or an umbrella give the necessary clues as to the nature of the contents. In fact, since symbols overcome language barriers as well they are replacing a number of the older types of wording (see Figure 5.6).

When using second-hand containers, care must be taken to remove or obliterate old markings and stencils. Waterproof paint or ink should be employed wherever possible, and the actual positioning of the marks on the cases should also be borne in mind to ensure that they are visible when the cases are stacked.

In most countries various government ministries cooperate with official bodies such as the British Standards Institution and the Institute of Packaging for example in the UK, covering the design and practice of export packing and marking. Naturally the EU is an example where there are moves to bring about a growing degree of international standards.

Packing can also be of considerable importance since in some instances duty might be assessed on the basis of the weight of the cases themselves. This type of duty is known as 'specific duty' and would depend very much on the nature of the commodity being encountered, more often in the case of certain bulky raw materials. Naturally, this is a vital marketing aspect because, if the duty is

assessed on *gross weight*, then it is of the utmost importance to ensure that as light a form of packing as practical is employed.
Remember that:

Gross   = weight of product + weight of packing cases, etc.
Net   = weight of product without packing
Tare   = weight of packing itself
Net, net = weight of product without either internal wrapping or outer transit packing.

It will also be important to ensure that the packing cases or containers are marked very clearly with the various weights and, of course, the metric system should be employed wherever applicable, certainly throughout Europe.

Free ports and customs zones

A vital factor gaining importance in the physical distribution process has been the evolution of certain geographical zones free of normal customs and duties procedures. These can greatly facilitate the shipping, transportation and handling of goods in international trade. Such international free trade zones as for example Margarita Island off Venezuela and Mersin in Turkey play a part, particularly in entrepot trade. The six main free zones or ports in the UK are Belfast, Birmingham, Cardiff, Liverpool, Prestwick and Southampton.

A free port is an area into which goods may move without paying duty to customs or similar import charges, including VAT, charged at importation in the normal way of goods entry. There is no special relief in the zones or ports such as company taxes, excise duties, and local rates. Users are subject to normal domestic laws within the zones or ports, for employment, health and safety and the environment on the same basis as outside the areas. Before listing eligible activity and benefits, it should be noted that customs and excise will not permit retail trade to be carried on, other than catering for staff canteens, or employee facilities.

Free-zone eligibility: activities permitted
- Loading, unloading and transhipment.
- Storage, including stockholding pending quota availability.
- Sampling, packing, labelling, and other minor handling for preparation of goods for marketing.
- Processing of most Third World country goods for export out-

side the European Community, subject to the 'protective test' applied by EC legislation.
● Destruction of, say, unsaleable or surplus goods.

Free-zone benefits
● Simplified customs procedures.
● Cash-flow advantages resulting from exemption of duties unless and until goods are released into free circulation.
● Secure environment provided by ring fence enclosing area.
● Economy of scale from physical concentration of facilities.
● Better potential for marketing/sales presentation.
● More flexible decision-making on quota goods, final destinations.

Before considering an application to use a free zone or port it is useful to sum up what is involved. In general, customs duty and agricultural levies are due only when goods are consumed either within the zone or port, or when they cross the boundary into UK markets or those of member states of the EC. VAT-registered traders may import goods into a free port without accounting for tax on them. Immediately those goods leave the free zone or port for use in the UK, VAT is chargeable. Normal VAT rules still apply to goods and services supplied to or within the zone. Relief from excise duty will be limited to bonded warehouse arrangements under existing legislation.

The first step towards using a free zone is an application to customs and excise responsible for the particular free port, who will grant a letter of authorization. A copy of this authority will be passed to the zone operator, who maintains security by controlling entry and perimeter patrolling. The operator must provide certain import statistics to customs on goods moving into the zone.

The development of free ports coupled with the growth of local export control facilities (LEC), as outlined in Chapter 4, will play an ever-increasing part in streamlining the flow of international goods and transportation and make a valuable contribution to the total distribution concept. It is very important to observe development of such professional institutions as the Institute of Physical Distribution and the resultant improvement of professional skills in this particular sphere of activity which is obviously so vital, particularly when applied to international trade.

6

Transport documentation and procedures

In no section of documentation and procedure has there been such widespread growth and modification as in that devoted to international transportation. There is now a very wide spectrum of different types of document that will play their part in monitoring the carriage of goods overseas, facilitate the obtaining of these goods by the importer, and relate various conditions of carriage between shipper, carrier and possibly forwarding agent.

Equally, this category of documentation will naturally play a large part in determining how the physical possession and title of ownership and property will pass from seller to buyer in the international scene. Consequently, the nature of the transport document and its deployment will often have to be related to the terms of payment involved in the export order.

Shipment and bill of lading practice

By far the largest volume of international trade is still carried by sea. Therefore, much of that trade, its commercial, legal and financial systems, revolves around ships and shipping practice.

When considering the shipment of goods, the exporter will take into account a number of factors. The first point will be whether use is to be made of a shipping and forwarding agent. When making this decision, a company will have to examine its own organization and personnel to see whether it possesses the expertise to carry out the many complex procedures that will be required. The total number of individual consignment shipments over a period of time will also influence the decision. A company with a considerable overseas business, involving a large number of shipments, may often find it preferable to develop its own shipping department, thus enabling it to have more direct control and making it possible to integrate the shipping function more closely with its internal production and despatch schedules. The experienced shipping staff employed by the company will also be charged with the task of studying the freight market and ensuring that wherever possible competitive freight rates and conditions are obtained. Different organizational patterns that may evolve in various companies have already been discussed in Chapter 2.

Shipping and forwarding agents

The services provided by a forwarding agent extend beyond the shipping function. Normally, most agents in the UK work within the framework of the standard trading conditions which are sponsored by the Institute of Freight Forwarders Ltd., the professional organization devoted to this sphere of activity. Some of the points covered by these trading conditions refer to the clarification that such agents are not common carriers, that subject to specific instruction they are free to select routes, entitled to retain all commissions, brokerages, etc. that they would be customarily entitled to receive; also, that all goods and documents held would be subject to a particular and general lien for any unpaid charges for freight handling, etc. Furthermore, no responsibility is accepted for any lack of accuracy in description of goods, or any fines, duties and taxes that may be levied by any authorities. Insurance cover will not be effected unless express instructions to do so are given. Agreements between the agent involved and his customer are governed by English law and come within the exclusive jurisdiction of the English courts. These conditions should always be carefully studied as they will be of great assistance to an exporter in helping to frame instructions clearly and concisely when instructing a shipping and forwarding agent to proceed with a shipment. When agents book freight space on behalf of a customer, they are, according to the custom of the London freight market (which has its headquarters at the Baltic Exchange), liable for dead freight should by any chance their customer should fail to produce the goods and the ship consequently has to sail with unfilled holds. The agent would normally look for indemnification.

At the international level there is a growing degree of international harmonization of practice and indeed of layout of certain documents such as bills of lading monitored by an international association known as Fédération Internationale des Associations de Transitaires et Assiniles (FITA). This is in fact a body of international freight forwarders.

To many companies, particularly the small organizations or those new to exporting, shipping and forwarding agents will be of tremendous value. They are experts in their field with an up-to-date and specialized knowledge of all the various methods of transport and relative freight and carriage rates. Their business keeps them in close touch with the constantly changing conditions at ports and the requirements of customs authorities. A not insignificant service also offered is the consolidation or groupage of a number of cargoes from different exporters into one consignment, which often makes possible economies of scale in the shape of preferential freight rates or at least the avoidance of minimum freight charges which might otherwise have been encountered on small shipments. Many such agents also operate road transport and can often include in their services the collection of the goods from the exporter's warehouse. Apart from charging their customer any direct costs encountered, such as transport, bills of lading, customs entry, etc., they will usually levy a service fee based on a percentage of the freight charge.

Many forwarding agents supply a printed form which lays out all the various permutations of instructions that the exporter might wish to give. Figure 6.1 shows a typical specimen, and it is interesting to note the categories of service that are available, ranging from collection from the exporter, and the arranging of insurance right through to customer, i.e. DDP. As will be seen from the above-mentioned standard trading conditions, it is essential that the instructions form be completed correctly. This underlines the fact that although an agent may be employed, the exporter must still understand enough of the procedure and requirements involved to formulate instructions in a clear and unambiguous manner providing all the relevant information.

Sea freight procedure

Whether the exporter is arranging the shipment directly with ship owners or utilizing the service of an agent, the following procedures will be encountered:

1 The selection of a vessel and shipping line for the required port of destination.

FORMECON
EXPORT FORMS
Tel. 0270 500800
Fax. 0270 500505

REF. 827 (SET)

SITPRO EXPORTSET

Seller (name, address, VAT reg. no.) Ⓐ

© SITPRO
1992

EXPORT CARGO SHIPPING INSTRUCTIONS

Invoice number	Date of purchase/acceptance of order
Invoice date (tax point)	Seller's reference
Buyer's reference	Exporter's identification code (USA only)

U N I C

Consignee (name, address, VAT reg. no.) Ⓑ

Buyer (name, address, VAT reg. no.) Ⓓ

Freight forwarder (name, address, VAT reg. no.) Ⓒ

Country of origin of goods | Country of destination

Terms of delivery and payment

To be despatched by (eg. road, sea, air) | From (pick-up point)

To (destination)

Please insure for

Shipping marks | No. and kind of packages; description of goods | Commodity code

Total gross wt (kg) | Total cube (m³)

Total net wt (kg) | Value £

Item/packages	Gross/net/cube	Description	Quantity/Home market value	Unit price	Amount

Certificate of shipment
Air, sea or other waybill
Bill of lading
Consular formalities/certs. of origin
Other documentation charges
Customs formalities   Export
  Transit
  Import

STATUS :
Enter T1/T2/MIX or T2L
(as applicable) →

Make out documents as indicated and dispose of as follows:

FREIGHT ▶
◀ DOCUMENTATION

Indicate services required and to whom charges should be debited, by entering
Ⓐ Ⓑ Ⓒ or Ⓓ
in check box.

Indicate who post enters if SCP →

Inland carriage to   Groupage depot/ICD
  UK port/airport
Depot/ICD or port charges including unloading
Freight to
Depot/ICD or port charges at destination
Oncarriage at destination to   Depot/ICD
  Place of delivery
Ocean freight payable at
No. of bills of lading required
  Original   Copy
I/We hereby declare that the above particulars are correct and agree to your published Regulations and Conditions, including those as to liability.

Exchange rate | Invoice total

Special instructions

Name of contact and telephone number

Signature

J357/001

Figure 6.1   Typical export cargo shipping instruction form

2 The procuring of space on board a specific vessel.
3 The consideration and calculation of the particular freight rates involved.
4 Payment of freight.
5 Preparation of the bills of lading.
6 Despatch of the consignment to the docks.
7 Utilization of appropriate standard shipping note form.

Shipping space may be booked with the shipping line direct, although it is more often the case that the loading brokers are used as an intermediate link. Basically, the broker in this case advertises dates of sailings, sends out notification or sailing cards, arranges the payment of freight and issues bills of lading. The broker's commission will be received from the ship-owner on whose behalf he has been operating

Lloyd's Loading List can be consulted for shipping details. This publication is issued weekly and enables exporters first of all to find the required port of destination. Listed against the port will be found the primary data regarding shipping availability.

A specimen entry is as follows:

ADELAIDE, Australia (AU) 34 56s, 138 36E

Vessel	*Flag*	*TEUs*	*DWT*	*Receiving dock/depot*
My 12 RESOLUTION BAY (FC)	GBR	2344	38757	LONDON–TILBURY

Receiving	XT	*ETD*
Ap 06		AP 09

FC = full container loads
TEU = maximum number of twenty-foot container equivalent loads
DWT = dead weight tonnage of vessel

Categories of carrier employees

Throughout this chapter various types of transport will be discussed so it is important at this stage to indicate the various types of contacts that will be made. *Lloyd's Loading List* indicates the following:

L Shipping Line/Accredited Agent: operates a ship or ships between advertised ports on a regular basis or a company which has been appointed agent on behalf of a shipping line.

N NVOC: does not own or operate the carrying ship but contracts with a shipping line for the carriage of the goods of the third parties.

Figure 6.2   Example of a sailing card

F Freight Forwarder: arranges the carriage of goods and the associated formalities on behalf of the shipper.

C Consolidator: groups together several compatible consignments into a full container load.

H Road Haulier: operates a motor vehicle licensed to carry goods.

R Rail Freight Operator: arranges the carriage of goods by rail.

A Airline: operates aircraft between advertised airports.

B Air Cargo Agent: arranges the carriage of goods on behalf of a customer.

NVOCC is a widely used abbreviation meaning a non-vessel owning common carrier.

Booking shipping space

Sailing cards will provide more detailed information and an example of a typical card is shown in Figure 6.2. It will be necessary to check if there are any restrictions on the despatch of the cargo to the appropriate loading point. Very often it is sufficient to arrange space booking in an informal manner. In some cases, particularly with high-frequency sailing to the Continent, an exporter will send the consignment to a specific shed and then arrange to notify the ship-owner, taking steps to prepare the appropriate bills of lading. Nevertheless, there may well be cases where prior booking or registration are required.

Sometimes, particularly when ports are congested and shipping lines are finding it difficult to clear cargo, it will be necessary for an intending shipper to provide the ship-owner with a cargo registration form giving full particulars of the consignment. This form generally comprises at least two parts, one of which will eventually be returned to the exporter instructing when to send that cargo forward. It is known as a 'calling-forward notice'.

Equally, if a cargo is a particularly heavy one, or includes unusually-shaped items, such as extra long lengths, special days are set aside when tackle and equipment are made available to handle them; the same applies for consignments such as explosives, corrosive materials or goods having low flash points, etc. Great care must be exercised in these circumstances; considerable inconvenience and expense might be incurred if a shipper ignored any of these prior requirements.

Further precautions might have to be taken if the goods in question are of a hazardous nature. As we have already seen in Chapter 5 on physical distribution, there is considerable legislation relating to dangerous types of goods, and special procedures and documentation are required. It will be seen later in this chapter that a special type of shipping note may be encountered. Cargo delivered without the correct description, or without compliance with the rules could result in heavy expenses and costs should any damage be done to property or other cargo due to the fact that the consignment arrives at a time other than that set aside for the reception of hazardous goods.

Ship categories

The prospective shipper will encounter different categories of vessels; for example the fast mail boat where freight rates are high but, of course, advantages of speed are obtained. Tramp steamers do not follow fixed routes or adhere to regular sailing timetables, but often ply according to the supply and demand for cargo space and take advantage of seasonal variations. The liner, on the other hand, sails regularly on advertised and specific routes and maintains a predictable service with fairly steady freight rates.

Attention will also have to be paid to the fittings and services offered within a particular type of vessel. Ships serving tropical climatic areas are invariably equipped with refrigerating machinery. From the point of view of product, special facilities will often be available to cater for the shipment of fruit, livestock or chilled meat, etc. One of the most obvious of advanced types of specialization is the oil tanker. Now, in addition, there is a rapid expansion in the construction of ships specially designed to carry containers and pallets. Indeed, today there is a very important differentiation between what are known as conventional 'break bulk' services and the employment of various forms of 'unit loads'. The RO/RO ferry for both container and straightforward vehicle transport is, of course, a widely used form of vessel for European and Scandinavian traffic.

Examples of conventional shipments might be:

200 drums of Oxitol Acetate
7 pieces Wooden cases Roughing Rolls

Forms of unitization might be:

Pre-slung cargo loads
Pallets
A TIR trailer roll-on/roll-off (RO/RO)
A standard 20 ft/40 ft container
Lighter Aboard Ship (LASH)

As an appropriate guide, a 20 ft container can cope with around 23 m³ and a weight of approximately 19 tonnes.

During the course of examining sailing lists and studying types of vessels, certain specialized terminology and units of measurement will be encountered. All ships are prefixed with abbreviations related to their methods of propulsion, such as 'ss' for steamship and 'mv' for motor vessel. An exporter may meet a type of classification clause associated with a specific ship. Such a clause will be linked with *Lloyd's Register of Shipping*, which covers thousands of vessels. The aim of such a record is to classify ships according to methods of construction, type of propulsion, navigational aids and the condition of general equipment. Symbols are allocated which indicate various characteristics and the term 'A1 at Lloyd's' has become a popular expression for reliability. These classification clauses can be of considerable importance when the question of marine insurance arises, since the risk cover and premium might at times be related to a particular type of classification.

The 'gross tonnage' referred to in ship terminology is obtained from a measurement, in units of 3 m³, of the number of tonnes enclosed in the total space of the vessel. This can be distinguished from the 'net tonnage' measurements, which excludes from the gross figure such things as spaces used for machinery, stores and crew. 'Under deck tonnage' is the measurement of all parts under the main deck. The net tonnage is a very important figure from the ship-owner's point of view because it is the basis for the payment of a variety of shipping dues and charges.

Types of cargo

Varieties of cargo are also met, the most common being 'general cargo' meaning that the vessel carries a variety of consignments of goods or materials, possibly all packed in different types of container. 'Full cargo' relates to the shipment of a similar commodity by a single merchant, or perhaps a number of merchants. Such cargoes are often found in seasonal commodity trading such as grain, cocoa or cotton. In such cases, these commodities may be packed either in some form of container or carried partly in bulk. 'Bulk cargo' applies to shipments of commodities such as coal or iron stowed loose in the ship's hold.

Conference system

We have considered the background factors encountered when seeking shipping space. We may now identify the considerations on which the exporter bases a selection of a particular ship or shipping line.

The basic choice will be made with reference to freight rates to be charged and services offered. A starting point would be the 'conference system' under which shipping companies operating liner services group themselves into associations known as 'freight conferences'. Such associations will normally consist of a group of shipping lines, all operating within more or less the same geographical area. An example would be the Australian and New Zealand Conferences.

Such conferences will maintain regular services, and fix freight rates and general conditions pertaining to the classification and carrying of cargo. The aim of the system is to achieve stability, assisting both the shipper, by providing a reasonably predictable system of freight rates and sailing schedules, and the ship-owner, by an assurance that there will be a steady flow of cargo available to fill the holds of his vessels between the various ports.

From the exporter's point of view the most important aspect of this system is the offer by the ship-owners of a rebate or some preferential freight rate in exchange for an assurance that the exporter will use only conference line ships. It is usual to identify two basic types of system, namely the 'contract system' and the 'deferred rebate system'. Under the former, the exporter will sign a formal agreement in advance, for a given period of time and will undertake to ship all consignments by conference lines' vessels. In return, there will be granted either an immediate cash discount, which is deducted from the freight account, or the exporter will be given a lower freight rate than that which would be charged to an exporter who was not a signatory to the agreement. The form of agreement may vary somewhat depending on the conference, but generally speaking, most agreements will contain a clause which obliges a shipper to pay as liquidated damages a sum equal to the rebate for failing to comply with the agreement by not confining the shipments to conference vessels. As a general rule, discounts given under this system will be in the region of 9.5 per cent.

Under the deferred system, no such formal advance agreement is undertaken. Instead, a shipper who has confined shipments to conference vessels for a stated period of time, completes and lodges a claim at the end of the period, usually some three or six months. The benefit is generally about 10 per cent of the net freight paid and is normally payable at the end of a further time period. Naturally there is something of a compromise between an immediate saving of money to an exporter under the contract system on the one hand, and the fact that, under the deferred system, a certain amount of the exporter's capital is tied up. This has to be related to the varying degree of flexibility of choice of ships that exists in the relation to the two systems.

The particular tariff conditions issued by conference associations must be carefully studied by the shipper as they lay down precise details of freight charges and classification of goods, etc., together with packing requirements and regulations for special cargo. An example is given below of an extract from such tariff conditions.

Where shippers are signatories to the UK Memorandum of Agreement or the XYZ Conference Outward General Cargo Agreement, rates of freight are net without rebate. For shipments made under rebate terms, 10 per cent is added to the freight, with the exception of livestock. With these exceptions a deferred rebate equivalent to the 10 per cent added to the net freight is returned on all shipments made under the terms of the Conference Rebate Declaration. Claims for rebates are made to the lines in two six-monthly periods from 1 January to 30 June and 1 July to 31 December each year, and rebates are payable six months after the end of the rebate period in which a shipment was made. Claims should be made to each line separately and appropriate per cent in full will be paid as interest on the amount of the rebate due.

Note that with regard to this type of condition there is a differentiation between general and other types of cargo, in this instance, livestock. It will be seen that there is also provision in this particular example for an interest payment on the deferred rebate that is eventually given. Also, in this case, both the contract and deferred systems are offered.

Conference terms

The exporter will now have made a fundamental decision as to the employment or otherwise of conference lines. From this point onwards there will be the checking with the appropriate shipping companies the actual freight rates offered for a particular export consignment, and at this stage comparing the advantages and disadvantages of possible charter party arrangements. For large and bulky consignments, charter party rates could in many cases offer considerable advantages to the shipper and therefore comparison between charter and tariff rates would be a worthwhile task. There is also much more scope for shopping around as, depending on the season and demand for shipping space, bargain freight costs are often possible. Chartered rates tend to show greater elasticity and can fluctuate from high rates when shipping tonnage is scarce to lower rates during idle tonnage periods.

Charter party agreements

As will be seen, the average exporter will be concerned mainly with normal tariff shipping companies, shipping goods under a bill of lading which is largely governed by statutory law, binding the shipper and ship-owner together in the contract of affreightment. Charter party agreements are more often governed by the rules of Common Law. We can generally distinguish three main classes of chartering agreement:

1 *Voyage* An agreement for the carriage of goods from one specific port to another, the ship-owner receiving freight for

cargo carried. The freight rate will be a part of the agreement in the terms of charter.

2 *Time* A contract whereby the vessel is actually hired for an agreed period of time and during this period the charterer usually has a considerable degree of freedom as to how the vessel is employed.

3 *Demise* In this case the ownership to all intents and purposes changes hands for the period of the contract.

Charter parties can be complicated but generally speaking the core of the agreement, and one which usually has to be defined very accurately when fixing a charter, revolve around the following points:

1 The ship-owner making the vessel available at the correct place at the agreed time and the vessel being in a seaworthy condition.

2 Correct agreement on the part of the charterer to provide the specific amount of cargo and the calculation of the appropriate freight rate.

3 Careful definition of time allowed for loading and unloading, these periods being known as 'lay days'. Also, an agreement for the payment of demurrage on days in excess of the lay days.

4 Whether the agreement covers a specific commodity and excludes all else or whether there is a more comprehensive range of cargo that can be carried.

The charter can be used in the sense of simply hiring a portion of the vessel, in which case an undertaking is usually made by the shipper to provide a certain quantity of cargo. This might bring into effect the concept of dead-freight, being the difference between the actual freight for the cargo shipped and the total freight originally agreed upon.

There are now certain complications in international shipping which may play a part in limiting the actual choice of vessel selection by an exporter. In the first place, of course, there are the terms of the contract. Strictly speaking as we have seen, in the case of an FOB contract the choice of selection and port of shipment would really be that of the overseas buyer, unless otherwise agreed.

Two other factors may have to be considered: first, that a GATT agreement laying down what is known as the '80/20 rule' will place limitations upon the amount of shipping space that can be operated by a shipping company between countries outside the nationality of that company. This could have the effect of giving national shipping lines a greater share of the shipping capacity to and from their own country.

Secondly, the exporter needs to be aware when considering selection of ships, that some markets lay down precise regulations to the effect that the importers of that country have to specify and ensure that their own flag vessels are utilized. In some cases where the appropriate flag services are not available certificates of exemption can be issued allowing the exporters to make their own selection. These latter types of requirement change a good deal from time to time and reference should always be made to the appropriate information sources. Croner's reference books and *Lloyd's Loading Lists* and *Supplements* are of particular importance in this connection.

Freight rates

A proportion of exporters in their everyday practice will be concerned with shipments and freight under the normal bill of lading. We will therefore now consider the question of types of freight rate and the methods of calculation which will be of interest to the shipper when contacting companies to arrange the shipment.

Three basic freight rates will be encountered, namely:

1 Weight
2 Measurement
3 Ad valorem (based on percentage of the value) – usually applicable to very high value producers
4 Box rates – tendency to charge a flat all-in rate for a full container or truck load

In practice, most shipping companies calculate freight rates on a weight or measurement basis, 1000 kg = 1 metric tonne, 1 m^3 e.g. $87.00 per tonne w/m (weight/measurement) ship's option. This usually means that the ship-owner has the option of charging the freight rate either on the overall measurement of the cargo or on the overall weight, whichever is the *higher*. A large proportion of freight rates are based upon volume for most types of general cargoes. It should be borne in mind that in many cases the actual freight rate will depend upon and vary with the *type* of commodity.

Therefore, shipping freight rates will at times be based upon certain tariff classifications. Freight All Kinds rates (FAK) would be rates irrespective of nature of commodity.

Freight calculations

Some specimen calculations are shown in Appendix A.

Nowadays, the exporter must be very careful when obtaining freight rates to allow for any freight surcharges that may be in operation. These surcharges are to meet unexpected variable costs and expenses that shipping companies may encounter due to circumstances beyond their control. Delays in discharging or loading cargo in certain ports, can lead to the levying of congestion surcharges. These charges should be carefully budgeted for because they can represent very high percentage additions on top of the basic freight rate.

Similarly, movements of exchange rates will sometimes lead to the inclusion of currency surcharges. Many shipping companies will base their freight rate quotations against a particular currency unit, say the American dollar, and apply this as a ratio when charging freight to shippers in other currency.

The term 'primage' is sometimes seen on freight accounts, generally being in the neighbourhood of 10 per cent. Originally this used to be a separate item added to cover special attention paid to the cargo by the master and was a common surcharge as far back as the eighteenth century. Nowadays, where met, this is usually the sum that is deducted for conference rebate, as mentioned earlier in this chapter.

Measurement of cargoes

It will be clear from our consideration of freight rates that a very important part of the shipping manager's responsibilities is that of packing and bundling consignments in order to achieve an optimum balance of cubic capacity against weight. Also for giving to the ship-owner or loading broker the specification of the cargo which will include weights and measurements ultimately to be used for the purpose of freight calculation. Care should be taken to observe the measurement requirements which are laid down by ship-owners. Usually they provide guidance as to how capacity or weight should be calculated with particular reference to rounding up of small dimensions. There are generally accepted methods in shipping circles as shown by 'case cube measurement'. A typical 'rounding off' stipulation would be as follows: 'Where parts of a centimetre occur, such as below 0.5 cm, these are to be ignored. Those parts over 0.5cm and over are to be rounded off to the centimetre above.'

Shippers should also check to see if any special allowances in freight rates are available from the ship-owner for the use of approved pallets or containers. It should also be borne in mind that often different freight rates will be quoted for various categories of cargo, e.g. machinery, bulk grain or bulk chemicals, etc.; this will have bearing upon freight tariff classifications as mentioned earlier.

When it comes to the actual payment of freight by the exporter, there may be several alternative methods operating in practice. Strictly speaking, from a legal standpoint, freight is not really earned by the ship-owner until the goods have arrived at the port of destination and ready to be delivered to the consignee. However, this rule is invariably qualified by the terms of the contract of affreightment set out in the various clauses on the bill of lading.

Payment of freight

It is usual for most shipping lines to require payment of freight by the shipper before the bills of lading are made available. The exporter, therefore, should be prepared to receive the freight account from the shipping company first. Much depends upon the size and continuity of the exporter's business and quite often the freight account will be sent to the shipper accompanied by the bills of lading with a note indicating that the freight must be paid, say within fourteen days.

Sometimes it is considered worthwhile for a shipper to provide a bond to the shipping line as surety in order to save time and trouble in paying each freight account separately. When employing a shipping and forwarding agent, it is usual for the agent to take care of the freight payment and send the bills of lading to the shipper, accompanied by the freight account, plus the agent's own charges.

Many export contracts require that the cargo should be shipped on a 'freight forward' basis and therefore freight becomes payable at destination by the consignee. In such cases the bills are often claused:

Freight payable at destination, ship and/or cargo lost or not lost.

Equally, it is common to find that some form of surcharge is made for collection of freight abroad. A typical example of such a charge would be as follows:

Freight 4 m³ @ £27.00 per m³	£108.00
Additional for collection abroad @ 2.5%	2.70
Disbursements 50p + 5%	0.53
Total freight charge	£111.23

The normal type of freight forward plussage is 2.5 per cent.

Whether the exporter or consignee actually holds the bill of lading, the ship-owner will always possess a lien on the cargo for any unpaid freight, etc. charges. Normally, to satisfy the lien on general goods they must be held for 90 days before being disposed of. Perishable goods obviously come in a different category as they may often have to be sold almost immediately.

The proceeds of such a sale will usually be disposed of as follows:

1 Settlement of freight.
2 Payment of any custom duties.
3 Payment of warehousing charges.
4 Settlement of any landing costs or dock dues.
5 Any expenses connected with the sale.

It is possible that bills of lading may contain clauses which permit the lien to be of a 'general' nature. This would mean that the carrier could exercise the lien on goods belonging to the trader other than those which actually incurred the charges:

● *Back freight*: a charge for the return of a cargo which has not been accepted at the port of destination. If a consignee should refuse to take delivery and freight has not been paid, we have seen that a carrier can exercise a lien, but might return the goods to the shipper; the amount of freight covering the return voyage would be known as 'back freight'. This category might also be applicable where goods have been overstowed or carried beyond the destination because of incorrect marking by the shipper.

- *Dead freight:* payment for space booked but not used.
- *Lump sum freight:* the agreed amount of freight charges for the shipment of goods which are not based on quantity. The freight is payable irrespective of the amount of cargo delivered. The ship-owner can claim freight from the shipper of the goods, the consignee or endorsee of the bill of lading, a seller who stops the goods in transit, or, of course, the charterer in the case of charter party agreement.
- *Minimum freight:* the charging of a minimum sum of freight irrespective of the actual weight or dimensions of the consignment.
- *Pro-rata freight:* in certain circumstances this would be a proportion of the freight paid in relation to the part of the voyage accomplished or to the part of the cargo delivered.
- *Groupage or consolidation rates:* here the shipper may receive a beneficial freight rate on the basis of the fact that the cargo is going to be grouped with those of other exporters to make up a block of freight for which the freight forwarder can in a sense receive a quantity discount.
- *FCL and LCL freight rates:* FCL would represent a freight rate based upon the fact that a Full Container Load of freight is being provided, as opposed to a Less than Container Load (LCL) where only a part cargo is being shipped.

Bill of lading and port procedure

So far we have considered the selection of an appropriate vessel or shipping line, the methods of procuring space and the various aspect of freight rates and calculations. The next stage will involve the exporter in the preparation of bills of lading and the actual forwarding of the consignment to the docks with a consideration of some of the documents and procedures involved in this process.

A preliminary outline of the various stages would follow the undermentioned sequence:

1 It has already been seen that some form of shipping instructions will need to be produced by the exporter for the forwarder/carrier and this will involve, amongst other things, detailing what sort of shipping documents (such as bill of lading) how many copies, etc., and all the necessary details to enable their completion.

2 When the consignment is actually forwarded to the docks, it

will be accompanied by a 'shipping note'. This will give details of the consignment and usually one copy will serve as a receipt. Nowadays most ports have fairly standard types of forms for this purpose: in the UK the standard shipping note is used and as this is based on the SITPRO layout it has an international connotation (see Figure 6.3).

3 When the goods/containers arrive at the docks, there is a tallying procedure, usually computerized, whereby the loading of the items is linked to the checking against bills of lading and the compilation of a ship's manifest; this also enables the preparation of freight accounts.

4 Sometimes at this stage, a 'mate's receipt' may be obtained by the exporter. This is, in a sense, a preliminary form of receipt given before the bills of lading become available and which, if issued, must be returned to the shipping company by the exporter in exchange for the actual bill of lading.

5 At this final stage, therefore, the bills of lading are signed on behalf of the master and made available to the shipper against payment of the freight account. A copy of the bill, known as the 'master's copy' goes with the ship to the destination port. The exporter will then make available the bill of lading to the customer, who will present this at the destination port and receive in exchange a delivery order in order to obtain the goods. The mode of actually transmitting bills of lading to the importer will very largely depend upon the method of payment being used. In Chapter 9 it will be seen that such documents as bills of lading might be presented against letters of credit or sent through banks with bills of exchange, etc.

6 The above sequences are essentially based upon fairly conventional types of shipment but the growth of container ports and ICDs (inland clearance depots) can impose a sequential difference so there has to be a degree of flexibility of interpretation.

Many of the processes outlined above would be taken care of by a shipping and forwarding agent. Nevertheless, a practitioner would still want to understand the various stages of operation in order to provide the agent with accurate instructions. The whole process is a vital one and it is unfortunate that delays in obtaining bills of lading are all too frequent. Accurate completion of bills, careful recording of measurements, marks and specifications and clear instructions will all help to improve the position. This will be achieved by a more professional approach by exporters and

© SITPRO 1991

STANDARD SHIPPING NOTE – FOR NON-DANGEROUS GOODS ONLY

IMPORTANT
USE THE
DANGEROUS
GOODS NOTE
IF THE
GOODS ARE
CLASSIFIED AS
DANGEROUS
ACCORDING TO
APPLICABLE
REGULATIONS
SEE BOX 10A

Exporter | 1

Customs reference/status | 2

Booking number | 3 | Exporter's reference | 4

Forwarder's reference | 5

| 6

Freight forwarder | 7

International carrier | 8

For use of receiving authority only

Other UK transport details (e.g. ICD, terminal, vehicle bkg. ref, receiving dates) | 9

The Company preparing this note declares that, to the best of their belief, the goods have been accurately described, their quantities, weights and measurements are correct and at the time of despatch they were in good order and condition, that the goods are not classified as dangerous in any UK, IMO, ADR, RID or IATA/ICAO regulation applicable to the intended modes of transport. | 10A

Vessel/flight no. and date | Port/airport of loading | 10

Port/airport of discharge | Destination | 11

TO THE RECEIVING AUTHORITY - Please receive for shipment the goods described below subject to your published regulations and conditions (including those as to liability).

Shipping marks | Number and kind of packages; description of goods; non-hazardous special stowage requirements | 12 | Gross wt (kg) of goods | 13A | Cube (m³) of goods | 14

FORMECON SERVICES LIMITED
SITPRO Approved Licensee No. 21

For use of shipping company only | Total gross weight of goods | Total cube of goods

PREFIX and container/trailer number(s) | 16 | Seal number(s) | 16A | Container/trailer size(s) and type(s) | 1.B | Tare wt (kg) as marked on CSC late | 16C | Total of boxes 13A and 16C | 16D

DOCK/TERMINAL RECEIPT   Received the above number of packages/containers/trailers in apparent good order and condition unless stated hereon
RECEIVING AUTHORITY REMARKS

Name of company preparing this note | 17

Haulier's Name

Vehicle reg. no.

Date

DRIVER'S SIGNATURE | SIGNATURE AND DATE

(Indicate name and telephone number of contact)

630   Non-completion of any boxes is a subject for resolution by the contracting parties

Standard Shipping Notes and Dangerous Goods Notes
obtainable from Formecon Services Ltd. 0270-500800   SSN   J 094/009

Figure 6.3   Standard shipping note

co-operation and understanding between shipping and forwarding agents, shipping lines and banks.

Characteristics of the bill of lading

A bill of lading can be considered under three headings, namely:

1 *Evidence of contract of affreightment.*
2 *A receipt for goods shipped*, and providing certain details as to the quantity and condition when placed on board.
3 *A document of title*, without which delivery of the goods cannot normally be obtained.

All three features are important to the exporter but from a practical point of view 3, which relates to the way the bill of lading can convey ownership of the goods, is probably the most important as this will have a crucial bearing on the way the documentary process is linked with methods of payment.

The background of the contract of affreightment in the UK is the Carriage of Goods by Sea Act 1971. This Act and further developments stemmed internationally from the Hague Rules which, at the International Convention in 1924, were recommended for submission to the governments of the major maritime nations for adoption and enactment into the law of their respective countries. Amendments and developments have led to the Hague–Visby Rules which, however, have been ratified by only a limited number of states. It is important to remember, therefore, that speaking internationally bills of lading with variations in the underlying contractual background may be encountered. On the back of a bill of lading will be found the *Clause Paramount* which will indicate if the particular Act is applicable. Also on the back will be found a number of clauses clarifying further the relationship between shipper and ship-owner. Broadly speaking, they cover such aspects as payment of freight, handling, stowage and general average provisions, etc.

As our primary concern is the actual completion and use of the bill of lading, we will consider the completion of the necessary details on a specimen such as that shown in Figure 6.4.

The factors which will determine the way the exporter completes the bill of lading will be determined by the following:

1 Any regulations in force in country of destination.
2 Requirements of customer.
3 Method of payment.

Shipper			B. L No
		Shipper s Ref	
		F / Agent s Ref	

شركة الملاحة العربية المتحدة (ش.م.ع)

UNITED ARAB SHIPPING COMPANY (S.A.G.)

Shuweikh,
P.O. Box 3636, Safat
KUWAIT

Consignee (If Order state Notify Party)

Notify Party (ONLY if not stated above otherwise leave blank)

*Local vessel	*From (place of acceptance or local port of loading)
Ocean vessel	Port of loading
Port of discharge	*Final destination (if on carriage)

Marks and Nos / Container Nos	Number and kind of packages description of goods	Gross Weight	Measurement

ABOVE PARTICULARS DECLARED BY SHIPPER

Freight details charges etc

Shipped either on board the local vessel named above or (if no local vessel be named) on board the ocean vessel at the port of loading thereof (or where this is a through transit bill of lading to which clause 3 (b) overleaf applies RECEIVED at the place of acceptance) in apparent good order and condition (unless otherwise stated herein) the goods above specified for carriage subject to the exceptions limitations conditions and liberties hereof to the port of discharge or final destination (as the case may be) and there to be delivered in like order and condition to the consignee or his or their assigns

The Tariff Conditions of the relevant Conference are (except insofar as they may be inconsistent with the terms and conditions set out herein) deemed to be incorporated in this Bill of Lading. A copy of the said conditions is obtainable from the Carriers.

IN WITNESS whereof the Master or Agent of the ocean vessel has signed the number of Bills of Lading stated above all of this tenor and date one of which being accomplished the others shall stand void

Number of Pieces or Packages (in words)

Ocean Freight Payable at	Place and date of Issue

Number of Original Bs/L	Signature

For the MASTER

SEE CLAUSES OVERLEAF   Rev 10/80   Printed in England by Rockliff Brothers Ltd , 2 Rumford Street, Liverpool 2

Figure 6.4   Standard bill of lading

4   Any regulations in force in exporter's country.

First of all, when beginning the completion of the bill of lading, the number of copies will have to be decided upon. Bills are issued in 'sets', a set consisting of a given number of originals with copies. The point to remember is that each original is by itself valid until one is presented to the ship-owner for the goods. A clause on the bill of lading will clarify this point as follows:

in witness whereof the agent on behalf of the master of the vessel in which the goods have been or are intended to be loaded and of the several carriers on the route severally and not jointly has signed the number of bills stated above, one of which being accomplished the others shall stand void. One of the bills of lading duly endorsed must be given up to exchange for the goods or delivery order.

Therefore, when completing the bill of lading, if we insert in the appropriate space, for example: 'Number of original Bs/L = 3', then the shipping company will sign and return three. The number of unsigned non-negotiable copies will depend upon our own internal record system or on what our customer has requested. To avoid confusion, some shipping lines issue original bills in one colour and copies in another. Some stamp bills 'Original' and others 'Non-Negotiable Copy'. The essential difference apart from this is, of course, the fact that only originals can be given in exchange for the goods. If in a particular transaction, the exporter is making the handing over of the goods dependent upon a method of payment (a documentary bill of exchange, for example), then all the originals must go through the banking mechanism and they alone go to the customer when payment has been received by the prescribed method. Although procedure varies somewhat between individuals, we generally find in shipping and forwarding agent circles that the terminology '3/3' would, for example, mean three original bills of lading and three copies. In banking practice, however, the tendency would be to interpret this as three originals of a set of three; in other words, '2/3' would mean two originals only out of the set.

The use of the different copies of the bills mean that some can be despatched by air and some by sea in order to minimize the chance of loss. If applicable, an original can always be sent with the carrying vessel in the 'ship's bag' and made available at the port of destination. Although there is no actual limit to the number of original bills of lading the ships will sign, it is most common to have two or three. No more than four originals are normally required.

Extensive use can be made of courier services today and one might quote the case of United Kingdom/West African Lines, UKWAL who with, say, a 10/11 day sailing period to Nigeria can have the bills of lading transmitted and in Apapa in about five days. Remember, however, all questions of the way in which bills of lading are distributed will in most cases depend upon the methods of payment being employed. The whole concept, however, must be kept firmly in mind as if the goods are arriving at overseas ports ahead of documents and the importer is kept waiting because of delays in bills of lading, then warehousing and demurrage charges will be incurred.

Negotiability of the bill of lading

Mention has already been made of the fact that the bill of lading can function as a document of title, and the manner in which it is completed will determine what is called the *degree of negotiability*. A glance at the bill will show that there are the following entries to be completed:

Shipper:
Consignee:
Notify party:

Against 'Shipper' enter the exporter's name. Let us assume an exporter is named K Contracts Ltd and the customer is Weston Carbons. The bill of lading is completed as follows:

Shipper: K Contracts Ltd
Consignee: Weston Carbons
Notify party: International Forwarding Agents Ltd

In this example, the exporter has made the bill of lading out directly to Weston Carbons. The shipping company has been requested to notify the forwarding agents at the destination port, i.e. International Forwarding Agents Ltd. In this case the bill can go to the customer without any endorsement by the exporter. Weston Carbons, upon receiving the document, could either present themselves to the shipping company for delivery of the goods, or, as would be more likely, endorse it (i.e. stamp their name on the back of the bill with their signature) and pass it to their agents (International Forwarding Agents Ltd) who would then arrange to obtain the cargo.

It will be seen that in this case the only party who can negotiate the bills of lading is Weston Carbons or the party to whom they endorse the bills. Assuming that the handing over of the bills of lading was not conditional upon some form of payment, i.e. through a bank, this method would be simple and would mean that such a bill could be sent forward direct to Weston Carbons without having to come back to the exporter for endorsement. This method is most suitable for countries where the bill of lading can be sent to the customer in the ship's bag, or an agent sends it direct by airmail. Delays often result when it is necessary to send it back to the exporter for signature. Speed is essential for exporting to Europe when often the vessel may arrive at the destination port in less than 36 hours. Consider another method:

Shipper: K Contracts Ltd
Consignee: To order
Notify party: Weston Carbons

In this case, for the bill of lading to made negotiable, it will have to be endorsed by K Contracts Ltd, the exporter. This will entail stamping the name of the company on the back of the bill of lading together with an appropriate signature. Weston Carbons would be notified by the shipping company and they would make the necessary arrangements. As will be seen in Chapter 9, where methods of payment are considered, this type of negotiability is suitable where the documents are being tendered against documentary bills or credit and where it is necessary for the shipping documents to be used as a form of security. This would be an example of 'ordering blank endorsed'.

Another possibility is for the bill of lading to be made out perhaps to a third party such as a bank. This may apply where, for example, Weston Carbons have received an advance of money and the bank require to have the bills made out to its order to give it some control over the transaction. Thus:

Shipper: K Contracts Ltd
Consignee: To order of Second International Bank Inc.
Notify party: Weston Carbons

Here, the bill would need to be endorsed by the bank before ownership could be transferred. As has already been mentioned, care must be taken to observe any special regulations which might have a bearing on the bill of lading. It will be seen that there are headings for 'pre-carriage' and 'final destination' and these will depend on the services offered by the particular shipping line in question. There is now a growing tendency for shipping lines to become more and more involved in arranging inland collection, shipment and delivery to final overseas destination. This is naturally very much the case when container traffic is being operated. In such instances, we meet a 'through bill of lading'. We might postulate the case of an exporter in Birmingham shipping from London to Hamburg for final delivery to a customer in Hannover. In such cases the exporter would fill in the bill as follows:

Pre-carriage by: Appropriate Shipping Company
From: Birmingham
Port of Loading Terminal: London
Port of Discharge Terminal: Hamburg
Final Destination (if on-carriage): Hannover

Care should be taken always to check whether appropriate services are offered by the shipping line; the terms of sale must also be borne in mind. If the contract was in fact CIF Hamburg, then any on-carriage arrangements should be cleared with the customer. On the other hand, if it were DDP Hannover, then the inland freight component part should have been included in the export's price.

When considering the marks and numbers entry of the bill of lading, accuracy is essential. As the bill of lading is the receipt for the goods, speedy identification between the document and the consignment is vital. Equally, an accurate description of the contents, and type and method of packing is required because the whole basis of the contract of affreightment will rest upon complete disclosure of the type and nature of the consignment which the ship-owner is undertaking to carry. As we have already seen the weights and dimensions should be completed in the correct units of measurement.

We also have to distinguish those cases where there are prescribed requirements for certain data to be included in the bills of lading in addition to the normal routing information. Chile, for example, requires the insertion of a Deposit Receipt No. or Registration Certificate No. on bills of lading. These numbers would obviously apply to the importer's currency and import regulations and therefore the exporter would need to ensure that the information had initially been obtained from the buyer. Many countries allow bills of lading to be made out 'to order' but require that the ultimate consignee's number be always shown.

Letters of credit are usually fairly precise as to the number of bills and the information to be contained thereon and these requirements must of course be scrupulously observed. The experienced practitioner will also know from experience that certain data, although not mandatory, can often assist the importer in obtaining a smooth trouble-free customs clearance, and details such as import licence numbers may often be included in the bill of lading data. Other cases might arise where goods are shipped under aid schemes or medical emergencies and special reference numbers are needed.

Types of bill of lading

It has been stressed that one of the characteristics of a bill of lading is its ability to serve as a receipt, and it is of some importance to consider what type of receipt this in fact represents. The kind of bill of lading which is normally required in commerce and, in fact, is specifically called for in most CIF contracts, is the 'shipped bill', sometimes known as an 'on board bill', and usually described in letters of credit as 'shipped in board'. The appropriate clause is shown on the bill and a typical one would be:

> *Shipped* in apparent good order and condition by the vessel first named above.

Thus, the issuing of a shipped bill is an acknowledgement by the ship-owner that the goods are in fact loaded on the vessel.

This can be contrasted with the 'received for shipment' type of bill which might be claused:

> *Received* for shipment at the place of receipt the goods mentioned above in apparent good order and condition.

In this case the ship-owner is merely confirming that the goods have been delivered into custody and might, for example, be stored in a warehouse under control. The 'received' bill is therefore of a lower order than the 'shipped' type. Nowadays, container lines, who undertake a considerable amount of inland collections, may not actually issue a shipped bill at the time of collection. Therefore the received bill is increasingly becoming acceptable. The ship-owner can always arrange later to clause a bill of lading indicating that shipment has been made. A number of shipping lines are now operating bills of lading with both 'shipped' and 'received' clauses in evidence and the appropriate deletion can be made when signature takes place.

Shipping companies always reserve the right to clause the face of a bill of lading giving rise to a 'dirty' or 'claused bill'. Again, this could prove detrimental to the exporter in the case of some contracts, especially if some stringent methods of payment such as a letter of credit was involved because, in the main, a 'clean, shipped on board' bill is in most cases the type that is essential. Some typical examples of clauses would be:

- Second-hand drums,
- Insufficient packing,
- Carried on deck without liability for loss or damage, however caused, or
- One case short, but if found on board to be delivered.

Such clauses could be of importance in the event of insurance claims so it is incumbent upon the exporter to ensure that there is a complete understanding with the ship-owner pertaining to descriptions and packing, particularly when employing a new type of packing material which might be perfectly sound but with which the ship-owner is unfamiliar.

As explained earlier, speed is essential in conveying the bill of lading, and therefore the ownership of the goods, to the customer; late arrival of bills is a serious inconvenience. It is often possible that the ship-owner will agree to release the goods without a bill of lading, against the issue of a guaranty for issuance of carriers certificate, and delivery of cargo without surrender of properly-endorsed negotiable bill of lading. The guaranty, countersigned by a bank and produced by either the importer or exporter, is to the effect that the bill of lading will be produced when available and that the shipping company will not be held responsible in any way for releasing the consignment without production of the original bill of lading.

In the case of bills being lost or destroyed, a similar procedure can be adopted, but usually when it is known that the bill has in fact been lost, the exporter can obtain a duplicate set of documents against indemnity. An undertaking will sometimes be necessary by the exporter to accept the charges for any cable or telex messages to the port of discharge.

Stale bills of lading

Sometimes, owing to delay, bills of lading which may be required for negotiation against letters of credit may not be received in time for them to reach the customer before the ship and cargo arrives at the port of discharge. The bank in question, noting the date on the bill and comparing this with the length of voyage, may fear that as the goods will arrive before the bill, some time may elapse before the consignee can clear at customs and obtain delivery. Consequently, warehousing and dock charges may be accumulating and we have already seen that the ship-owner can exercise a lien on the goods for these expenses. Such bills are therefore described as 'stale' and can be extremely troublesome where short sea voyages are involved. Hence the indemnity procedure which is often resorted to as outlined above. It will be seen later, when considering letters of credit, that this often leads to the insertion of 'presentation dates'.

Groupage bills

Sometimes a forwarding agent will consolidate a number of consign-ments from different exporters on one bill of lading in order to simplify shipment, save charges and avoid minimum freight or obtain preferential rates. In such cases only one bill of lading is in existence and each individual exporter cannot, therefore, obtain a separate bill of lading. 'Certificates of shipment' are issued, or sometimes agents issue bills of lading known as 'shipping and forwarding agent's' bills or 'house' bills. It should be stressed that strictly speaking these documents are not sufficient to satisfy a CIF contract and sometimes lead to difficulties with letters of credit. Again, the progress in transportation methods and growing use of containers, together with increasing efficiency on the part of shipping agents consolidating consignments, are bringing about a greater degree of acceptance of shipping certificates and house bills. Mention was made earlier in this chapter of FITA and their bills are normally recognized world-wide and acceptable by banks as fully negotiable documents.

Short form bills of lading

Basically, as the name implies, the short form of bill is an abbrevi-ated type of document, smaller, and not containing the long list of detailed clauses that generally appear on bills of lading. In certain circumstances it may not, therefore, be considered a suitable form of evidence of contract or affreightment. Letters of credit and contracts of sale should always be checked carefully to see if there is any mention that short form bills will not be accepted so that the necessary type of bill of lading can be obtained from the shipping line. Based upon a United Nations Recommendation both the General Council of British Shipping (GCBS) and SITPRO have developed the use of what is known as the 'common short form bill of lading' and this has largely overcome the reluctance that has in the past been shown to the use of this type of document. Unlike the more standard 'long form' or previous 'short form' types, the common short form bill does not bear individual shipping line logos. These can be inserted by the exporter or freight forwarder and their omission at this stage simplifies stockholding. It is now generally accepted that the bill retains the three essential characteristics of the more conventional bill of lading as mentioned on page 115.

Sea waybill

Because of the speeding up of transportation and therefore shorter voyage periods, use is now being made of this species of document shown in Figure 6.5. It serves as a receipt for goods and evidence of contract of carriage but does not act as a document of title. Because of this the consignee does not usually need to possess this document in order to obtain the goods on their arrival. The importer may well be able to be provided with a complete set of other documents such as invoices, certificates of origin, etc., thus being able to arrange clearance much sooner than if negotiable bills of lading were awaited.

It must be stressed that this whole question of transfer of title will hinge upon the attitude of the exporter towards security of payment. It will be seen in Chapter 10 that the new banking rules in ICC Brochure No. 500 have broadened their approach to the spectrum of transport documents acceptable against letters of credit. Similarly mention will also be made in this chapter of a Midland Bank/SITPRO survey which examined the administration of letter of credit and discrepancies encountered during their administration. Amongst the various reasons for rejection by banks of documents, one section devoted to bills of lading listed the under-mentioned problems:

Discrepancies in bills of lading	*% of total admin errors*
Absence of full set	1.3
Absence of 'on board' notation	0.7
Bills of lading requiring endorsement	0.7
Claused/dirty bills of lading	0.8
Goods consigned to wrong party	1.5
Port of shipment/discharges incorrect	1.0
Others	4.9
Sub-total	10.9

Figure 6.5 Non-negotiable sea waybill

The above will give some idea of the importance of the exporter's awareness of the details of the various aspects of bills of lading as it can be seen that errors in this field can lead to 10.9 per cent of all rejections of credit due to incorrect documentation.

Ship-owner's liability

The original Carriage of Goods by Sea Act 1924 basically limited the ship-owner's liability.

In 1968 there took place a reform of the rules relating to bills of lading by means of the Hague–Visby Rules. The amendments to the original Hague Rules proposed by the Brussels Protocol were enacted in the UK by the Carriage of Goods by Sea Act 1971. Included in this Act was the provision for the ship-owner's liability to be increased to £401 approximately per package or unit. This figure was related to the gold franc so that in the course of time changes in various currency equivalents could be encountered.

Shipping note

The standard shipping note developed by SITPRO replaces many different kinds of existing shipping notes by a standard form, for use when delivering export cargo to the receiving authority at any British port, container base or other freight terminal. Stocks are available either in gummed sets for completion by ball-point pen or typewriter, or loose, for use in spirit duplicating, xerographic or offset litho machines. The forms may also be produced on to blank Baron self-copy paper by means of xerographic or other plain copiers, using a film overlay – in this case, the second, third, fourth and fifth sheets of the set should be coloured or marked pink, yellow, blue and green respectively.

The distribution of the standard six-part set is normally as follows:

retained by docks or terminal
returned by ocean carrier as a
   'received for shipment' return
HM Customs
truck driver as receipt
ocean carrier as 'shipped on board' return
retained by shipper as administrative copy

Figure 6.3 shows a standard form which should always be completed carefully. Attention is drawn to some of the box numbers as follows:

Box 2   Very important, as here we would expect to see references to such items as the ECI number or reference to pre-entry, etc., in other words, linking the shipment with the particular customs procedures involved (see Chapter 4).

Box 3   For some destinations the process of booking shipping space may involve registration and the obtaining of a number. If this is the case, it is most important that it should be quoted as goods may be shut out if arriving without details of the registration.

Box 8   Name of shipping line, container or combined transport operator.

Box 9   A reminder that there may be a facility available at the port of terminal for àrranging appointments for the delivery lorry, and therefore there may be a booking reference number required.

Box 10A   Very important because it indicates that this form can only be utilized for non-hazardous cargo as otherwise the Dangerous Goods Note (DGN) should be employed. This contains much the same information but in addition certifies the nature of the hazard and indicates, where applicable, the IMO (International Maritime Organisation) Hazard Class UN No., etc. The form is printed in red with bold, diagonal striped edging.

The note must be lodged *either* with the vehicle at the receiving point or at the receiving authority's designated office *before* arrival of the goods, according to local port practice. Only goods for shipment to one port of discharge on one sailing and sometimes relating to only one bill of lading, may be grouped on one shipping note.

Port practices

It will have been seen in Chapter 5 on distribution that there are various patterns and structures of ports and container depots both in the UK and overseas. There will always to some extent be the possibility of variations in practice and procedures. The development of such documents as the SITPRO standard shipping note and DGN, etc., have brought about a greater degree of standardization internationally in port/shipping operations.

Containers

A brief consideration of the above will show that the mechanics of the container process will influence considerably the question of the nature of the bill of lading encountered in container shipments. Emphasis will be placed by container operators on the concept of a 'through delivered' service in order to extract the maximum benefits from container operations. Therefore, the exporter will encounter more frequently:

1 groupage bills of lading,
2 through bills and lading, and
3 'received for shipment' bills of lading.

Operators often consolidate several exporter's cargoes into one container which will be shipped under a main bill of lading. The individual shippers will receive either *certificates of shipment* or *house bills of lading*. Container operators are more likely to arrange to collect shipper's cargoes in order to enable them to control the whole process. They will therefore handle the 'pre-carriage' and often final inland delivery to overseas customers. This will frequently enable the exporter to receive 'all-in' freight quotations which will be a tremendous boon, and enable delivered prices to be quoted with more accuracy and precision than in previous cases when often an exporter would have to build up the costing on the basis of several prices covering inland transport, dock charges, handling, loading and unloading, ocean freight and charges involved in the overseas country. The more orthodox type of shipment would have often meant that some four or five separate organizations might have been involved in a shipment, with all the associated difficulty of obtaining from each one a particular cost quotation.

As to the bill of lading itself, the exporter will have to consider the nature of the receipt to be obtained from a container operator and the type of negotiability of the bill of lading with its resultant title of ownership and acceptability by the banking system when documentary bills or credits are involved and where the bill may perhaps, on occasions, be presented as security for an advance or for discounting of bills of exchange.

As in many cases, containers will be loaded at exporter's premises or at an ICD, the operator will provide the equivalent of a 'received for shipment' bill of lading. This is understandable, because, at this stage, as actual 'shipped on board' bill is just not a possibility.

When presented as security for an advance, such documents will be evaluated with due regard to all the relevant circumstances in the same way as any document presented as collateral.

The banks emphasize that the use of containers implies that some goods inevitably will be carried 'on deck' and that suitable and adequate insurance must be arranged.

The *Uniform Customs and Practice for Documentary Credits*, ICC Brochure 500 has introduced fresh articles which provide much wider scope for the utilization an acceptance of these more 'anticipatory documents' as they are obviously now in very wide usage.

The question of the liability of the ship-owner in terms of value per package or unit has already been discussed and the definition of such units when shipping by container can be important. If, for example, a liability figure was applied to a whole container load as a 'unit', there would be some concern both for exporters and insurance regarding the level of recourse against a ship-owner.

The amendments to the Hague Rules have as their main objectives the readjustments of liability limitation in order to counteract monetary depreciation since 1924 and also the adaptation of the rules to suit the new transportation techniques such as containerization and other methods of unitization of cargo. A container clause has been developed to cover consolidated goods when containers, pallets or similar articles are used. The number of packages or units enumerated in a bill of lading as packed in the container will form the basis for calculation of liability. For example, if a bill of lading indicated 2000 cartons of whisky loading into Container No. 2356, then the carton would be the basic unit for liability. There is also provision for a weight limitation of liability to cover general merchandise which cannot be expressed clearly in units or cases.

It is felt in may quarters that the importance attributed to the level of liability on the part of the ship-owner is somewhat exaggerated as, in any case, freight rates are adjusted to cover such liabilities and in practice there often results a certain amount of double insurance.

Another expression increasingly encountered with container traffic is that of the twenty-foot equivalent unit, TEU. This is employed as a unit of measurement equivalent to one twenty-foot shipping container. It would follow that two TEUs could be equal to a forty-foot container, etc. This can be used to express the container capacity of a ship and the number of containers carried on a particular voyage or over a period of time. It could also be expressed as a unit for freight calculation.

Container insurance

The other important aspect is, of course, the application of insurance to container consignment. Much has been written about this and there are a number of different viewpoints as to how insurance cover and the resultant policies and premiums are affected. Experiments with combined insurance certificates and bills of lading have so far not succeeded because the adoption of such cover might mean the companies with advantageous premiums owing to their sheer size and business might find themselves faced with higher insurance costs which might result from container companies issuing their own insurance cover. Nevertheless, there is very little doubt that further developments will solve this type of problem and that such combined documents will eventually be developed.

There are a number of special factors which will influence the outlook of insurance companies with regard to container risk cover. For example, it represents a 'concentration of risk' and it is possible that certain types of damage such as sea or rainwater might take place and not be detected at all throughout the voyage, whereas such damage might be easily noticed in an orthodox consignment of a number of separate wooden cases. Such damage, in a container, might slowly and steadily affect the entire contents of a container. Insurance companies also point out that a container is like a miniature hold of a vessel and needs specialized personnel to handle packing, loading and stowage. This may not always be possible, for example when, as in some instances, exporters load containers themselves.

There is also the vital question of on-deck stowage. It is calculated that the payload of a container ship consists of approximately 40 per cent of deck stowage. In many cases, where computerized documentation is being employed, it is not possible for the container operator to indicate on bills of lading that particular containers are either below or above deck. This might well mean that insurance premiums have to be averaged out to cover the possibility of on-deck risk exposure. Close attention is being paid to these problems by the container committee of the International Union of Marine Insurance (IUMI).

The other international body deeply concerned is the Comité Maritime International (CMI) and the aim of the April 1969 Convention (known as 'the Tokyo Rules') was to lay down a framework for the provision of a suitable combined transport document giving a satisfactory document of title which will enable each combined transport operator to work efficiently and at the same time provide suitable receipts and title for the exporter.

The need for inter-modal transportation backed by a suitable CTO (Combined Transport) document has led to the formulation of a set of provisions and rules for the satisfactory operation of such a document. These rules have found expression in Brochure 298 of the International Chamber of Commerce entitled *Uniform Rules for a Combined Transport Document*. Such a document should be a great step forward for CTOs (Combined Transport Operators) who provide start-to-finish delivery services.

Air freight

We can envisage much of the mechanics of shipping as being applicable to air freight except that obviously the overall tempo is much faster. The Carriage of Goods by Air Acts, 1932, 1961 and 1962, based upon the Warsaw Convention Rules, provide the background legal framework establishing the relationship of the trader to air carrier. The Acts set out basic definitions, regulate the documents relating to air carriage, and establish the liability of the carrier.

Most exporters will employ forwarding agents and the latter's activity in the sphere of consolidating cargoes to obtain better freight rates is of great importance due to the need to minimize the comparatively high freight costs of air transport. In the field of aircraft charter there is a growing number of brokers in the Baltic Exchange who specialize in this work and they collectively form the Airbroker's Association. Because of the speed of transportation, air forwarding agents will often offer many services including, in many cases, delivery of goods to the ultimate consignee on COD basis.

Air freight rates

The exporter can keep in touch with the various scheduled airline flights to all parts of the world by referring to such publications as *Cargo by Air*, a supplement to *Lloyd's Loading List*. This can, of course, be supplemented in greater details by the schedules and other information issued by the airlines themselves. The various permutations of air freight rates can be a little more complex than sea freight and be summed up briefly in the following categories:

Freight classification and calculation

Airline rates are based on the kilo. Volume does not normally become a factor until it exceeds the $6m^3/1000kg$ ratio (6 cubic

metres to the tonne). The most common practice encountered in
air freight is to employ the ratio of 6000 cubic cm to a kilo and is
described as a chargeable kilo/volumetric unit; the freight rate is
based upon the highest figure. Thus:

> A consignment weighing 75 kilos and measuring $100 \times 100 \times 60$ cubic cm a freight rate of £8.00 per chargeable kilo/unit.
> Total consignment therefore measures: 600,000 cubic cm divided by 6000 = 100 volumetric units.
> Ratio therefore 75:100. Consequently freight rate of £8.00 multiplied by 100 (the higher of the two figures) = £800.

The shipper of air freight will encounter several different types
of freight classification, such as:

1 General Cargo (GC)
2 Specific Commodity Rates (SCR)
3 Unitized Load Device (ULD)
4 Container Rates
5 Classified Rates
6 Freight All Kinds (FAK)

'Classified rates' represent a percentage discount or surcharge
based upon a general cargo rate and apply normally to specialized and
high cost items such as furs, precious metals and live animals, etc.

'Freight all kinds' represent a more simplified structure where
freight is charged at a set rate per kilo irrespective of the commodity. This was originally based upon the assumption that a shipper
could offer a guaranteed volume of cargo during a twelve-month
period. Many FAK rates are now, however, available without this
contractual stipulation.

Mention has been made of COD deliveries and these are available
for most European destinations. The charge for such consignments
is usually 1 per cent of the COD amount, excluding freight. COD
is not usually accepted where consignments involve onwards carriage by other airlines. Similarly, it cannot be used on UK domestic
routes, and perishable cargo, livestock and newspapers are excluded. 'Charges forward' represent the charging to the consignee
at the point of destination, the cartage, export fees, freight and
insurance premiums.

An exporter would normally commence the air transaction by the
completion of a 'shipper's letter of instruction' which corresponds

basically with a shipping and forwarding agent's instruction form used for sea freight. This would call for information pertaining to:

1 Method of despatch to airport and the party responsible for making arrangements
2 Instructions to prepare or obtain air waybill
3 Consignee's full address
4 Notify party, if applicable
5 No. of packages, type of packing
6 Nature, quantity of goods and markings and numbers
7 Weight and measurement details
8 Value for customs and value for carriage
9 Instructions regarding insurance
10 Details of charges to be paid by shipper
11 Details of charges to be paid by consignee
12 COD details, if applicable
13 Details of any documents attached, e.g. export specifications or documents for customs entry, consular invoices or certificates of origin
14 Instructions in case of non-delivery, e.g. hold and notify shipper or abandon

Preparing the air waybill

The next stage after this is for the air waybill (see Figure 6.6) to be prepared. This document is approximately the equivalent to the sea freight bill of lading inasmuch that it functions as a receipt and evidences a contract of carriage. However, the air waybill is not a negotiable title to goods in the same way as is a sea bill of lading although, of course, it is widely used as a valuable receipt and evidence of despatch and can be utilized within the framework of letters of credit, etc. When the sets of waybills issued by the various airlines are studied, *three originals* can be distinguished. These, however, do not function as a set of bills of lading would to a sea transaction. They would cover the following stages:

IATA Specification
Original No. 1 for issuing carrier
Original No. 2 for consignee
Original No. 3 for shipper

The actual numbering sequence may vary with HAWB (House Air Waybill)

Figure 6.6　Air waybill

Under normal conditions, the exporter would receive No. 3; No. 1 would be retained by the airline and No. 2 would automatically go forward to the consignee to enable the goods to be collected at the destination point. The passing of ownership by a transfer of documents against payment can in consequence follow a different pattern compared with that relating to sea deliveries. Sometimes an exporter might consign the goods and address the air waybill to an overseas bank or agent who can then, in turn, arrange to hand over a delivery order to the importer when appropriate payment is made. On other occasions, a COD method might be possible.

Apart from the above three copies, airlines issue a number of extra sheets for purposes such as the following:

● Delivery receipt
● Airport of destination
● Third carrier (if applicable)
● Second carrier (if applicable)
● First carrier (if applicable)

Normally IATA recommend a set of nine air waybills although most carriers seem to provide ten or twelve which provide extras for local inward clearance and payment of charges, etc.

The details inserted in the air waybill would consist of all the routine description of cargo, etc., and are largely an extension of the particulars mentioned in the letter of instruction. In addition, the following points would be of particular importance to an exporter.

Declared value for carriage

Within the framework of the General Conditions of Carriage, the liability of the carrier is normally restricted to approximately £16.00 per kilo (this is only a very approximate figure and will vary over time with gold and currency rates), or to the value which might be declared by the exporter on the air waybill. In the event of a higher figure being inserted, a valuation charge would be made by the air carrier. The insertion of the letters 'NVD' (No Value Declared) in this particular section would indicate that the normal carrier liability would prevail and no valuation charge would be incurred. The latter case is most likely to be encountered in practice as shippers will normally cover through their own insurance operations. There can sometimes be problems when shipping very high-value cargoes and an insurance premium may be based on the assumption that a shipper is, in fact, inserting value declarations thus increasing the carrier's liability cover.

As in cases of sea shipment where groupage/consolidation services are utilized, the agents arranging despatch may issue House Air Waybills (HAWB) in place of the normal airline Master Air Waybill (MAWB).

Rate class

Various code numbers applying to certain aspects such as the particular freight rate being applied, e.g. SC, GC, FAK, etc. would usually be encountered.

Restricted articles

The IATA lays down certain regulations for articles of a dangerous or hazardous nature and there exists a Restricted Cargo List which defines the commodity, gives it Class Code Group classification and prescribes packing and suitable labelling. The exporter must indicate on the air waybill the relevant particulars as per the list and provide a certificate. Such a certificate is on a printed form not unlike the shipping note but with a bold red diagonally-striped border.

Rail systems

The exporter to Europe is served by a constantly-growing rail system. This provides a variety of services enabling the exporter to send goods to Europe. In many cases, through deliveries can be made. The through railway wagon is an excellent method of transport and British Rail have accumulated a vast amount of experience in handling procedures and documentation and offer some of the simplest methods available by the use of various *consignment notes*.

Normally, a shipper is likely to utilize the railways either simply to convey goods to the docks for subsequent shipment by vessels not operated by BR, or, via one of the systems of rail ferries, to convey the goods to a Continental port or even, at times, to carry the consignment right through to a customer's address.

For sending the goods to the docks for subsequent shipment outside the railway system, it is likely that a BR number, BR 20105, consignment note would be used. This is a very simple form and requires only basic details of cargo, dock to which goods are to go and name of carrying vessel, together with wagon number and specification of consignment. The relationship of the railways to the particular dock in question should always be checked by the exporter as this may affect the manner in which charges are made.

If the goods are being consigned to a Continental port, then for most goods a form of 'Declaration and Consignment Note' should be completed for destinations entailing carriage by water and the passing through customs. Such consignments could be forwarded from the Continental port to the final destination, of course, but for this last segment of the journey the terms and conditions of the particulars in question would apply. Some salient details required by the consignment note would be as follows:

1 Type of service, for example for the Continent:
   - Mail service (express parcels)
   - Grande vitesse (fast goods)
   - Petite vitesse (ordinary goods service)
2 Any document attached, i.e. customs entry, invoices and certificates of origin or export licences, etc., and instructions regarding the issue of bills of lading.
3 Full specification of goods, including accurate trade description and units of quantity.
4 Whether there is any question of duty relief or goods under bond, etc.
5 FOB value.
6 Origin of merchandise.
7 Payment of charges: if BR do not require payment, are charges for sender or consignee?
8 Type of risk cover.

For deliveries right through to a Continental destination, one of the best methods is the use of a CIM (Convention Internationale de Marchandises). This form is known as a 'consignment Note/ Lettre de voiture' or 'Frachtbrief'. Goods so carried are subject to the provisions of the International Convention concerning the Carriage of Goods by Rail 1961. The details of the consignment note are very much as per those covered above.

Sheet 1: Consignment note (to be handed to the consignee when the goods are delivered)

Sheet 2: Invoice (for accountancy purposes and where all charges are shown; retained by the destination railway authority)

Sheet 3: Arrival note (goes forward to, and is retained by destination station)

Sheet 4: Duplicate of consignment note (given to sender after consignment has been accepted)

Sheet 5: Duplicate invoice (retained by forwarding station)

The movement of railway wagons is covered by the TIF (Transports Internationaux par Chemin de Fer) Convention which prescribes a TIF International Customs Declaration to facilitate the crossing of frontiers for goods carried by rail. When shipping to the Continent under a CIM consignment note, it is necessary to utilize a TIF BR Form. Two copies of this declaration are normally required for every Continental country involved in the consignment journey.

TIR road transport

One of the problems facing road transport was of course the complications, in relation to customs examination and possible duty payments, facing a haulier when a vehicle was involved in crossing several frontiers. There were also the problems involved with the actual vehicle, which was sometimes regarded as being exported and then re-imported with all the associated complications and paperwork. To cope with these emerging problems the TIR (Transport International Routier) Convention was formed. This is an international convention established by the Economic Commission for Europe, to which the UK is a party. Other countries in which the convention operates include:

Austria; Belgium; Bulgaria; Czech Republic; Denmark; Federal Republic of Germany; Finland; France; Greece; Hungary; Italy; Liechtenstein; Luxembourg; Netherlands; Norway; Poland; Portugal; Republic of Ireland; Romania; Slovakia; Spain; Sweden; Switzerland; Turkey; United States of America and the former Yugoslavia.

In essence, the purpose of the Convention is to make it possible for goods packed in customs-sealed road vehicles or containers to travel across one or more international frontiers with the minimum of customs formalities. This avoids the examination of goods at each frontier post and means that the carrier does not have either to pay duty or give security for these payments. The operation of this procedure hinges upon three main requirements:

1   That prior approval has been received for road vehicles or containers which have to fulfil certain requirements laid down by the Convention.
2   That a TIR carnet is used as the basic documentation.

3 That this carnet is issued by an approved association and that adequate control of this document is undertaken.

Prior approval of vehicles or containers

Application has to be made to the appropriate licensing authority for examination. Such approval will depend upon a number of factors, for example:

1 That customs seals can be easily and effectively used.
2 That goods cannot be removed from, or introduced into, the sealed part of the vehicle without obvious damage or breaking of seals.
3 That possibility of concealed areas where goods may be hidden exists.

After inspection and approval, the carrier will receive a GV 60 or certificate of approval which is usually valid for two years. There is also the 'certificate of type approval' which is given to a manufacturer covering a particular design which enables the operator to affix a metal plate to the vehicle approving the design. Plates measuring 250 × 400 mm showing in white the letters 'TIR' on a blue background must be fitted to the front and rear of the vehicle in question. Three photographs of the vehicle – front, rear and one side – should be carried to assist the customs authorities in their control. Great care must be taken by the carrier that all vehicles are maintained up to the TIR standard and that no damage or modification takes place that might adversely affect this compliance.

TIR carnet issued by approved association

Application may then be made to some approved guaranteeing association such as the RHA (Road Haulage Association Ltd) for admission to the scheme and for the necessary carnet. Various types of carnets are available, e.g. a six-volet (voucher) or a 14-volet type. A pair of vouchers is necessary for the country of departure, the country of destination and each country traversed. The main component parts of the carnet consist of:

1 Guaranteeing association (the RHA) and the international organization to which it is affiliated, in this case the IRU (Union Internationale des Transports Routiers)
2 Declaration and undertaking by the carrier to abide by all the necessary regulations and requirements

 3 Goods manifest
 4 Details of carnet, e.g. offices of departure; vehicle certificate number and date
 5 Stipulated itinerary; seals and identification marks
 6 Detachable vouchers

The validity period (two months from date of issue) will also be shown.

The carnet obtained from the RHA will include a loose-leaf form which can be used as a schedule of the movements and whereabouts of a carnet. This form has the following headings for completion:

Carnet No.	Volet
Expiry date	Date issued
Sent to	Destination
Trailer/vehicle No.	Job No.
Returned from	Date returned

Plus a space for any other explanatory notes

Great care has to be taken with the handling and use of the TIR carnet as loss of this document or infringements can result in suspension from the scheme or the need for an exporter to stand indemnity for any violation of customs authority which might result from the loss.

Damage to the vehicle due to accidents or any other emergency must be reported to customs or police who may be called upon to fill in a declaration or carnet. Otherwise, the carrier will be liable for duty, etc. payments which may become due as a result of seals or canvas being broken or torn, or if the TIR regulations are in any other way infringed.

The carnet itself is printed in French but additional pages may be inserted giving a translation in the language of the country of issue. Translation may also be required by countries en route.

Another form of document encountered is the ATA Carnet, essentially designed to cover temporary admission into and out of a country and possibly involved in transit across other territories, rather along the lines of the TIR system discussed above. This carnet, however, mainly caters for taking goods abroad for exhibition, demonstration and other business reasons and then bringing them back into the country of origin. It is obtained from and administered by appropriate Chambers of Commerce for a fee and guarantee charge. The carnet is made up of a number of coloured vouchers, white, yellow and blue and the various pages are stamped and one is eventually returned to the Chamber of Commerce for clearance. A large number of countries recognize this procedure under an International Convention Admission Temporaire – Carnets.

Obviously, the main purpose is to avoid the complications at customs and possible tax or duty payment and consequently it is no longer of any great importance in single market operations.

Standardized international road consignment note

The IRU (International Road Transport Union) have developed a consignment note satisfying the requirements of the CMR (Convention de Marchandises par Route). This can be obtained from the RHA and is normally issued in English, French and German with some other translations being available, and acts as a waybill.

There are four main parts to a CMR consignment note set, namely:

1 for consignor
2 for consignee
3 for carrier
4 copy

In addition, there are some six other copies which may be used for such purposes as internal accounting and record keeping. Altogether there are some 31 items for completion covering such data as names of consignor/consignee, specification of goods, metric volume, by whom charges are made payable, currency special requirements, etc. Items 1–12 inclusive are completed by the consignor. The consignee's signature for receipt is obtained on the carrier's copy.

It will be seen in Chapter 7 the development of the EU and the single market can in many ways influence transit operations. For say, road operations within and around the Community, there will really be no need for example for TIR documentation. Nevertheless, it must be borne in mind that the above-mentioned waybills and consignments will still be needed as they establish a relationship between seller, carrier and purchaser.

Postal services

For many exporters the use of parcel post for their exports can be of considerable advantage, as a very efficient system of overseas parcel post exists covering a wide variety of markets. Essentially, it should be borne in mind that goods sent by parcel post are liable to customs examination at point of destination or any appropriate payment of duty, etc. Reference should be made to the current *Post Office Guide* to obtain all the applicable regulations such as the maximum weight, types of items that cannot be sent, for example hazardous or dangerous goods, etc. Reference should also be made to the particular destination in order to ascertain what appropriate documentation is required.

It is likely that the following types of documentation will be encountered:

1 An adhesive form to be affixed to the parcel.
2 An alternative tie-on version of the above for small parcels or where it is not practicable to use an adhesive form.
3 A non-adhesive form of which one or more copies may be required.

Reference should be made to the regulations governing the particular market, in order to see which specific category is involved. For certain letter-post dutiable items a 'green label' system is operated.

The value and nett contents should be shown on the above documents, together with all other relevant information which will facilitate customs clearance. Equally, any certificates of origin should accompany the parcel, if necessary, and this should be stated on the customs declaration under the list of contents. To some countries services such as 'Franc de Droits' (Free of Charges) exist whereby delivery may be made to a customer free of customs and other charges. This system is indicated by the initials 'FDD'. Such parcels as a rule must be posted at a head or branch office and the sender must pay a deposit on account and undertake to remit any balance on demand. Many of the organizations involved in parcel and post despatch have developed their own specialized documentation. Fig. 6.7 shows a typical Parcel Force combined set of documentation clearly showing the permutation of customs declarations, despatch notes, etc. Provision is made for FDD or COD services.

It has been the task of this chapter to examine some of the main

Figure 6.7 Parcel Force combined set of documents

categories of transport documentation and procedure in addition to the more orthodox bill of lading/title of ownership transactions. It is in this former category that the greatest changes have occurred particularly in relation to container and road transport. The task has been for UK commercial practice to adjust the transfer of ownership and payment methods to suit the new form of through delivered/combined transport operator type of consignment. A very encouraging factor is that great strides have been made by the various international institutions and organizations, coupled with real progress towards standardization of documents and procedure, particularly in road and rail transport, and showing great potentialities when applied to international trade.

7 *International trading areas*

One of the most interesting aspects of international trade today is the growth and rapidly changing patterns of trading groups and areas. Most countries today, particularly with the re-orientation of many of the hitherto centrally planned economies are anxious to expand trade with each other. This has led to a process of two kinds. Firstly, bilateral agreements whereby two countries negotiate tariff and trade agreements usually leading to reduction in duties and the creation of either FTAs (Free Trade Agreements) i.e. removing tariffs or PTAs (Preferential Trade Agreements), whereby any duty adjustments may be selective and proportional. Secondly, and most important today, is the formation of groups of countries for trade and even political and social harmonization. Examples can be seen with the LAFTA (Latin American Free Trade Agreements), the USA/Canada and of course, the very advanced example of the EU/single market.

This is, of course, a highly specialized subject by itself but essentially the concern in this chapter is to identify the way the various agreements and arrangements impinge upon trade practice, movement of goods, and very often resultant patterns of documentation and procedure. In order to administer trade relationships with each other, countries usually have to formulate certain requirements and rules of origin and call for the provision of information and values, etc., to be provided. Often this results in special invoices, certificates of origin and movement certificates which will be considered more carefully later in this chapter.

An initial distinction must be made between:

Figure 7.1　Bilateral agreement

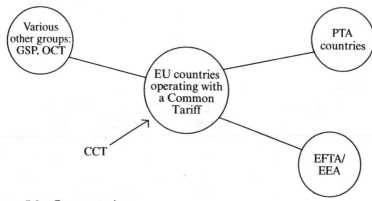

Figure 7.2　Customs union

1 **The bilateral agreement**

This is where two countries will enter into a tariff agreement between themselves but each remain free to maintain their own duties to the rest of the world (Figure 7.1). In this case, each country normally formulates underlying rules of origin and requires certificates or statements to this effect. This will be necessary to avoid any deflection of trade. Negotiations and arrangements known as MFNs (Most Favoured Nation Agreements) attempt to widen and smooth out such relationships between countries.

2 **The customs union**

A more advanced development whereby a number of countries collectively adjust and harmonize their tariff with the rest of the world and create a common market. Obviously the EU is a classic example and we see the grouping together of a number of countries within a Common Customs Tariff (CCT), Figure 7.2.

The situation becomes even more complex when the trading

groups then enter into relationships with other countries and gradually a network of trading agreements emerges. Into this picture comes the United Nations Institution, GATT, (General Agreement on Tariffs and Trades) which periodically brings about international discussions aimed at reducing both tariff and non-tariff obstacles to trade. The latest Uruguayan Round has resulted in a massive boost to world trade. We have also seen the recent development of the new WTO (World Trade Organisation) designed to regulate global trade.

The growth and development of the European Community (EU, European Union), has naturally had considerable impact upon international trade and has brought about a series of re-alignments of relationships between many countries. Taking the UK for example, not only is there the dimension of operating between the Community but also the second dimension of that Community's relationship between other trading groups and individual countries.

The Community at present consists of the following full member countries:

Austria	Holland
Belgium	Italy
Denmark	Luxembourg
Eire	Portugal
Finland	Spain
France	Sweden
Germany	UK
Greece	

Turkey is an example of an Associate Member.

Some of the more important administrative developments of the Community can be categorized under the following headings:

1 *Transport*. Procedures both within and sometimes outside the EC.
2 A whole series of *regulations and directives* which face the exporter depending upon the type of product and markets.
3 The series of *trade agreements* concluded between the EEC and other countries and trading groups resulting in preferential and free trade agreements.

Most companies in the Community are concerned to a greater or lesser extent either directly or indirectly with the following:

1 The Common Customs Tariff (CCT), see Chapter 4.
2 Moves towards certain areas of political and social harmonization, e.g. labour policy, transport policy, etc.
3 Free Circulation Common Agricultural Policy (CAP) with levy and subsidy systems, etc.
4 The adoption of rules of competition which will have a bearing on marketing and distribution policy and structure.
5 A relationship between EU/UK and other trading groups and areas such as the old EFTA (European Free Trade Association) system, Commonwealth preference and GSP (General System of Preference) areas, and a number of specially-negotiated relationships with other countries such as, for example, the Mediterranean area. EFTA countries such as Austria, Finland and Sweden, etc., have now moved into a membership with the EU, and for countries such as Switzerland and Norway there is the EEA (European Economic Area). Similarly Central and Eastern European countries such as Poland, Hungary and Romania are entering into PTAs and seeking ever closer association with the Community. From 1995 Latvia, Estonia and Lithuania are moving from the GSP into a closer PTA relationship with the EU.

It will be seen, therefore, that the above five headings considerably influence the activities within a company's export department. The export sales function now has to keep abreast with tariff matters and their impact upon cost and pricing strategy. The many complex and individual arrangements between 'third countries' need to be studied, together with new definitions of origin criteria. The shipping and transport specialists need to familiarize themselves with new procedures, etc. As always, the company will be in many cases employing outside specialists, such as forwarding agents and other transport operators.

Background of the EU

It is not proposed to go deeply into the origins, history and institutions of the Common Market since much has already been written and published on this subject. However, one thing that must be established at this point is the basic terminology because the reader will no doubt have noticed over the past few pages a somewhat confusing usage of words – EEC, EU, Community, etc. First of all it should be borne in mind that basically there were three communities, namely the EEC, the lesser-known ECSC (European Coal and Steel Community) and Euratom (European Atomic Energy Community). The terms EEC, Common Market, Community became commonly used expressions. At an intergovernmental conference in 1985, the Foreign Ministers of the member states finalized their Agreement on the Single European Act ratified by governments in the following year. By this Act the Community set itself a target of creating a truly 'European' Union with a market free of internal frontiers by the end of 1992. This proceeded really in two stages, the first in 1988 when a major simplification of customs procedures was undertaken, with the introduction of the Single Administrative Document and a drastic reduction in the need for the then existing T2 and T2L forms, followed by the formulation of the Single Market in 1993 and the ratification of the Maastricht Treaty, and so we now have the generally accepted term: the European Union (EU). Figure 7.3 shows the relationship between the institutions of the EU.

Criteria governing trading areas

In Chapter 4, we examined some of the control mechanisms needed by customs authorities to administer and monitor exports and imports. So far in this chapter we have noted the growth and development of agreements between countries, the emergence of trading groups and some implications of the resultant relationships. It is necessary now to focus on the criteria involved, and in Chapter 8 the sequence can be completed by an examination of some of the actual procedures and documents that ensue.

1 Duties and taxes
2 Quota systems
3 Any political implications
4 Preferential schemes (PTAs)
5 Free Trade Agreements (FTAs)
6 Common or Single Market situations

It is important to bear in mind that we are essentially limiting our examination to the normal movement of goods, both imports and exports, and must remember that all Customs authorities throughout the world have other formidable demands upon them in the administration of immigration and the control and policing of drugs, smuggling, arms and ammunition, etc.

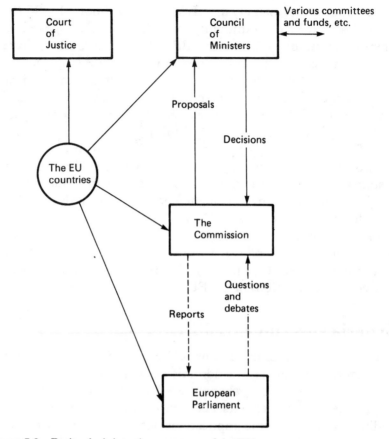

Figure 7.3   Basic administrative structure of the EU

Duties and Taxes

In a straightforward situation where a country is levying an import duty we find the following types of duties and taxes:

Ad valorem: Normally levied as a percentage upon the monetary value of the consignment. In which case there will be a particular method of valuation, e.g. the CIF value or in some cases the FOB (as, for example, with New Zealand). The question may arise regarding the inclusion or otherwise of packing costs, royalties and commissions, etc. Normally these calculations will be based upon a straightforward contract price but in the case of say, inter-company dealing, the authorities may seek some other criteria such as an 'open market value', etc. There may be variations of the standard duty rates such as Anti-Dumping

(ADD, or Countervailing Duties) where it is felt that imports are coming at prices below those charged domestically in the country of export. The Tariff No./Commodity Codes will be employed to link appropriate duty rates.

Specific duties: For various reasons it might be the case where the actual duty assessed is based not upon the value as above, but on a specific unit of measurement such as a kilo or a pair, etc. A case may be encountered of a composite nature where the two methods are combined.

Taxes: In many countries, apart from actual tariff duties, various sales, VAT or special excise duties such as on alcohol or tobacco may be encountered. Care has to be taken because there can be such a wide variety of rates and differing methods of computation. Most of these will be encountered at the point of importation so care must be taken when linking the responsibilities to the various contract and delivery terms such as CIF, DDU and DDP, etc.

Quota systems

As part of regulating international trade, most countries at times will operate quota systems and impose certain value and/or quantitative limits on particular product categories, which can be operated usually within certain periods of time. Sometimes where some form of imbalance is feared, there might be voluntary quota systems; for example, Japan may undertake to limit export of automobiles or electronics to certain countries. Tariff quotas may be encountered which allow certain quantities of a commodity to enter at different rates of import duty. In such cases as these, the various customs authorities will issue TQ details of the various types of quantities and values involved.

Political implications

There will always be the possibility of countries being obliged to impose sanctions or discriminate against what might be considered unfriendly powers, although happily, with the growing number of peace initiatives the position has and will continue to improve a good deal.

PTA/FTA relationships

The existence of trading relationships has been considered and the following can be seen as a few examples encountered, for instance, with some of the EU agreements:

1 *Association Agreements*, such as with Turkey dating from 1963 and envisaging eventual full membership.

2 *Preferential Trade Agreements (PTAs)* concluded, or in process of being concluded, between the EC and certain Mediterranean countries (e.g. Egypt, Cyprus) and Africa, Caribbean and Pacific (ACP) countries (e.g. the Bahamas, Nigeria and Tonga).

3 *Free Trade Agreements (FTAs)* Now merging into the European Economic Area (EEA), cover trade between the EC and all individual members of EFTA/EEA. The agreements will allow free trade in the great majority of industrial products covered by Tariff Chapters 25 to 99 from the HM Customs Tariff. This relationship is now mainly found with countries such as Norway and Switzerland.

4 *Generalized System of Preference (GSP)* covers certain developing countries belonging to the UNCTAD Group of 77, and allows many goods from these countries into the EC either duty free or at reduced rates.

The above relationships, resulting from preferential and free trade agreements, have to be based on some fairly precise rules of origin in order to enable products to qualify for favourable treatment and at the same time to avoid 'deflection of trade' – that is to say, where products might simply be shipped via a third country to obtain a tariff concession to which they might not be entitled. Basically, running like a thread through most of the trade agreements, the following criteria can be detected:

1 Whether or not the products in question do actually originate, or are wholly produced, in the country in question, (EC Regulation 802/68 sets out the definitions of originating products);

2 The concept of 'sufficient transformation' which is based on tariff heading, i.e. a finished product from a number of imported items has a different tariff heading compared with the imported items;

3 The satisfying of some value-added percentage or qualifying process.

The above criteria can be checked against various publications as for example HM Customs and Excise Notices 827/828/829. It should also be borne in mind that the expanding relationships within the EU and the European Economic Area (EEA) absorbing most of the old EFTA promises a growing simplification of origin rules.

Single Market situations

Obviously a number of countries operating a common or single market situation aim at simplifying the movement of goods between countries belonging to the group. A concrete situation can be considered with the European Community where the concept of Free Circulations has been formulated. Community status can be considered as:

Status: Whether the goods qualify for a nil duty position within the community which will mean that they must be goods originating wholly in the community, or any imported items from outside the EU which have paid all appropriate (if any) import duties. Care must be taken that there is no conflict, for example, with claiming any duty drawback, etc.

Free circulation: If the above requirements have been met, then goods can be expected to enter the community country in question free of duty.

Transit: Basically, the nature of the possible movement of goods over a number of frontiers or customs posts within the EU area. Now a very limited requirement.

The above degrees of status initially received as a series of designations, prefixed 'T' originally manifesting in a series of 'T' Forms and then in 1988 largely being absorbed by the SAD Form (see Chapter 4). The most important designations were:

T1 Goods not in free circulation and therefore subject to an import duty upon entering a community country.
T2 Goods in free circulation and not subject to a community duty.
T5 A designation relating to some special control requirement such as CAP.

There may still be situations with trade with Portugal or Spain where the designation T2 PT/T2/ES are encountered.

Since the advent of the Single Market in 1993, some 85–90 per cent of transactions within the Community need no formal entry processing at the customs points, and indeed it is customary to no

Value Added Tax Return
For the period
to

HM Customs
and Exclse

For Official Use

Registration number

Period

You could be liable to a financial penalty
if your completed return and all the VAT
payable are not received by the due date.

Due date:

For
official
use
D O R
only

Before you fill in this form please read the notes on the back and the VAT leaflet *"Filling in your VAT return"*. Fill in all boxes clearly
in ink, and write 'none' where necessary. Don't put a dash or leave any box blank. If there are no pence write "00" in the pence column.
Do **not** enter more than one amount in any box.

For official use		£	p
VAT due in this period on **sales** and other outputs	**1**		
VAT due in this period on **acquisitions** from other **EC Member States**	**2**		
Total VAT due **(the sum of boxes 1 and 2)**	**3**		
VAT reclaimed in this period on **purchases** and other inputs (including acquisitions from the EC)	**4**		
Net VAT to be paid to Customs or reclaimed by you (Difference between boxes 3 and 4)	**5**		
Total value of **sales** and all other outputs excluding any VAT. **Include your box 8 figure**	**6**		00
Total value of **purchases** and all other inputs excluding any VAT. **Include your box 9 figure**	**7**		00
Total value of all **supplies** of goods and related services, excluding any VAT, to other EC Member States	**8**		00
Total value of all **acquisitions** of goods and related services, excluding any VAT, from other EC Member States	**9**		00
Retail schemes. If you have used any of the schemes in the period covered by this return, enter the relevant letter(s) in this box.			

If you are enclosing
a payment please
tick this box.

DECLARATION: You, or someone on your behalf, must sign below.

I, ... declare that the
(Full name of signatory in BLOCK LETTERS)

information given above is true and complete.

Signature .... Date ....19............
A false declaration can result in prosecution.

CD 2650/N3(04/92)   F 3790(   )

VAT 100

Figure 7.4   VAT return form

INTRA EC TRADE STATISTICS **Supplementary Declaration**

Trader.	VAT No.	Branch ID	Official Use Only
Agent.	VAT No.	Branch ID	

H M Customs and Excise

INTRASTAT

DISPATCHES | Period | No of items

#	1. Commodity code	2. Value £'s Sterling	3. Delivery terms	4. Nature of transaction	5. Net mass (kg)
1	6. Supplementary units	7. Country of destination	8. Mode of transport	10. No. of consignments	11. Trader's reference
2	1. Commodity code	2. Value £'s Sterling	3. Delivery terms	4. Nature of transaction	5. Net mass (kg)
	6. Supplementary units	7. Country of destination	8. Mode of transport	10. No. of consignments	11. Trader's reference
3	1. Commodity code	2. Value £'s Sterling	3. Delivery terms	4. Nature of transaction	5. Net mass (kg)
	6. Supplementary units	7. Country of destination	8. Mode of transport	10. No. of consignments	11. Trader's reference
4	1. Commodity code	2. Value £'s Sterling	3. Delivery terms	4. Nature of transaction	5. Net mass (kg)
	6. Supplementary units	7. Country of destination	8. Mode of transport	10. No. of consignments	11. Trader's reference
5	1. Commodity code	2. Value £'s Sterling	3. Delivery terms	4. Nature of transaction	5. Net mass (kg)
	6. Supplementary units	7. Country of destination	8. Mode of transport	10. No. of consignments	11. Trader's reference
6	1. Commodity code	2. Value £'s Sterling	3. Delivery terms	4. Nature of transaction	5. Net mass (kg)
	6. Supplementary units	7. Country of destination	8. Mode of transport	10. No. of consignments	11. Trader's reference
7	1. Commodity code	2. Value £'s Sterling	3. Delivery terms	4. Nature of transaction	5. Net mass (kg)
	6 Supplementary units	7. Country of destination	8. Mode of transport	10. No. of consignments	11. Trader's reference
8	1. Commodity code	2. Value £'s Sterling	3. Delivery terms	4. Nature of transaction	5. Net mass (kg)
	6. Supplementary units	7. Country of destination	8. Mode of transport	10. No. of consignments	11. Trader's reference
9	1. Commodity code	2. Value £'s Sterling	3. Delivery terms	4. Nature of transaction	5. Net mass (kg)
	6. Supplementary units	7. Country of destination	8. Mode of transport	10. No. of consignments	11. Trader's reference

When complete return to:-
HM Customs and Excise, Tariff and Statistical Office,
Sort Section, Portcullis House, 27 Victoria Ave.,
Southend-on-Sea,
Essex, SS2 6AL.
Your declaration must be received by the 10th. working
day after the period end.

Place and date

Name of signatory (in BLOCK LETTERS)

Signature

C1501   CD3380/N4/(11/92)   F6640 (Dec 92)

Figure 7.5 INTRASTAT SSD

longer describe inter-Community trade as exports and imports but rather Dispatches and Arrivals. The actual need for accompanying documentation such as the SAD is now limited to such special cases as where goods move across the community and into say, another country such as Switzerland where transit documentation may be needed and therefore the 'T' designations on the SAD will still be employed. It is likely that in the near future further simplification with the EEA is very possible.

Bearing in mind the above, it will be seen that with regard to inter-Community trade, the various EU customs authorities will not be able to monitor or record the flow of goods at the EPUs but they still need the data such as tariff classification and other relevant statistical information. Since 1993 therefore, new procedures have been introduced. First of all, traders have been called upon to supply with their VAT return the total value of all their supplies and acquisitions of goods to other EC member states. Figure 7.4 illustrates a typical UK quarterly return form and boxes 8 and 9 can be seen to show the appropriate information. In addition, depending upon annual threshold turnover figures which are adjusted from time to time by customs, a monthly Statistical Summary Declaration (SSD) INTRASTAT is required to provide more detailed data of Dispatches and Arrivals. Figure 7.5 shows a typical dispatch SSD and the various boxes indicate the type of information required. A similar form would be utilized for Arrivals.

Having considered the wide spectrum of requirements that must be one way or another observed in order to satisfy the different criteria, we can now turn to the next chapter where examples of the various types of documents and procedures that manifest themselves can be seen.

8

International invoices and certificates of origin

Some of the most important categories of international trade documentation are represented by various types of invoices and certificates of origin. These documents in themselves are often called upon to satisfy a whole range of international trade agreements and import and export customs authority regulations.

Invoices

To any form of trader, the basic commercial invoice is a document of fundamental importance since it fulfils the following functions:

1 It is a supplier's bill for goods and services.
2 It is a detailed list showing unit prices, totals, weights and other specifications, and certain other elements of the total price such as packing and delivery charges.
3 It provides a checklist for the customer and generally enables a particular˙ consignment to be identified against a specific order.
4 On occasions it may be a key document inasmuch as it will be used as evidence of value in, say, an insurance claim. Equally, to a bank, it may prove to be an essential part of the shipping documents which it may be holding as security.
5 Although the invoice, as such, may not be a contract of sale, it can in certain instances act as evidence of the contract.

Invoices for duty payment purposes

So far, the above data is of general application to all invoices, whether employed in normal domestic trading or in international business transactions. It is when we consider *export invoices* that we realize the very wide variety of the types that may be encountered, and also the different requirements that they might be called upon to fulfil. In the first place, the overseas buyer will invariably need a supplier's invoice to present to the customs authority. This will, in fact, be a key document because the value and description shown on the invoice may provide the basis for any duty or tax assessment and indeed, the description of the goods on the invoice may play a part in their identifications as to whether they are allowed to be imported or not, i.e. subject to any import licensing. At all times, therefore, the invoice must be made out clearly to enable correct assessment to be made and to enable the importer to obtain speedy customs clearance and take delivery of the goods. One of the key pieces of information that the importer will require, therefore, is the basis upon which the particular overseas market in question assesses import duty. See Chapter 4 for various types of duties and Chapter 7 for the various trading groups.

It would be impossible to attempt an identification and examination of every type of invoice that might be encountered because these are so numerous. Nevertheless, it is hoped that the following comments will enable a practitioner to make an analysis of a given market and to decide upon which principles invoicing should be based.

First of all, when the question of *ad valorem* duty is considered, it is most important to find out the actual value to be assessed; for example, is the *ad valorem* percentage to be levied on the FOB or CIF price? It is probably true to say that in most cases the CIF contract price is chosen as the basis of duty assessment. However, it must be borne in mind that certain variations may be encountered in different markets. If for example, *ad valorem* rates are operating, there may sometimes be questions of royalties, agent's discounts or other component parts of the price structure. Similarly, cost of packing or computation of freight might play a part in determining the ultimate dutiable figure. In the case of *specific* duties the number of units, gross or net weight might all influence duty assessment.

It will be seen, therefore, that considerable thought must be given to the layout and completion of an export invoice. A simplified example is shown in Figure 8.1.

Of course, much more information than that shown would often be needed but essentially this example shows some of the basic elements of the export invoice structure.

Bought of:
Southern Exporters Ltd.,
Winchester, Hants, England

9th August 19...................

EX 7051

Customer:

Invoice No. ....

OY Bemberg AB
PO Box 101
Helsinki 10
Finland

Customer's
Order No. ......571...........

Invoice of ONE CASE CONTAINING ONE HEAVY-DUTY
COMPRESSOR
Shipped per mv 'BALTIC MERCHANT' from London to
Helsinki

Marks:	Description of Goods	£ p	£ p
B.A.B.	ONE WOODEN CASE		2000.00
571	CONTAINING ONE MK		
HELSINKI	11-B COMPRESSOR		
	380V INDUSTRIAL		
Specification:	Charges:		
1.5 × 1.5 ×	Case including packing	25.00	
1.5m	Carriage to docks	14.00	39.00
cu.m. =			
3.375			
Gross wt: 100 kilos	FOB	39.00	2039.00
Net wt: 90 kilos			
	Freight, incl B/L,	50.00	
	etc., charges		
	Marine insurance, incl	15.00	
	policy stamp, etc.		65.00
	CIF Helsinki	65.00	2104.00
		*Finnmarks 15.500.00	

Figure 8.1 Example of an export invoice

Internationally-speaking there has been a steady move towards a degree of harmonization in the methods of valuation for customs purposes based upon the Brussels Convention on the Valuation of Goods for Customs Purposes, known as the 'Brussels Definition of

Value'. Emerging from the 'Tokyo Round' of the GATT Multilateral Trade Negotiations has been a new package of agreements on valuation. This agreement was accepted by the EU and a number of the other more important countries; it is expected to be progressively adopted by most other countries. The new valuation code was accepted by the UK and other Community countries in 1980.

Whereas the Brussels definition of valuation adopted the 'notational' system whereby the criterion is the price the goods would fetch on a sale in specified open market conditions, the later GATT agreement employs a 'positive' system employing a range of specified methods of valuation. The broad classifications of this system are:

Transactive value
Transaction value of identical goods
Value derived from selling price of goods in importing country
Computed value based upon build-up cost

It will be borne in mind that the relationship between buyer and seller may play a part in the choice of valuation method. Sales between associated companies may mean that the actual transactive value, as evidenced by the contract sales invoice, is not applicable; there may be the need for the customs authorities to take into account a comparison of other prices. Similarly, the computation of the price may have reference to any tools, designs or other factors supplied but not included in the actual invoice price.

A vital point to remember is that goods always have some value in the eyes of the importing customs authorities even if they are supplied genuinely free of charge. In such cases it is always wise to indicate on the invoice a value for customs purposes even if no charge is being made to the overseas importer.

Different types of export invoice

So far, the commercial invoice has been considered and emphasis placed upon the information it should contain, with particular stress on duty assessment. It is necessary now to look at all the possible categories of invoice encountered in exporting. These can be considered under the following headings:

1 *Commercial invoice by itself*
2 *Commercial invoices plus some form of declaration* which the exporter is responsible for signing.

3 *Commercial invoice plus declaration* as above but requiring some form of independent verification by, say, a Chamber of Commerce.
4 *Consular invoice* Either the supply of an invoice form by the Consulate/Embassy which is rare nowadays, or much more likely, the stamping, signing and legalization of the seller's own invoice. It should be borne in mind that this process will cost money in fees and may also take a little time to process.
5 *A specific invoice form* which is required by some countries. In a case such as this, the exporter may obtain the requisite invoice form which is laid down by the appropriate authorities.

The reasons behind the various types of invoice set out above can be seen to stem from:

1 The possible need for the invoice actually to contain a signed declaration by the exporter that the invoice is showing the correct price structure and other data.
2 The need at times for some independent verification to ensure that the prices actually shown on the invoices are bona fide, that no attempt is being made to show inaccurate prices to avoid customs duty.
3 Sometimes an invoice is designed to show a comparison between the domestic selling price and the export price. This may very often be conditioned by a country's desire to avoid any form of dumping activities by exporters, or where it wishes to foster and protect infant industries.

Bearing in mind the above classification of the various invoice types and some of the main reasons behind them, some examples can now be considered.

Commercial invoices with declaration

'Sweden does not actually call for a declaration as such, on the invoice, but apart from the normal data it requests the inclusion of the Harmonized Commodity Description and Coding System (HS) and the provision for customs of three copies. Facsimile signatures are accepted.

The signatory would normally be a director, secretary or partner.

When completing declarations such as this, the exporter should be careful to note whether facsimile signatures can be used. In some cases this is so but some countries prohibit facsimiles and require that signatures be original. This point can be of some importance when simplified systems of documentation are being produced by reprographic or computerized systems, or if carbon copies are being utilized. Sometimes coloured inks are required when signing.

An example of an *independently verified declaration* would be the case of Iran which requires that a commercial invoice should show the following types of declaration:

> We hereby certify this invoice to be true and correct and in accordance with our books, also that the goods are of ... origin.
>
> We hereby certify that the prices stated in this invoice are the current export market prices for the merchandise described therein and we accept full responsibility for any inaccuracies or error therein.

Normally, such invoices will need counter-signing by a Chamber of Commerce and sometimes (although rarely), by the Iranian Embassy.

Care may have to be taken on invoices with regard to geographical place names, etc. With Iran no mention should ever be made of the 'Arabian Gulf' but rather 'Persian Gulf'. Obviously, to certain other countries the reverse could be true.

Consular invoices

This type of invoice is distinctly different, being a particular set of forms which have to be purchased from and used in conjunction with the appropriate embassies or consulates. Their use has diminished dramatically over the years and they represent nowadays a rather specialized requirement. An example is given below in order to gain some idea of the type of detail encountered.

Honduras
Five copies, to be completed in Spanish, obtainable at London Consulate at £6.00 per set of five: must show values in US dollars and 8 per cent of total FOB value at the foot of the invoice to facilitate calculation of charge in Honduras; must not be included in CIF value.

To be presented to the Consulate: Legalization fee £12.50.

Letter of correction £12.50.

Immediate legalization may be obtained for additional fee of £12.50.

Consular invoices not required for shipments of a CIF value less than US dollars 25 or for air freight shipments irrespective of value.

The charges shown are for example only and should always be checked.

Specific invoice forms

As has been mentioned, these are usually encountered when some special form of duty preferential system is in operation, or when there is a need to scrutinize very carefully the relationship of the export price to the exporter's current domestic value. Examples of such forms would be the customs invoice called for by Canada (see Figure 8.2). This form was introduced on 1 January 1985, aligned to the UN/ECE (United Nations/European Commissions on Economy) and takes into account the GATT valuation system referred to earlier in this chapter.

Similarly, many countries may require this specific type of form which can be purchased from commercial stationers and used by the exporter. Or, in a large number of cases, it may be possible for the shipper to employ their own basic commercial invoice but to ensure that all the required data is incorporated to satisfy the particular country's customs requirements.

Much progress has been made over recent years towards this growing international standard of invoicing, but care must always be taken to ensure whether ordinary commercial invoices plus specialized data can be used, and if it can, is any prior approval of the invoice format required?

Many of the above-mentioned types of specific invoice incorporate declarations of the origin of the goods and indeed are often referred to collectively as 'Certificates of Value and Origin' (CVO). It is here that SITPRO systems can be of immense benefit since they have developed a wide variety of 'overlay' systems. By this means, specialized invoices can be produced *within* the framework of the exporter's own documentary systems as the overlays can contain the specific text and data required by individual countries (see Chapter 11).

Set out below is a list of the main categories of information that may be required in these types of invoices.

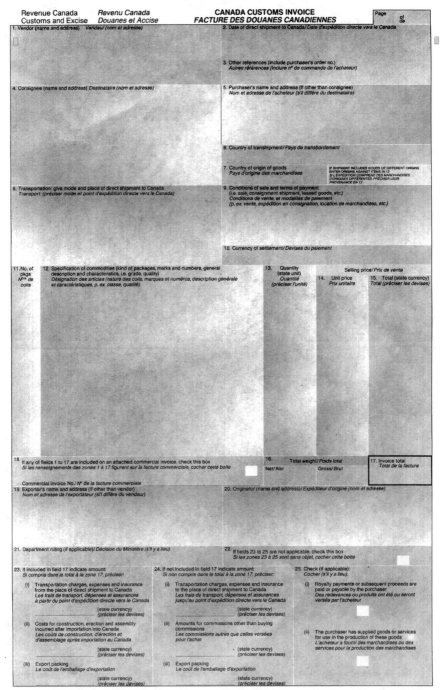

Figure 8.2   Customs invoice (Canada)

1 Importer (name and address)
2 Purchaser – if other than importer (name and address)
3 Vendor (name and address)
4 Exporter – if other than vendor (name and address)
5 Consignee (name and address)
6 Description of the imported goods, including marks and numbers, number and kind of packages and characteristics
7 Quantity
8 Total weight (net and gross)
9 Unit selling price
10 Current domestic value or open market value in exporting country at factory/warehouse/port of shipment and details of any export subsidies or similar benefits received in the exporting country
11 Conditions of sale and terms of payment (i.e. sale, consignment shipment, leased goods, etc). Whether prices are FOB, CIF, duty-paid, etc. Details of discounts and other special arrangements
12 Currency of settlement
13 Place of direct shipment to overseas market
14 Date of direct shipment to overseas market
15 Transportation charges, expenses and insurance to the place of direct shipment
16 Transportation charges, and expenses from the place of direct shipment
17 Insurance costs from the place of direct shipment
18 Amount for packing costs incurred by the buyer

There is a growing tendency also for many international invoices to require the insertion of the appropriate trade classification of the merchandise. The most widely used now is, of course, the HS. Some thought may have to be given to this aspect; there can at times be differences in interpretation of the particular classification heading which could lead to incorrect duty assessment because, it will be remembered, the tariff number is not merely statistical but also indicates a linkage to a given rate of duty. Consequently, there may be the need for some liaison between exporter and importer concerning the correct application of the tariff heading.

Of all areas where it is essential to have accurate reference material, the invoicing sphere is perhaps the most outstanding as requirements change so quickly and are of such vital importance. The following are three major works of reference which, apart from providing much valuable information in many spheres, are of particular value in checking the invoicing requirements of an importing country: Croner's *Reference Book for Exporters*; Tate's *Documentation Guide*, *Formecon Factfinders Sheets*, and National Westminster Bank's Monthly *Exporter's Bulletin*. *Consular Requirements* – a supplement to *Lloyd's Loading List*, is also a useful reference point.

Such works of reference enable constant watch to be kept on a country's documentary requirements and for an accurate profile to be maintained.

In addition to the relationship of the invoice to duty calculation and payment, there will, in many cases, be the question of taxes such as VAT. In the majority of cases in international trade, VAT is levied at destination and therefore the importing authorities will use the supplier's invoices amongst other documents to assess the actual duty due. As far as the supplier is concerned, they will normally be allowed to zero rate their exports and their export invoice copy. Appropriate proof of exportation such as a bill of lading or waybill, etc. will be retained for proof to their tax authorities that VAT is not due.

Since the coming of the Single Market, there has been the need for new thinking on this point by EU customs authorities because, as we have seen, in the vast majority of cases there will be no export and import customs clearance procedures. At the same time, EU VAT is still destination based. In order to enable the control and monitoring of liability and payment of VAT, the following procedures have been introduced for VAT registered traders.

Examples of VAT liability are given below:

1 UK company supplying goods to a German customer and subsequently invoicing:

In order to zero rate the *supply* the invoice must show

(a) The supplier's VAT number
(b) The purchaser's VAT number

    e.g. UK VAT No. GB 975 4219 15
    Germany DE 775149034

It will be noted that the numbers quoted on the invoice are prefixed with the EU country code.

The identifier codes are:

| Austria | AT | Denmark | DK |
| Belgium | BE | Finland | FI |

France	FR	Luxembourg	LU
Germany	DE	Netherlands	NL
Greece	EL	Portugal	PT
Ireland	IE	Spain	ES
Italy	IT	United Kingdom	GB

UK company retains copy of invoice as proof for VAT authorities, preferably together with certificate of shipment or similar document.

It is the responsibility of the German company upon *acquiring* the goods to account for any VAT payment to their authorities.

2 UK company acquires (purchases) goods from a French supplier.

Must provide supplier with the appropriate UK VAT No. prefixed GB and receive from supplier invoice indicating both French and UK VAT numbers.

At the time of arrival in UK at buyer's premises no actual tax payment takes place as there will be no import formality.

UK company is obliged to *account* to customs on their next quarterly VAT return indicating VAT due. In most cases this will be largely a book-keeping transaction as payment will be cancelled out by the input/output procedure. In fact this is almost the equivalent of the Postponed Accounting System (PAS) whereby the trader is actually relieved from any actual payment. This system was at one time employed on UK imports but was largely replaced by the deferred payment scheme. In this case, the importer was called upon to actually pay the VAT but was normally given a month under the operation of the Trader's Unique Reference No. (TURN). Note that this is still the case for imports from countries outside the EU.

3 At the end of each quarter, the UK supplier provides customs authorities with a VAT EC Sales List (ESL) listing sales under the various customers' registration numbers (Figure 8.3).

Whilst on the subject of VAT operations in the UK, it should be mentioned that many quite complex relationships can occur between say, associated companies or those servicing orders in one EU country but drawing from different community supply points.

Figure 8.3　VAT EC sales form

This can lead to cases of 'triangulation' and care must be taken to check with the authorities. Some situations may lead to a company finding it advantageous to register for VAT purposes in several Community countries.

Also, if a trader pays freight accounts to carriers domiciled in the same member state, then VAT will be charged and paid against the invoice. If the carrier employed is not in the same member state, and provided the carrier is given a VAT number, then the tax is not actually charged and paid on the freight account. The trader would instead simply have to account for it by a reverse charge procedure when making the next return.

A point to remember in general regarding VAT rates in the EU, is that they vary considerably. The next intergovernmental conference in 1996 envisages a move towards harmonization of rates and indeed to make VAT (in the case of EU operations) 'origin based'. This will mean that goods in this case will move forward always tax-paid.

Certificates of origin

As has been seen above, some export invoices may in fact require some indication of the actual origin of the goods being shipped. The concept is an important one and it must be confessed that there can often be many uncertainties. There is much virtue in the exporter having a firm grasp as to the particular reasons lying behind the need for a country to insist upon certificates of origin or at least some form of declaration from the exporter when goods are being imported into an overseas market.

First of all let us consider the particular formats in which questions of origin can materialize, namely:

1 A simple statement on the export invoice prepared by the exporter, remember the example given earlier for Iran.
2 Some official form such as the standard type available from Chambers of Commerce (see Figure 8.4).
3 A geographically-specialized standard form such as the Arab British Chamber of Commerce (ABCC).
4 One of the specific type of Certificates of Value and Origin (CVO) referred to above.
5 Although perhaps not strictly comparable, forms such as EUR 1/ 2 which in their own specialized way have a bearing upon origin. The EUR 1 is generally classified as a Movement Certificate.

170 *International Trade Procedures and Management*

1 Consignor	No. FG 482150	ORIGINAL
	EUROPEAN COMMUNITY	
2 Consignee	CERTIFICATE OF ORIGIN	
	3 Country of Origin	
4 Transport details (Optional)	5 Remarks	
6 Item number; marks; numbers; number and kind of packages; description of goods		7 Quantity

8 THE UNDERSIGNED AUTHORITY CERTIFIES THAT THE GOODS DESCRIBED ABOVE ORIGINATE IN THE COUNTRY SHOWN IN BOX 3

CHAMBER OF COMMERCE & INDUSTRY

Place and date of issue; name, signature and stamp of competent authority

Slough

............19

Chamber of Commerce & Industry

DTI/XP 13026

The John Oldham Printing Group, Huddersfield

Figure 8.4   Chamber of Commerce certificate of origin

Another point which may have to be borne in mind is also the possible distinction between 'originated in . . .' and 'manufactured in . . .'.

There is really no basic international definition as such pertaining to origin, although the gradual process of harmonization is constantly taking place. Certainly between trading groups such as EU, FTA, LAFTA, and GATT there must of necessity be a large degree of coalescence of basic understanding and systematization of rules of origin, but as has been said, much depends on the reason behind the need for this information.

Some main reasons are:

1 In order to qualify for some form of preferential treatment regarding the levying of duty.
2 To administer the application of a quota agreement.
3 Backing up a political sanction.
4 To link the purchasing of goods to some form of financial assistance.
5 Statistical purposes.

The degree of importance and precision of the rules will therefore depend to some extent upon the relevance of the above-mentioned reasons.

For the purposes of tariff preference the most widely encountered basic rules can be illustrated by those formulated by a series of EEC directives which can extend origin from either 100 per cent origin in the country concerned, or for goods processed or utilizing components and materials from other outside countries, can nevertheless certify that substantial economically-justified process has in fact been carried out in that exporter's country. In some cases the criteria may be based upon a simple percentage, e.g. 50 per cent or 75 per cent, etc.

On the other hand, if it is a question of political boycott or economic sanctions then the definition of origin may be much more exacting and relate to materials or components that, although substantially processed in the exporting country, may nevertheless be excluded since they contain items obtained from a country which itself is on a 'black-list'.

In the case of say, developing countries which are recipients of financial aid, loans or lines of credit, it is becoming customary in some cases to link that aid to purchases from the donor country and thus bring about the need to identify origin.

With regard to the types of certificates of origin by approved Chambers of Commerce, it is customary for companies to lodge undertakings with their local offices worded along the following lines:

FORMAL UNDERTAKING

To be given by an applicant when first applying for Certificates of Origin or certification of international trade documents and to be renewed whenever the Chamber so requires.

In consideration of the Northern Chamber of Commerce and Industry from time to time granting or certifying Certificates of Origin or other documents I/we hereby agree to accept and be bound by the Standard Rules for the issue of Certificates of Origin, etc., in force at the time of certification, and further that I/we will at all times keep the Chamber and its officials indemnified against any claims or demands whatsoever which may at any time be made against them, or any of them, by reason of any fault, defect, omission or inaccuracy in the content of the Certificates or other documents, or in the manner of their issue, this indemnity being subject to all statutory provisions to the contrary.

Signature: Date:

* (Proprietor, Partner, Director or Secretary)

Name, address and telephone number of Company or Firm:

. . . .
. . . .
. . . .
. . . .

*Delete as appropriate

This is usually backed up by a number of specimen signatures indicating the personnel authorized to sign such certificates. The certificates are then official and a fee normally paid.

Another document is the 'movement certificate'. This certificate has to be completed, verified by the customs authorities and a copy made available to the exporter's customer so that the latter can claim whatever tariff benefits may exist under a particular agreement. An example of such a certificate is the EUR 1 (customs reference C1299, see Figure 8.5), which is used for trade between EU countries and EEA/FTA/PTA areas. The EUR 1 form is also being used in trade with a variety of countries embraced by the preferential trade areas mentioned earlier in Chapter 7. Simpler forms such as the EUR 2 are used for low-value consignments in some cases for postal dispatches. The EUR 1 movement certificate consists of four pages (plus a duplicate sheet for countersignature by Chamber of Commerce if required). The top copy (page 1) is presented to HM Customs for certification and endorsement. It is this copy that must eventually be transmitted by the exporter to the customer. Page 4 represents the exporter's declaration, to the effect that the goods qualify for the particular benefit in question, e.g. wholly produced, sufficient transformation, or satisfying some process or added-value criteria. The tariff heading number should be given. In certain circumstances, the exporter can make special arrangements with HM Customs to use instead a signed prescribed declaration on the invoice to the effect that the goods fulfil the required rules of origin. In this case the exporter must obtain, and show on the declaration, a Customs Authorized Number (CAN).

For those without authorization, an invoice declaration can be used for certain countries for low-value consignments. An example is shown below:

The exporter of the products covered by this document declares that except where otherwise clearly indicated these products are of EEA preferential origin.

Constant reference must be made to the appropriate sources of reference, as for instance, HM Customs publication Notices Nos. 827/828 in order to keep abreast with changing requirements and values as this is a pretty dynamic area of procedure. Also, it may be borne in mind that relationships are in a state of flux on account of the movement towards closer union of, for example, the EEA.

As will have been seen in Chapter 7, the need for the EUR 1 for

APPLICATION FOR A MOVEMENT CERTIFICATE

EUR1 No.   Q   676370

See notes overleaf before completing this form.

1. Exporter *(Name, full address, country)*

2. Application for a certificate to be used in preferential trade between
THE EUROPEAN ECONOMIC COMMUNITY
and

....
(Insert appropriate countries or groups of countries or territories)

3. Consignee *(Name, full address, country) (Optional)*

4. Country, group of countries or territory in which the products are considered as originating
EEC

5. Country, group of countries or territory of destination

6. Transport details *(Optional)*

7. Remarks

(1) If goods are not packed indicate number of articles or state "in bulk" as appropriate.

8. Item number: marks & numbers

Number and kind of packages (1): description of goods

9. Gross weight (kg) or other measure (litres, cu. m., etc.)

10. Invoices (Optional)

(2) Complete only where the regulations of the exporting country or territory require.

11. CUSTOMS ENDORSEMENT

Declaration certified   Stamp

Export document (2):

Form....................................No. ....

Customs office ....

Issuing country or territory:
UNITED KINGDOM
....

Date...

....
(Signature)

12. DECLARATION BY THE EXPORTER

I, the undersigned, declare that the goods described above meet the conditions required for the issue of this certificate.

(Place and date)

....
(Signature)

Figure 8.5   Movement Certificates (EUR 1 Type)

countries such as Austria, Sweden and Finland has disappeared, but on the other hand the need for this movement certificate now arises with the Baltic States, Poland and Romania, etc. Also, we must expect to encounter variations of a theme, for example with Turkey, which has a somewhat specialized associate membership with the EU resulting in the employment certificates known as the ATR 1 or ATR 3 depending on whether the consignment is shipped on the basis of a through consignment or whether via transhipment. The form is similar in appearance and use to the EUR 1 but the origin criteria is based more upon the basis of the 'free circulation' concept.

All in all, the permutation of invoices, certificates of origin, movement certificates and other associated documentation is a vital one. Therefore, this segment of documentation usually linking up with the invoice, will in most cases play an important role in the importer's clearance of goods and any mistakes could lead to quite severe penalties or sanctions, and in any case delays or problems with the buyer's authorities.

Another type of invoicing/documentary procedure that may be required by some countries e.g. Indonesia, Nigeria, Philippines etc. is where pre-shipment inspection is specified. Then it will be necessary for the exporter to co-operate with such agencies as Cotecna International, SGS Inspection Services or similar organizations. They will normally arrange for quality/quantity inspection and price comparison based upon pro-forma invoices. Upon satisfactory completion of such processes a CRF (Clean Report of Findings) is issued. Such documents are normally required to complete the payment process i.e. againt a letter of credit.

9

Methods of payment and finance

The payment risks

No export transaction can be said to be successful until payment has been received for the goods delivered overseas, and the proceeds have been safely credited to the exporter's account. Many of the problems of payment, such as length of credit period, checking the financial stability of a customer, or debt recovery, are similar to those that any business person would face in the home market of the UK. In exporting, however, we are bound to be faced with a number of extra risks, the main elements being associated with the following:

1 Distance: even if not geographically distant, the market is nevertheless across a frontier.
2 Different legal systems provide varying frameworks within which the exporter must decide a payments policy.
3 Currency differentials: fluctuating rates of exchange.
4 Greater difficulty involved in the recovery of goods.
5 As export markets tend to become more competitive, there is a greater demand by customers for longer credit periods and discounts, etc.
6 As most exporters usually find themselves dealing with a number of different countries, so there must be more risk of their sales contracts being upset by political disturbances or sudden unexpected foreign legislation.

Bearing in mind the above considerations, it would seem that the broad background of export finance which it is our task to consider can be examined under three main headings, namely:

1 The mechanics of arranging for and receiving payment.
2 Foreign exchange and its relation to the sales quotation, and the receipt of the proceeds.
3 The institutional aspect: the operations of the banking mechanism, factoring and credit support facilities.

Bound up with the mechanics of payment will, of course, be the process of invoicing, but this is a specialized aspect dealt with separately in Chapter 8. Also, the export practitioner will have to be very flexible in outlook, as there are many different ways in which companies handle their export payment. In many, the accounts departments look after the drawing of bills of exchange and preparation of invoices, whereas in other organizations shipping and payment functions are linked directly together within the framework of a self-contained export department; again, Chapter 2 dealt with this aspect.

There is little doubt that many potential exporters are dissuaded by payment problems. Time and time again companies relate difficulties they have experienced in getting their money, and often a first venture into the export field results in either a number of bad debts, or payment being made over so protracted a period that all the profit has disappeared. Again, failure to allow for variations in rates of exchange or banking charges results in a severe shock when the money is finally credited to the exporter's account.

Many of these problems are due to a complete lack of appreciation of the technology of overseas payment and a failure to adopt a systematic approach and a well defined export price and payments policy. In many cases, companies complain that long credit periods are required by their overseas customers and that to grant them would completely 'kill' their business because of the cost involved. Often this type of problem can be solved by the skilful use of bills of exchange and co-operation with bankers or one of the many excellent export houses. Certainly there is no lack of basic information on this subject. The banking system in particular produces excellent booklets giving advice on methods of payment and showing how they themselves can assist. It would appear that the main need is for a really integrated approach. This approach should start right from the quotation stage when the price and conditions are being formulated for presentation to the potential overseas buyer.

A vital point to bear in mind is that it is not merely a question of a passive response to a customer's enquiry, such as deciding whether or not we can concur with their wishes. For example, a customer's enquiry or order may stipulate payment 'thirty days after acceptance of the goods' on an open account basis. In this case, the export manager must judge whether this is possible or not and respond accordingly. But many enquiries from overseas do not in themselves mention any payment terms and therefore the reaction to this aspect, and what payment terms are put forward, is going to have an important bearing on a company's competitive position. This will call for a dynamic and creative response. Thus the payment terms and conditions will function as vital marketing tools in their own right.

Formulation of a payments policy

A checklist covering the salient features of a payment policy could be as follows:

1 Financial position of country of import.
2 Any exchange restrictions in importing country.
3 Any restrictions applying to methods of payment in importing country.
4 The credit standing and financial status of the buyer.
5 Type of product involved in the transaction, e.g. consumer-products, consumer durable goods, capital equipment or perishable goods.
6 The amount of money involved in the transaction.
7 The particular customs of the trade in question.
8 Competitive conditions.

It is not suggested for a moment that the above represents the exact order of priority, but, broadly speaking, this should represent the various stages to be checked when deciding payment policy. Items 1, 2 and 3 listed above are largely outside the control of the exporter, but success or otherwise in export transactions will depend to a great extent upon knowledge and assessment of all the relevant factors. Whatever the financial standing of the overseas customer may be, and however glowing the credit status report is, the financial and political position of the importer's country will be a controlling factor. The buyer may have the funds and be only too anxious to meet the commitment, but should a country experience economic, political or exchange difficulties, it may be forced to impose restrictions on payment abroad. This could lead to delay in settlement or even complete loss. Therefore, it is essential that consideration be given in the first place to the financial, economic and political standing of the importer's country, before deciding on the credit terms and methods of payment that are to be extended. Obviously, the larger the sum of money and the longer the period of credit involved, the more vital becomes the factor of country and exchange risk. This aspect is known as the *transfer risk*.

Credit status enquiries

Having analysed the position of the importing country, exporters' policies will then be determined by the knowledge of the customer's financial and credit status. To this end they may enlist the help of:

1 a bank,
2 overseas agent,
3 a fellow manufacturer (trade references),
4 a professional institution specializing in the credit status,
5 organizations concerned with the exporter's business, such as factors and credit insurance companies.

Banks offer help to an exporter by using their extensive overseas intelligence networks in order to check the financial standing of prospective buyers. Most banks possess a vast amount of information about the standing of traders and agents in all parts of the world and, in addition, can always make further enquiries through their numerous overseas correspondents. Reports can generally be obtained at very short notice and banks can be assisted in their efforts by the provision of the name of the bank where the overseas importer keeps an account, if this information is in the possession of the exporter. The bank should always be given a clear idea of the extent of the actual monetary value and length of credit involved. A potential customer may be perfectly sound for business up to say, £10000 every three months, but should an exporter begin to speed up the tempo of business with this particular account, the customer may be tempted to exceed financial resources. If the course of business extends over a long period of time, it is advisable to renew the enquiries periodically, at least once every twelve months.

If a good agency system has been built up by the exporter in various overseas markets, this too should be a source of information about customers. An agent can supplement banking information by knowing how the prospective customer is paying bills, stock levels, the quality of customers' products and services and how the business is being affected by the prevailing economic climate. As in all agency relationships, a great degree of care is necessary when selecting agents and acting on their advice. It is imperative in the field of financial status enquiries that the exporter has the utmost confidence in the agent. It might be very tempting for an unscrupulous agent, thinking only of commission, to introduce a wide circle of customers, some perhaps of doubtful financial stability. On the other hand, with a *del credere* type of agent, it is an integral part of their duty to ensure that business is done only with financially sound and reliable companies.

A very good source of information, and one which is not always exploited, is the mutual exchange of information between fellow manufacturers and exporters. Often this can be done without either party revealing any secrets or betraying any confidences. Sometimes it is possible to obtain more intimate details which can be of help in framing credit policies. For example, an exporter might learn that a particular importer is very sound and highly respected in the trade, but simply has a bad habit of invariably taking a long time to settle debts, even though eventually discharging obligations. This might help in making decisions as to whether to offer cash discount incentives or to employ documentary bill systems.

The UK is also very well served by professional institutions which specialize in credit reporting services. This is usually done on a subscription basis and provides such information as company history, management, operations, reputations, affiliations, financial structure, payments record and credit opinions. Most of these organizations also offer a specialized consultancy service particularly suitable for unusually large initial orders or contracts or where heavy capital commitments are likely to be incurred. For rapid, on-the-spot decisions, which are so necessary for the present-day export manager, there are a number of registers and directories produced by such organizations which give a lot of background information on a wide range of companies throughout the world.

Such organizations as NCM and Trade Indemnity Ltd incorporate credit status checks as an integral part of their insurance facilities.

The skilful use of these services is becoming an essential part of modern management technique and the investigation of customer financial standing is as important to corporate strategy as the forecasting of production and sales schedules.

Having therefore considered the importing country and the status of the overseas customer, the exporter will begin to investigate the alternative methods of payment and relate them to specific transactions in order to achieve a balance between on the one hand making the offer attractive and competitive to the customer and on the other, minimizing the risk and ensuring the maximum profit return obtainable.

Methods and mechanics of payment

There are six basic methods of obtaining payment for export orders and in order of preference for the *exporter* they are

1 Cash with order,
2 Documentary letter of credit,
3 Documentary bills,
4 Open account,
5 Payment against goods shipped on consignment, and
6 Compensation or barter trading.

From the trader's point of view, the ideal method of payment would be by cash, either on confirmation of order or when the goods are ready for shipment. This state of affairs is only likely in a sellers' market as it is naturally very unpopular in the eyes of importers. Nevertheless, in cases where specialized products are being made to suit an individual customer, it may be essential to ask for at least part of the purchase price with the order. This would apply particularly in instances where the exporter may be locking up considerable capital in the preparation of the goods. In practice, compromises are often sought. As an example, a scientific instrument manufacturer, with an order to equip a whole medical laboratory in France, might arrange to receive one-third of the purchase price with the order when the contract is signed, one-third when the consignment is ready for shipment and the balance when the apparatus has arrived, been installed, and is operating satisfactorily. Many variations of this theme will be found in different trades. The other extreme is presented by the methods of *payment against consignment* or *open account* and these are the most favourable methods from the point of view of the importer.

Goods shipped on consignment enable the exporter to place

stocks in the importing country (usually through an agent) without actually giving up the title of ownership. For certain categories of goods, particularly fast-moving consumer and consumer-durable products, the maintenance of stocks will be essential. Normally, the exporter will not receive any payment until sales are made in the overseas country and the goods may always be sent back without liability on the part of the importer/agent. Stocks therefore might represent a considerable amount of capital locked up in the overseas market and exposed to all the normal commercial, plus political and climatic risks. Consignment operations are best based on a well-established and trusted agency system. It must also be borne in mind that where the EU is concerned, care has to be taken regarding possible variation in VAT liabilities. Fiscal agents may need to be appointed.

Open account

The open account system is a common method of settlement in today's international trading practice. The mechanism is simple. The exporter dispatches goods, sends the appropriate documents of title, e.g. bills of lading, together with an invoice, and then has to wait for payment. The goods thus pass into the customer's possession before payment is made and the exporter has only the protection of the particular contract of sale. Should anything go wrong it is always difficult and expensive to enforce this by methods of litigation. There is no special procedure or documentation, however, and therefore the open account system has the advantage of simplicity; terms and methods of settlement need attention. Very often some form of discount incentive is offered for prompt payment and might be phrased as follows:

$2\frac{1}{2}$ per cent discount for payment within seven days, or terms net monthly account.

Sales on this basis are usually settled by periodic remittances against statements. With open account the actual mechanics and speed of remitting money is of vital importance.

Transmission of funds

It is important that the method of transmission of the proceeds be allowed for, and to a large extent this applies to the operation of *all* methods of payment. Funds might be transferred in the following ways.

1 TT (telegraphic transfer): this is a speedy method of settlement as the importer's bankers will send to their correspondent in the exporter's country a coded message ordering that the seller's account should be credited accordingly.
2 AMT or MT: in this case funds would be transferred either by Air Mail Transfer or ordinary Mail Transfer.
3 SWIFT messages: a computer network at present utilized by about 800 European, North American and Hong Kong banks. The initials stand for The Society for World-wide Inter bank Financial Telecommunication.
4 Cheque: the importer, depending upon the exchange control regulations of the country, may be able to discharge the debt by simply sending a cheque to the exporter for payment into the bank.
5 Banker's draft: this is really a cheque drawn by one banker on another.

It is really important that these methods of transmission of funds should be considered because the cost of each method will, of course, vary. The quicker methods of transmission will obviously cost more, but at the same time they will have a bearing on the time period during which the exporter is out of funds. It could make a big difference as to whether the proceeds of an export transaction are received in a day or so by cable or perhaps take up to three or four weeks to arrive by ordinary mail. In times of high interest rates this might amount to a considerable out-of-pocket expense for the importer.

This 'float time' therefore will have an impact upon the cash flow aspects of an exporter's business and needs to be carefully monitored. The starting point of such control might utilize the following type of calculation:

$$\text{Break-even point} = \frac{\text{TT cost} - \text{MT cost} \times 36\,500}{\% \text{ interest rate} \times \text{days saved}}$$

(*Source:* SITPRO Check List for International Money Transfers)

Circumstances suitable for 'open account methods' are as follows:

1 If the exporter knows the overseas customer very well and has had previous commercial dealings.
2 Inter-company relationships.

3 The importing country is politically stable and financially sound.
4 Where one is selling in competitive, sophisticated and demanding markets such as department stores in France and Germany, to compete in terms of price and methods of payment as well as quality and delivery.

So far then, we have considered two extremes, namely 'cash with order' on the one hand, and 'open account' and 'consignment' on the other. We have seen how they affect both importer and exporter, the relative risk on either side and the fact that none of them needs any complicated documentary procedure. Between these two extremes many export consignments are paid for by 'documentary bills' or 'documentary letters of credit'. Banking experts calculate that about 30 per cent of international business is still conducted by these methods of payment. The essential characteristic of these documentary systems is that the exporter in one way or another makes the handing over of the appropriate documents (such as bills of lading, air waybills, etc.) dependent upon payment by the importer. With this characteristic is usually coupled the employment of bills of exchange and the close liaison of the exporter and importer with the banking mechanism.

Documentary bills

In outline, the exporter dispatches goods, assembles the appropriate documents (in most cases consisting of bills of lading/transport documents, invoices and insurance certificate – a typical set of documents for a CIF contract); then draws a bill of exchange on the importer and this 'documentary package' is then transmitted through the exporter's own bank (known as the 'remitting bank') and presented to the customer through a bank overseas in the buyer's country (known as the 'collecting bank') on either a D/P (documents against payment) or a D/A (documents against acceptance) basis. In the former case, the customer will usually receive the documents and therefore title to the goods, upon payment to the overseas correspondent bank the appropriate sum of money. With documents against acceptance, documents of title will be received accepting the bill of exchange, namely signing the name and date across the face of the bill undertaking to pay the sum involved at some specific time in the future. For example, a 90-day bill duly accepted would mean that it would mature (become payable) 90 days from the date of acceptance.

The basic mechanism of the documentary bill is illustrated in

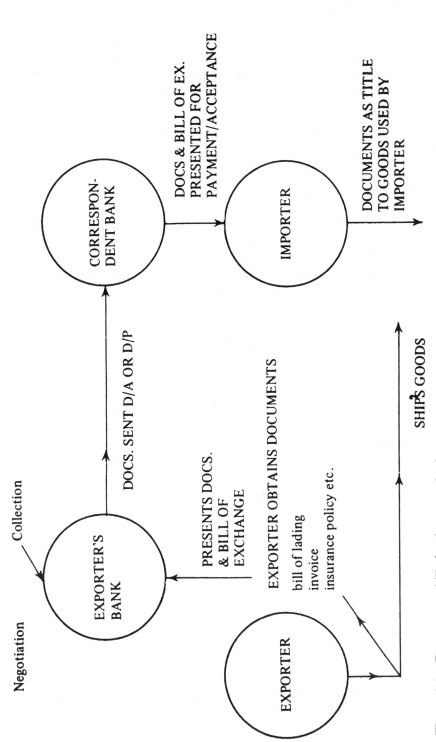

Figure 9.1. Documentary bill of exchange mechanism

Figure 9.1 but before we consider the processes and procedure more closely, it would be useful to study further the bill of exchange.

Although the term 'bill of exchange' is mainly employed in the text it should be appreciated that in commercial practice the term 'draft' is often encountered.

The bill of exchange

This document has a very long history and was widely used in international commerce in the Middle Ages. It is defined in the Bills of Exchange Act 1882 as

> . . . an unconditional order in writing, addressed by one person to another, signed by the person giving it, requiring the person to whom it is addressed to pay on demand or at a fixed or determinable future time a sum certain in money to or to the order of a specified person, or to bearer.

This must be closely adhered to in order to ensure that a fully negotiable instrument is produced and, indeed, the wide use of bills of exchange (or drafts as they are also called) stems from their negotiability which enables them to be passed from hand to hand.

At this stage it must be borne in mind that this type of bill can be used in other fields of trade but here we are concerned principally with the bill of exchange linked to the handing over of shipping documents, in other words, a 'documentary bill'. Bills can be employed without being so linked and are then known as 'clean bills' but care must be taken not to confuse these with clean bills of lading.

There are three parties to a bill of exchange, namely the drawer, drawee and payee. Applying this to a typical export transaction we have:

> Exporter (drawer) draws bill on drawee (importer), usually instructing that the sum of money should be paid into exporter's account (payee).

In most cases, the drawer is also the payee but this need not necessarily be so; it might be that instructions are given for the proceeds to be placed to the account of a third party.

The terms 'documents against payment' and 'documents against acceptance' have already been mentioned and these provisions would decide whether the bills were 'sight' or 'period' or 'time bills'.

The 'tenor' of the bill is the period of time involved. This can be clarified by looking at the following specimen:

```
                              No. 1246

LONDON, 5th September, 19 . . . For £25 000
At . . . . Sight . . . . pay this . . . . .              SOLE BILL of Exchange
.....................................................................................to the Order
of ...................................... OURSELVES ...........................................
                  TWENTY-FIVE THOUSAND POUNDS
Value Received...............................   for on and behalf of
A. B. PEINTURE                                 Silcometer Instruments
                                               Ltd


To ....................................................
LILLE, FRANCE
                                               ....................................................
                                               Secretary/Accountant

....................................................
```

In the above case, the drawer and payee is, of course, Silcometer
Instruments Ltd; the drawee is A. B. Peinture. The sum of money
which is shown in both figures and words is £25 000.

The specimen indicates that the 'tenor' of the bill is 'at sight'. If
the bill had been a time bill (sometimes referred to as 'usance
bills') for a period of, say 60 days, then the wording could have
been 'At sixty days after sight'. In the absence of any other
arrangements, the 60 days would run from the date of acceptance
or 'sighting'. Note that the wording is 'Pay this sole bill' which
means that in this case only one copy of a draft is actually being
drawn. It might well be that two copies are, in fact, needed and in
this event, one copy would have the wording 'Pay this *first bill* of
exchange, second of same date and tenor unpaid'. The second copy
would read 'Pay this *second bill* of exchange, first of same date and
tenor unpaid'. Note that each copy is by itself negotiable but once
one has been paid or accepted, then the other one is void. In
practice this operates in much the same manner as sets of bills of
lading. It is still sometimes the policy of banks to send two sets of
documents by separate posts.

The wording 'value received' suffices to indicate the aspect of
'consideration' which is necessary for a contract between the exporter and the customer. Sometimes a note can be put on the face of
the bill which identifies more specifically the nature of the transaction, e.g. 'Shipment of 20 compressors per the ss *Arabella*'. The bill
is normally signed by the parties empowered by the individual
company to sign cheques, i.e. secretary, accountant, or director and
should be endorsed by the drawer on the back of the draft itself.

When completing bills, the following additional points should be noted:

1 Bills may be printed by companies rather like their cheques, or pads of forms can be obtained from commercial stationers. The number shown on the specimen, 1246, would be an identification number which would be entered on a counterfoil for retention. If necessary, a bill can be typed on a plain piece of paper.
2 UK bills no longer need stamp duty at home but an exporter should not overlook the possibility of some form of revenue stamp charge being incurred in some overseas countries.

In the above example of the 60-day draft, it was seen that the bill would mature 60 days after the date upon which the drawee made formal acceptance. In practice, however, there could be other options. For example, a bill could be drawn payable at 60 days from date of bill of lading or some other reference point such as date of ship's report. This approach can, of course, inject a greater degree of flexibility, but when employing such maturity periods, the legal definition of 'at a fixed or determinable future date' must not be overlooked. Any unacceptable vagueness in the wording could weaken the legal character of the bill of exchange.

The drawer must balance a degree of precision when considering the degree of time involved. A bill dated, say, 20 September drawn at 90-days' acceptance may well find that the bill does not get presented to the customer until, say, 30 September. The 90 days is therefore going to run from the actual date of acceptance, i.e. an extra 10 days have been added to the period. The alternative would be to draw the bill at 90 days 'from date hereof'. This would mean that whenever the bill was accepted, the period would run from the date of the face of the bill, in this case 20 September. In other cases the date could be linked to say, 'date of bill of lading' or 'date of shipment'. Care must always be taken to ensure that the time period can be accurately determined.

Looking back on our definition, therefore, we find: 'requiring the person to whom it is addressed to pay on demand *(sight)* or at a fixed or determinable future time *(time)*'.

Negotiating and discounting bills of exchange

An important by-product of the use of bills of exchange in export transactions is the possibility of utilizing them with the objective of obtaining advances of money. This is usually carried out by the widely used process of 'negotiation' and also in some cases the 'discounting' of bills. Care must be exercised in the use of the term negotiation because obviously it is a widely-used term in a general commercial sense, i.e. negotiating a contract or negotiating a set of documents, etc. In the sphere of negotiating bills of exchange we normally mean that when, say, sending drafts and documents on either a D/P or D/A basis through the bank, arrangements are made whereby the bank in question actually pays the exporter immediately. Subsequently, when the bills have been appropriately honoured, the bank will debit the exporter with the cost of interest, etc., involved in the time taken for them to obtain reimbursement, and the time they initially credited the exporter. Naturally, there will be a relationship between the prevailing rates of interest and other charges and the exporter's cash flow needs.

The second, perhaps more formal term 'discounting', implies that a term bill, duly accepted, is discounted by a bank or other financial house. This means that the exporter will receive the value of the bill *less* a discount rate. The bank will hold the bill and then present it to the drawee (acceptor) for due payment. It is probably true to say that formal discounting tends to be more applicable to large-value transactions involving larger companies and not so widely encountered as negotiation operations.

Discounting is very often linked with the term 'acceptance credits' whereby a bank agrees to have the bill drawn upon it for acceptance. For this they charge an acceptance commission which can vary. The accepted bill can then be discounted in the financial market through banks or specialized discount houses who will, of course, charge a discount rate. Such bills will generally be referred to as 'bank bills' and may of course attract rather more favourable rates (from the point of view of the exporter) as compared with 'trade bills' drawn up and accepted by commercial companies. With the latter, of course, there will not be any acceptance commission.

Discount rates are usually based on a straight per annum basis and this is calculated on a 365-day period for sterling bills and 360 for foreign currency drafts.

A typical basic formula therefore used by the exporter when viewing discounting financially, might be as follows:

£50 000 sterling draft at 90 days
Prevailing per annum discount rate 14.5 per cent
Acceptance commission 1.2 per cent per annum

Therefore:

$$£50000 \times \frac{14.5}{100} \times \frac{90}{365}$$

	£
= amount of discount	1787.67
less acceptance commission	150.00
	− 1937.67
Amount received	by £48 062.33
exporter	

The above may serve just to give a very approximate idea of the magnitude of the discounting process. Of course many fluctuating factors will affect the rate itself depending upon the prevailing cost of money market rates, parties involved and underlying creditworthiness of the drawer and acceptor, etc. Another important factor for consideration is the question of 'recourse'. A bill discounted 'with recourse' means that should the holder of the bill find that on maturity it is dishonoured (i.e. not paid by the drawee) then recourse may be had to the drawer (i.e. exporter) for reimbursement of the money. 'Without recourse' would mean that the discounter would accept the credit risk in the event of non-payment by the drawee. The Bill of Exchange Act allows for such bills to be drawn *sans recours*. Naturally, bills with such clauses have less attraction for a discounter and have limited use in normal bill discounting.

When considering such instruments as bills of exchange it should be borne in mind that promissory notes may also be encountered and are provided for by the Bill of Exchange Act. In essence, instead of the exporter drawing a bill for acceptance, the importer issues a promissory note making a legal promise to pay a sum of money in a prescribed period of time.

Nowadays, in international trade there is considerable use of 'forfaiting' which is a rather specialized international type of financing against bills and notes. This will be referred to later against the background of finance and credit institutions.

Banks, when making advances of money or negotiating bills may sometimes require a degree of security over, say, shipping documents. This may lead to the exporter providing the bank with a 'letter of hypothecation'. This, in a sense, provides the bank with a degree of rights against the documents and goods in the event of non-payment. Reference is usually made to 'general letters of hypothecation' lodged by the exporter to cover the whole of the export business being transacted over a prescribed period of time, or a 'specific letter' which will apply to one particular transaction.

Of course, no form of bill can give the exporter absolute security. The customer can go bankrupt before the bill is presented or matures. We have seen that if it is discounted, the drawer may be liable to ultimate recourse by the bank. Nevertheless, a customer who has accepted a bill of exchange and wishes to keep a good reputation will have a much more difficult job in delaying payment compared with, say, an invoice and statement on open account terms. It is said that a trader dishonours a bill 'at peril'.

Before considering the final procedural stage of the documentary bill, namely presenting the documents to the bank and the completion of the appropriate bill lodgement form let us sum up the type of situations suitable for D/P and D/A payment.

Situations suitable for documents against payment are:

1 Exporter may not be wholly satisfied with the financial status of the customer and therefore retains control of goods by keeping the documents (in the banking channel) until payment is received.
2 It does at least provide the importer with the opportunity of obtaining the documents (and title to the goods) at the time payment is made. In fact, it is almost like a COD transaction.
3 Markets where it may be relatively easy to dispose of goods may exist in the overseas country.
4 The sight draft, together with shipping documents, will often enable an advance to be obtained from the bank.

Situations suitable for documents against acceptance are:

1 Competitive selling conditions; customer wants to obtain, use or dispose of goods before actual payment.
2 A compromise for the exporter. The goods have gone to the customer but exporter holds an accepted bill which may be discounted at a discount rate.
3 The exporter can always reserve the right to unload the cost of credit on to the customer by putting an interest clause on the bill, which means, in effect, that although the importer will be getting credit for the period of 30, 60, 90 days, etc., an interest rate will have to be added to the principal sum shown on the bill when it arrives at maturity.

4 It might be considered that as the exporter holds an accepted bill, this represents an unconditional promise to pay by the buyer. Should the buyer subsequently not pay, then the bill could be considered 'dishonoured' and legal action taken. Litigation against an unpaid bill in this sense may be more effective than, say, against breach of the sales contract but this is a very debatable issue and the seller will always take great care with regard to policy in this connection. This matter will be discussed further a little later in the chapter.

Charges incurred on bills of exchange

These charges include:

1 Possible overseas stamp duties.
2 Negotiation charges by bank in UK.
3 Collection charges by correspondent bank overseas.
4 Cost of transmitting proceeds, air-mail, SWIFT message, etc.
5 Interest charges between time when money is paid in to bank overseas and time it is received in UK.
6 Sometimes question of exchange rate conversion.

A typical structure of a banking charge might be as follows:

Documentary Bills for Collection/Negotiation
0.25 per cent (0.25 per £100). Min. £20, max. £80.

For negotiations, interest to cover the period until the bank receives reimbursements from its correspondents will also be charged.

Again, these figures are intended only to provide some comparative idea of potential costs and could vary between banks and customers.

Wherever possible, the various charges and interest rate, etc., should be made quite clear when conditions of sale are being arranged. Nothing is more conducive to a bad customer relationship than for there to be misunderstanding on this point. Equally it is important when calculating the selling price and profit margin, that these types of charges be included in the computation. There has grown up a practice of inserting various types of clause on the bill of exchange which clarify the position as to the party bearing responsibility for the particular charges involved.

Examples are:

1 'Payable at the current rate of exchange for sight drafts on New York.'
2 'Payable at banker's selling rate for telegraphic transfers on London.'
3 'Payable with stamps and all charges for collection.'
4 'Payable with interest at . . . per cent per annum from date hereof until the appropriate date of arrival of remittance in London.'
5 'Payable with exchange and stamps as per endorsement.'

It will be seen that the above provide a number of permutations to cover the various charges, and some, such as 2, actually specify the mode of transmission of proceeds. Some clauses are traditionally used in certain countries, e.g. 4 which is often called the 'Eastern Clause'. Clause 5 is used where bills are going forward for negotiation mainly to Australia or South Africa, and in these cases the negotiating bank will insert an exchange figure endorsement on the bill so that the importer has to pay sufficient currency to cover the various charges incurred, including possibly an interest element as well.

The point must be emphasized that clauses should not be used unless both the exporter and importer understand them completely and are in agreement. Equally, they should only be used when it is appropriate for the specific country or customary for a particular trade. Banks should be consulted as to the suitability of a clause and, as will be seen, there are plenty of facilities for clarifying these instructions when the lodgement form is completed and handed to the bank with the documents.

Collection order or bank lodgement form

A form is obtained from the bank and although it may vary from one bank to another, it will require basically the same treatment. The layout for a typical bank collection order is shown is Figure 9.2. This form is completed, (generally in duplicate), and handed to the bank, together with the bill of exchange duly drawn and accompanied by the appropriate documents (usually bills of lading, invoice, insurance policy and perhaps other peripheral documents such as certificates of origin). A glance at the form will show that in the light of our above analysis we should know what instruction to issue, i.e. D/A or D/P charges, the mode of transmitting the documents and how the proceeds should be remitted. These are just a few points which deserve mention. Most important is the instruction regarding 'protesting'. If a customer refuses to accept

©BBA/SITPRO 1976/1981/1987/1992

FOREIGN BILL AND/OR DOCUMENTS FOR COLLECTION

AUTHORISED BY BRITISH BANKERS' ASSOCIATION

Drawer/exporter

Drawer's/exporter's reference(s) (to be quoted by bank in all correspondence)

Consignee

Drawee (if not consignee)

To (bank)

For bank use only

FORWARD DOCUMENTS ENUMERATED BELOW BY AIRMAIL. FOLLOW SPECIAL INSTRUCTIONS AND THOSE MARKED X

Bill of exchange	Commercial invoice	Certified/consular invoice	Certificate of origin	Insurance policy/ certificate	Bill of lading	Parcel post receipt	Air waybill

Combined transport document

Other documents and whereabouts of any missing original bill of lading

RELEASE DOCUMENTS ON	ACCEPTANCE	PAYMENT		protest	do not protest
			if unaccepted ⟶		
If documents are not taken up on arrival of goods	warehouse goods	do not warehouse		telex/cable	airmail
			and advise reason by		
	insure against fire	do not insure		protest	do not protest
			if unpaid ⟶		
				telex/cable	airmail
Collect ALL charges			and advise reason by		
				telex/cable	airmail
Collect correspondent's charges ONLY			Advise acceptance and due date by		
				telex/cable	airmail
Return accepted bill by airmail			Remit proceeds by		
In case of need refer to				for guidance	accept their instructions

SPECIAL INSTRUCTIONS   1.   Represent on arrival of goods if not honoured on first presentation.

Date of bill exchange

Bill of exchange value/amount of collection

Tenor of bill of exchange

Bill of exchange claused

Please collect the above-mentioned bill and/or documents subject to the Uniform Rules for Collections (1978 Revision), International Chamber of Commerce, Publication No. 322. I/We agree that you shall not be liable for any loss, damage, or delay however caused which is not directly due to the negligence of your own officers or servants.

Date and signature

J725-001

Form No. 882   Published and Sold by FORMECON SERVICES Ltd, Gateway, Crewe CW1 1YN   Tel. 0270 500800   Fax. 0270 500505

SITPRO Approved Licensee No. 21

Figure 9.2   A typical bank collection order

or pay a draft correctly drawn and in conformity with the agreed contract, then this bill is technically dishonoured. Should litigation be resorted to, then it would be necessary for the bill to be 'noted' by a public notary in the overseas country and then officially 'protested', which is a legal process. This whole question is a delicate one and needs very careful handling as the processes can vary considerably from country to country. It is also quite easy to cause a perfectly sound customer considerable annoyance by protesting a bill. A typical cause of trouble is the synchronization of presenting bills with the actual arrival of a carrying vessel. Suppose a consignment of materials has been shipped to a customer in Italy who is going to use this in the process of manufacturing rubber. The terms of payment may have been agreed at 120 days to enable the importer to obtain the raw material and complete the manufacturing process. What may happen, is that the documents pass through the banking system and are presented to the importer immediately for acceptance. It may well be that because of unexpected delay the ship is not due to arrive for some time, and perhaps it might be up to 14 days before the Italian importer could hope to obtain delivery. As the 120 days would usually begin to operate from acceptance date, it would, in effect, cut down the period in which the importer would have the goods before payment is due. For voyages to more distant markets the effect would be even more noticeable. This can be taken care of by instructing the bank to re-present on arrival of ship and therefore no protesting at this stage is required. In any case, most exporters would instruct a bank to notify them if the draft has not been honoured, giving the reason and asking for fresh instructions before there was any question of protestation.

The question of possible protesting and notation does need to be considered carefully because in some countries there are specific time limits within which a bill has to be officially protested. Should this not take place, and some periods are very short (sometimes a few days), then the bill could not be officially processed and subsequent legal rights are lost should litigation be considered. Normally exporters will still not let this worry them unduly but it should be borne in mind that sometimes, as we shall see, an exporter may be operating under some form of credit insurance cover and it is just possible that on occasions the cover may be dependent upon a particular form of payments terms. If these, for example, are 90 day bills, and the drawee had dishonoured the bill, then it might very well be necessary to ensure that the dishonoured bill was legally processed promptly so that the credit insurer can retain all full legal rights of any future legal action.

With regard to charges, it will be noticed that there is an opportunity to waive them if they are refused by the drawee. When small sums are involved, and where perhaps the question has not been clarified in the order, this is often a common-sense way of avoiding troublesome correspondence and a disgruntled customer.

For some time, the banks in a large number of countries have been interpreting documentary collection procedures in accordance with 'Uniform Rules for Collections' laid down by the International Chamber of Commerce. The rules state together basic definitions, methods of presentation and payment, acceptance, protesting and charges, liabilities and responsibilities. They will form an ideal reference point between the exporter, the remitting and collecting banks and the overseas importer.

When considering the collection order form it is important to remember that in some cases for various reasons, the exporter may instruct the bank to send forward documents but without actually drawing a bill of exchange. This may be quite common when, perhaps, dealing with a well-known regular customer. Both parties might be quite content to rely upon payment against the invoice and handing over of the documents without the formality of the bill of exchange. This is sometimes referred to as 'Cash Against Documents' (CAD). Care must always be taken to distinguish this from 'Open Account Terms'.

Looked at from another angle, bills could be drawn and sent through the bank *without* any shipping documents, namely a 'clean collection'. The *documentary* collection is of course the synchronization of the handing over of documents only against a prescribed mode of payment or acceptance of drafts.

It may be seen that clean drafts might make a lot of sense in certain conditions. From what has been said in general regarding documentary bills, it will be appreciated that in order for this method to operate in a classical sense there is the assumption of passing title and ownership through the banks by the transfer of documents. This is perfectly satisfactory when we envisage shipment by sea and the utilization of negotiable bills of lading. However, in the case of fast moving traffic such as air freight and the employment of waybills, then the transfer process may not be quite so simple. In such a case as this, one could envisage quoting a customer, say, on a 90 day basis, sending a draft 'clean' first to the customer, upon receipt back of the accepted draft the exporter is then free to dispatch and ensure that the appropriate shipping documents, i.e. air waybills, etc., can go straight through to the customer.

Another variation with documentary bills, and one commonly employed, is to have the appropriate documents made out to a bank as consignee who can subsequently obtain payment from the customer against an invoice. The customer can then be given a release note or delivery order on the particular airport/seaport/ depot, etc.

Documentary commercial letters of credit

As has been seen, next to cash-with-order the most favourable method of payment for the exporter is a form of Letter of Credit (L/C). With many qualifications, which will be considered, the letter of credit places a sum of money in the UK to be made available upon presentation of the required documents. Compared with the documentary bills already discussed, it will be seen that the L/C provides for payment to be made in the *exporter's* country and also that the *importer* is responsible for undertaking all the necessary initiative and procedure in establishing the credit (although this would often be done in close consultation with the exporter).

The parties to an average L/C transaction will be: (1) the importer (applicant), (2) the bank in the importer's country (issuing bank), (3) the bank in the exporter's country (advising/correspondent bank), and (4) the exporter (beneficiary).

The loose term 'credit' can at times be a little confusing and should not be confused with private letters of credit provided by banks for persons travelling abroad. In banking terms, a commercial documentary letter of credit has been defined as:

> ... a promise given by bankers to accept or honour bills of exchange if drawn on them, or, if drawn on the buyer or the issuing or paying bank by the seller, to negotiate them, security for the payment or acceptance of the obligation to pay reposing in the pledge of the documents of title to the goods exported in the special property thus obtained.

The above definition reveals a factor of fundamental importance to major areas of export documentation, namely the use of the documents as title to the goods. It is this which makes the manner in

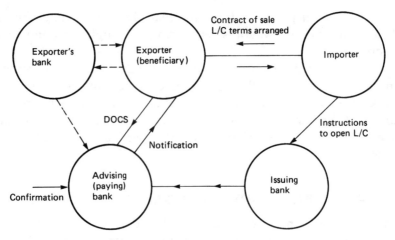

Figure 9.3   Letter of credit diagram

which bills of lading are made negotiable so vital, i.e. to order and endorsement. Indeed, it also highlights the question of whether any non-negotiable document employed such as waybills are made out to the consignee or the bank.

The security offered by letters of credit has to be earned because, as we shall see, this method must by the very nature of the relationship between importer/exporter demand a great degree of precision of procedure, with particular reference to the type and description of the shipping documents required.

Figure 9.3 can be used to trace the main mechanism of the L/C process which goes through the following stages:

1 Importer completes a bank form which contains full instructions on how the L/C should be constructed, see Figure 9.4.
2 Importer's bank transmits the L/C to its correspondent bank in the exporter's country.
3 Correspondent bank notifies exporter, sending the detailed L/C containing all the requirements, and showing the value of the credit and length of time for which it is valid.
4 Exporter then proceeds with shipment and careful collection of all the required documents, ensuring that they conform one hundred per cent with the L/C.
5 When documents are complete, exporter presents them (usually together with a draft) to correspondent/advising bank who checks them for conformity and then pays according to the terms of credit.

Application to Open a Documentary Credit
(To be completed in triplicate. Typescript or Block Capitals. The
Applicants attention is drawn to the notes overleaf. If necessary
further guidance may be obtained from your Account holding Branch.
Where applicable boxes should be marked by an 'x')

Original
(for despatch by
Branch to
Overseas Branch/IBC)

Leave this space blank

To be completed by Branch (NWB29)

To: National Westminster Bank PLC

Tel No
and ext

1 Please open an ☐ **Irrevocable** ☐ **Revocable Credit**
  by ☐ Airmail ☐ Tele-transmission.
  If tele-transmission, send ☐ Brief Details ☐ Full details.
  (If contact cannot be made, despatch will be effected by Cable unless otherwise instructed in Section 23)

2 For Bank use only

3 Applicants full name and address _____

  _____ Account Number _____

4 In favour of (Full name and address) _____

5 Currency and amount (Figures and words) _____

6 Available either by (A) Drafts at ☐ sight ☐ ___ days sight ☐ ___ days from date of _____

  Or (B) By Deferred Payment (without drafts) ☐ ___ days from _____

7 Expiry date _____ In (Country) _____

8 Documents must be presented within ___ days from On Board Date of the Marine Bill of Lading or from the
  date of 'Taking in Charge' as indicated upon any other Transport Document but in any event not later than the expiry date of the
  Credit. (If left blank 21 days will be applied)

  Documents Required

9 ☒ ___ Signed Invoices

  Either number 10 or number 11 must be completed

10 ☐ Insurance ☐ Certificate ☐ Policy in negotiable form dated not later than the On Board Date of a Marine Bill
   of Lading or the date of 'Taking in Charge' as indicated upon any other Transport Document covering the ___
   ☐ CIF or ☐ CIP value plus ___ % and the following risks: 'War, Strikes, Riots and Civil Commotions'

   ☐ Institute Cargo Clauses 'A' (All Risks)
   ☐ Institute Cargo Clauses 'B' (WA)   **These alternatives will be accepted**
   ☐ Institute Cargo Clauses 'C' (FPA)   **unless otherwise instructed**

   Any other risks required:

11 ☐ Insurance will be cared for by the undersigned and I/we undertake to keep the Merchandise adequately covered by Policies
   of Marine, War, Fire and other usual risks in approved companies and to lodge with you or produce upon demand the policies if
   called upon to do so and in the event of failure to do so you may insure the Merchandise at the expense of the undersigned.

12 ☐ Full set (if issued in more than one original) Clean 'On Board' Marine Bills of Lading issued to order and Blank Endorsed
   marked ☐ Freight Paid ☐ Freight Collect ☐ Notify (Full name and address)

13 Full set (if issued in more than one original):
   ☐ Combined Transport Bill of Lading issued
     to order and Blank Endorsed
   ☐ Railway Consignment Note
   ☐ Roadway Bill
   ☐ Other Document of Movement _____

   Evidencing goods consigned to (Full name and address)

   Signed by the Carrier or signed on behalf
   of the named Carrier by his Agent marked
   ☐ Freight Paid
   ☐ Freight Collect ☐ Notify
   (Full name and address)

Figure 9.4 Application form to open a letter of credit

6 Note that in the diagram, the exporter's bank is also shown. This
  is because many exporters pass the documents through their
  own bank for checking and presentation. There is no absolute
  necessity for this, but it is sometimes more convenient for the
  exporter to have their own bank's assistance and guidance.

7 The credit will be opened for a sum of money with a period of
  validity.

A point of some significance is the fact that the overseas customer has to complete their instruction form for the bank and it is important to remember that the professional exporter will, wherever possible, ensure that when the details of the transaction are being formulated, every assistance is given to the customer by advising of any details which streamline the credit requirements. In practice, many orders get off to a bad start by insufficient co-operation on this point and, as soon as a L/C arrives, the exporter finds it contains requirements which are impossible to fulfil and immediately correspondence, delay and expense can result. A simple example is that of part shipments being permitted. Broadly speaking, and all other things being equal, an opening bank would tend to favour a L/C for a complete shipment but if there is a possibility that the exporter may have to ship more than one consignment, then advance information on this point to the customer might lead to their deleting 'not permitted' in the letter of credit under 'partial shipments: not permitted/permitted'.

So far, the credit has been referred to in general terms but it is important that the practitioner is able to identify the main types that are encountered in trade, and to distinguish between their relative advantages and disadvantages. Letters of credit can be classified as follows.

Types of letters of credit

(a)   Revocable credit

As the name suggests, this type can be cancelled or modified by the customer (the opener of the credit) without prior approval of the exporter. Obviously this leaves much to be desired since, although the credit is opened and notified by the bank, by the time the goods have been shipped and the documents presented, the customer may have cancelled the credit. The exporter, who has shipped the goods, is therefore left with the documents. This type of credit is really only a mere mechanism for providing payment and guidance to the exporter as to the form the documentation should take.

(b)   Irrevocable credit

This is far more common to letters of credit and constitutes a legally binding agreement between beneficiary/issuing bank and importer to the effect that (amongst other things) the credit cannot be revoked or modified without prior agreement of the beneficiary. Here the exporter has the degree of security that is more usually associated with credits.

There remains one important aspect which has a bearing upon the above types of credit, namely that of 'confirmation'. We have seen that an irrevocable letter of credit establishes a bond between the issuing bank and the exporter, but this bond will not extend to the notifying or paying bank in the UK unless the credit is confirmed. We may therefore expect to see clauses on the L/C, such as:

Revocable
We have no authority from our clients either to confirm this credit or to guarantee the acceptance/payment of drafts drawn there against. The credit is therefore subject to cancellation without notice and the above particulars are for your guidance only.

or

Unconfirmed
We have not been requested by the above named (issuing) bank to confirm this instrument, and consequently this advice conveys no engagement on our part.

It is important that there should be no misunderstanding on this point. If the letter of credit is not confirmed, then the UK bank which has notified the exporter is not itself a party to the credit but is acting merely as an agent, authenticating the origin of the credit instructions, but not automatically obliged to negotiate drafts drawn. Supposing some political or economic crisis should arise which prevents, at the last moment, the issuing bank (in the importer's country) from transferring currency to the UK advising bank; then if the L/C was unconfirmed, the advising bank would not necessarily be obliged to pay against the credit when the exporter presents the documents.

Confirmation of a L/C by the advising bank is, then, normally desirable and we would look for a clause such as:

The above credit carries our confirmations and we hereby agree with the drawers, endorsers and holders in due course of drafts drawn under this credit that such drafts will be duly honoured on presentation provided that all the terms and conditions of the credit have been complied with.

Therefore, provided that the exporter meets all the conditions of the credit, and produces the necessary documents within the period of validity, the advising bank will ensure that the money is there to honour the draft without recourse to the drawee. The exporter will then always hope to receive wherever possible an 'Irrevocable Confirmed Letter of Credit Without Recourse' and this would represent, as far as is ever humanly possible, one hundred per cent certainty of obtaining payment. The validity of the confirmation must, however, always be considered. The mere description on a letter of credit to the effect that it is confirmed may not always be sufficient if the bank does not possess the correct status. If there is any doubt, an appropriate bank should be consulted.

Naturally, the varying degrees of security of letters of credit will mean a scale of charges which vary accordingly. Some specimen charges are:

For confirming a credit (inclusive of the fee for advising)
0.25% minimum £80 each three months or part thereof, charged for full period of validity at time of confirmation. Payment commission 1% minimum £35.00

Amendment fees £30.00 per amendment.

The whole question of confirmation has to be considered very carefully. Obviously from the seller's point of view, it is desirable, but it involves charges and therefore buyers may not look upon it so favourably. In practice, therefore, exporters receiving confirmed credit frequently have to budget for the fact that they will eventually bear the cost. Nowadays there is a rather more liberal outlook on this subject and many of the well-known international banks do not consider that there is really any need for confirmation by the bank through which they are corresponding.

There are cases when an exporter receives a credit which they cannot get confirmed through the advising bank and as perhaps they feel uneasy about the overseas country's financial or political position, they may seek to get an external confirmation through a well-known bank in their centre. This is sometimes known as 'silent' confirmation and, of course, can sometimes be quite costly.

Although *prima facia* charges are for the account of the opener, that is, of course, the customer, the exporter must be prepared for sometimes having these charges or at least a part of them debited to themselves. It is a point therefore that must be considered both in relationship to pricing and costing and customer relations.

The above are only intended to give some idea of magnitude as far as possible charges are concerned, and detailed reference should be made to individual banks where charges will often vary.

It is important to remember at this juncture that the aspects considered against D/P and D/A bills of exchange have certain factors in common with letters of credit, namely drafts drawn against credits can also be at sight or term and may be paid, accepted, negotiated or discounted. Clearly the major difference is that in credit operations various banks are more directly implicated in the various financial undertakings. The degree of involvement as has been seen will vary with such aspects of irrevocability and confirmation.

In the general course of export trade, a number of different variations on the letter of credit theme may be found, all designed to fit in with special types of transactions and trading patterns. The following represent the main categories likely to be encountered.

Transferable credit

Can be transferred by the beneficiary to another party. Often used by brokers or merchants where they can assign part of the credit to the primary supplier. Where the credit is split, it would be known as a 'transferable and divisible credit'.

Revolving credit

One which is automatically renewed as the amount of credit used by drawing of bills. Very useful in a case where a buyer places a contract for regular, say monthly, shipments. If normally buying £5000 monthly, then the revolving credit would be opened for £5000 and, as the draft is drawn and honoured, another £5000 would automatically become available. These are very suitable where it is necessary to span a rather long period, e.g. a 2-year revolving credit.

Countervailing or back-to-back credit

Used in triangular or entrepot trade. For example, a UK merchant may receive an order from Sweden for some heavy machinery and is buying from Germany. The Swedish customer opens a L/C in London in favour of the merchant. If the German supplier requires cash against documents, to avoid being out of funds the merchant may arrange with the bank to use the existing L/C as a security for the opening of a credit in Germany in favour of the supplier. The bank is able to keep control of the operation, maintaining shipping documents throughout as security and charging the merchant accordingly when final settlement has been made.

Anticipatory or packing credits

In this case, the credits permit payment (usually partial) against documents obtained early in the shipping process; for example, warehouse receipts, dock receipts, wharfinger's receipts. Final payment is generally made when the bill of lading is produced. Used a lot in raw materials, commodity and livestock transactions. In the wool trade there is usually a clause in the credits known as the 'red clause' which enables such advances to be made to the beneficiary.

Stand-by credits

This type of credit can be a little confusing and care is needed in its interpretation. In one form, it represents a credit which is opened through a bank in the normal way and can be made irrevocable, etc. When reading through the provisions however, it might transpire that the conditions of the credit indicate that it only becomes operative if something does *not* happen. An example could be where a supplier ships goods, sends the documents to the customer and invoices directly on, say, a 30-day basis just like an open account transaction. The stand-by credit sets out details of the product, a sum of money and validity period and goes on to state:

> Your statement signed by an Authorized Officer to the effect that payment of the subject invoice for delivery of the above-mentioned goods is properly due to them and that such payment has not been paid . . .

In this case the bank will make good the payment under the credit.

Another use of the expression stand-by credit is where it is issued by the *seller* to the buyer to become operative only if the seller fails to meet some provision of the contract. In this sense it is more akin to a *performance guarantee*.

Deferred credits

There has been a growing use of deferred payments being made a condition of a credit without the drawing of a time draft. Instead of a period of time being, say, geared directly to a bill maturity date, i.e. 90 days from sight, it could be 90 days from receipt and installation of goods and issued of an acceptance certificate by the buyer. There are many variations possible.

UCP Brochure No. 500

Mention has been made several times of the high degree of precision which is necessary when attempting to fulfil the requirements of a letter of credit. Because the documents represent the goods called for by the opener of the credit, the bank has no alternative but to reject any documents which do not conform precisely to the credit. This is known as the doctrine of 'strict compliance'. We have seen that for documentary bills, the ICC has formulated a series of internationally-accepted rules. Similarly, for letters of credit, we have Brochure No. 500, the *Uniform Customs and Practice for Documentary Credits*. In a series of 49 Articles it defines terminology and sets out the rules and procedures to be adopted by banks which conform to these rules. In practice, this represents the main international trading countries. Usually there will be a note somewhere on the credit to the effect that 'I/We agree that, except so far as is otherwise expressly stated, this Credit will be subject to the uniform Customs and Practice for Documentary Credits (1993 Revision) International Chamber of Commerce Brochure No. 500'.

This brochure should be studied in detail by the practitioner since, quite apart from the formulation of procedure and terminology, it is a mine of information about letters of credit and the usual type of documentation used against such credits.

Let us take a look at a specimen Article.

Article 13

Standard for Examination of Documents

(a) Banks must examine all documents stipulated in the Credit with reasonable care, to ascertain whether or not they appear, on their face, to be in compliance with the terms and conditions of the Credit. Compliance of the stipulated documents on their face with the terms and conditions of the Credit, shall be determined by international standard banking practice as reflected in these Articles. Documents which appear on their face to be inconsistent with one another will be considered as not appearing on their face to be in compliance with the terms and conditions of the Credit.

Documents not stipulated in the Credit will not be examined by banks. If they receive such documents, they shall return them to the presenter or pass them on without responsibility.

(b) The Issuing Bank, the Confirming Bank, if any, or a Nominated Bank acting on their behalf, shall each have a reasonable time, not to exceed seven banking days following the day of receipt of the documents, to examine the documents and determine whether to take up or refuse the documents and to inform the party from which it received the documents accordingly.

(c) If a Credit contains conditions without stating the document(s) to be presented in compliance therewith, banks will deem such conditions as not stated and will disregard them.

Article 14

Discrepant Documents and Notice

(a) When the issuing Bank authorises another bank to pay, incur a deferred payment undertaking, accept Draft(s), or negotiate against documents which appear on their face to be in compliance with the terms and conditions of the Credit, the Issuing Bank and the Confirming Bank if any are bound: (i) to reimburse the Nominated Bank which has paid or incurred an undertaking and (ii) to take up documents.

This example will indicate the precision and detail required but reference should be made to the full brochure when administering credits. This should also be supplemented with Brochure 511 which gives a detailed interpretation of the Articles and compares them with the previous 1984 rules which were superseded in January 1994.

A checklist for letters of credit

1   Type of letter of credit: irrevocable, confirmed, etc.
2   Period of validity: expiry date.
3   Are there any other limiting time factors? Does bill of lading have to be dated before a certain time? Is there any expiry date of import licences or currency permits?
4   Are description of goods, names, etc., correct?

5 Check total value of credit. Is it sufficient? What currency? Are there any tolerances?

6 What documents are called for, such as bills of lading, air waybills, certificates of shipment, etc? Are clean shipped-on-board bills required? Should they be made out 'to Order'? Is part shipment or transhipment allowed?

7 If insurance is involved, is a policy or certificate called for? What value should be covered for insurance purposes? Where should claims be made payable and in what currency? And, of course, what risk cover is required?

8 Are there any special peripheral documents called for such as quality certificates or inspection notes? Check to see if inspection by an outside authority is specified.

9 Check port of departure and port of destination.

10 Ensure that the advising bank's instructions, also the manner in which the draft should be drawn and presented, are carefully noted and adhered to.

11 Pay particular attention to any specialized documents, such as consular invoices and certificates of origin, that may be required. Remember that many of these will have to be obtained from outside sources such as consulates and chambers of commerce. The cost and time involved in obtaining them must be borne in mind. Check most carefully to see if there are any obligations as to the dating of these documents. For example, it may sometimes be the case that a certificate of origin must be dated prior to the date of a dispatch document such as bill of lading or air waybill.

12 Remember that a letter of credit should be checked immediately it is received. Any discrepancies or confusing items can often be easily rectified by contacting the customer via the bank. This is often easy if done in the early stages but becomes expensive and annoying to the customer if left to the last moment.

13 Finally, is there a presentation date mentioned? If not, we have 21 days from date of shipment.

It will be seen from the above that, when the letter of credit is being analysed, reference to the *Uniform Customs and Practice* brochure (where applicable) will enable many points to be clarified.

Dealing with discrepancies

Naturally, the experienced exporter will expect transactions to proceed smoothly and for the draft and documents to be negotiated without difficulty. There will, however, always be the possibility that some problem or discrepancy will arise and it is necessary, therefore, for the various techniques of overcoming these problems to be studied.

The following sequence should be followed, wherever possible, when the exporter is faced with documents which contain some irregularity or discrepancy which has resulted in the bank refusing to meet the draft.

1 First of all, the discrepancy should be rectified by the exporters, themselves, if at all possible.
2 On many occasions it might be preferable to contact the customer requesting an alteration in the terms of credit to enable the paying bank to meet the draft or to request the bank to request permission to pay. It is often possible to ask the paying bank to telex for permission to pay.
3 The exporter may use a form of indemnity countersigned by their own bank against which payment is made.
4 Payment is made under reserve.
5 The documents are sent forward for collection.

Some examples of the conditions which might give rise to the above courses of action are as follows:

1 When presenting the documents, a mistake might have been made on the exporter's commercial invoice. It is usually a simple task for a fresh invoice to be prepared and re-presented.
2 A bill of lading may have been 'claused' when the credit calls for 'clean shipped on board' bills. In this case, the exporter cannot rectify the position and, if time permits, might be able to contact the customer asking for the claused bill to be made acceptable under the credit.
3 Very often there is not time to take the necessary steps to rectify discrepancies and the possibility of using a letter of indemnity has to be considered. This document, signed by the exporter and countersigned by the exporter's bank, would be submitted to the paying bank with the documents. The draft

could then be paid but, of course, when the documents arrive the overseas importer would be free to reject them if the discrepancy in question ran counter to requirement and was perhaps regarded as of fundamental importance. In such a case as this, the paying bank could then return to the exporter and ask for reimbursement under the terms of the indemnity.

In many cases the use of a letter of indemnity can act as a very useful form of 'lubrication' and help considerably in certain types of discrepancies. It might be the only possibility in a case where a 'stale' bill of lading is involved. After all, the customer will still normally want the goods, but the indemnity might well protect the importer's interest should heavy warehousing or other expenses be incurred due to the delay.

It should, however, be realized that in practice the raising of a letter of indemnity must to some extent weaken that 'without recourse' concept which is, as we have seen, of paramount importance to the exporter in letter of credit transactions.

4 'Payment under Reserve' is basically the same approach as the letter of indemnity but in this case there is no formal document and the payment is made under a verbal agreement and represents a high degree of trust between exporter and banker.

5 Should the case arise where a set of documents contain numerous serious discrepancies, then it may be impossible to employ any of the above techniques. In this event, the bank will not pay against the exporter's draft but simply send the documents forward to the issuing bank overseas in trust, who will present them to the importer, who will then have the choice of either accepting or rejecting them and paying or not paying. This in effect has reduced the original letter of credit to the status of documents against payment.

It must again be emphasized that banks, when handling and paying against letters of credit, are really bound within very precise limits to observe the doctrine of strict compliance and therefore the requirements called for by the letter of credit must be precisely observed.

Over the years, SITPRO and leading banks, particularly the Midland Bank, have carried out surveys and monitored the performance of exporters in handling letters of credit. Progress has certainly been made but although it is not possible to be absolutely accurate there seems little doubt that just over half of all documents presented against credits are rejected on first presentation. This, of course, is an average figure and there would be many variations between different companies and their degree of efficiency.

A very useful contribution has been the activities of SITPRO and the ICC in improving the standardization of Letter of Credit formats and also the improving technology of banking communications.

So far we have examined the various mechanisms of payment encountered in international trade, from the viewpoint of security, competitiveness and cash-flow considerations. This, however, was really only half the story and the exporter needs to be familiar with other elements of the overall financial background to overseas payments. Essentially, these fall under two broad headings, namely: the possibility of foreign exchange units entering the picture; plus the need to appreciate some of the financial, credit insurance institutions and other sources of finance that may be available. In some high-level and sophisticated transactions there may even be the question of barter/compensation deals.

A knowledge of the existence of various schemes of credit insurance and availability of lines of credit and inter-government financing may, in many cases, make all the difference to penetrate export markets. Perhaps no other field in exporting has seen such a rapid development as the financial operations devised and operated by banks, governments, state trading organizations, factors and varieties of merchant banks, etc.

Let us first of all consider some of the salient features encountered with the possible involvement with foreign exchanges.

The mechanism of foreign exchange

A feature of foreign trade is that in many cases the question of foreign currency and exchange rates will arise at some time during the transaction. It may of course transpire that exporters will transact orders expressed in their own currency, i.e. dollars, francs or pounds, and of course some currencies do not take upon themselves international roles. Consequently, from say, a UK exporter's point of view, the sterling unit will often be employed. In other cases, however, overseas importers will pay in their own currency which the exporter will normally (but not necessarily) use to purchase their own currency units.

On the other hand, the exporter could quote in the buyer's currency and normally use the currency so earned to purchase sterling for subsequent crediting to an appropriate domestic account.

Choices facing exporters when dealing with such a situation are as follows:

1 How will quotations be expressed? In sterling or in the overseas currency?
2 Is an exchange variation possible and, if so, how much risk is there of losing money owing to this variation?
3 What steps can be taken to remove the risk?

It should be borne in mind at this early stage that in some countries various forms of exchange control may operate and needless to say these will have a profound effect upon the currency options open to both exporters and importers.

Before considering the above in detail, let us look briefly at the mechanism of exchange rates. In a sense, a foreign exchange transaction, resulting from trade between countries, is a system which operates by inter-bank settlements. Let us assume a UK exporter has sold goods to a customer in Paris. That customer, in order to pay the exporter, will arrange to have a franc account at the French bank debited to the value of the invoice for the goods. The UK exporter will expect in due course to have a sterling account credited by the corresponding amount. By one method or another, therefore, the francs debited from the importer's account have to be transmuted into sterling credited to the exporter.

Usually this will, of course, be arranged between, in this case, the French and UK banks and this could be done in two ways:

1 The French bank could literally use the importer's francs to buy the necessary amount of sterling to meet the needs of the UK exporter, or
2 the French bank could credit the account of the UK bank in francs, which would mean that in effect the UK is holding francs in Paris.

In the latter case, the UK bank might credit the sterling account of the exporter and itself hold francs in Paris. Thus, we might represent the position graphically, as in Figure 9.5.

Now suppose that at a later stage a French exporter secures an order from a buyer in the UK. In this case, the UK importer's sterling account in francs will be credited. What could well happen

Figure 9.5 International exchange mechanism

is that the UK banking system could utilize francs from the account it was holding in the French bank. Should the UK banks hold no francs in this way, then they would have either to buy francs in the foreign exchange market, or the French bank could elect to hold a sterling balance to its credit in, say, London. In other words, in the case of a French export, the procedure would have been reversed.

Naturally, inter-banking operations nowadays are much more complicated due to the existence of the currency markets which in essence means that foreign currencies will often move out of their own countries to be borrowed and utilized in overseas financial systems. Such movements, against varying interest rates in the money market, will naturally exert a marked influence on exchange rates.

Nevertheless, the simple example outlined above is sufficient to show that, in order to support international trade, the banking system will find itself either buying or selling foreign currency or at times holding foreign currency balances in other countries. When one enlarges upon this and thinks of the volume of trade throughout a large number of different countries, all involving the exchange of many different units of currency, it will be seen that the net effect of these transactions will have an impact upon the demand for, or supply of, a particular currency unit.

If one regards a unit of currency in the same way as any other commodity, then one could postulate that if the demand for, say, the French franc increased (perhaps because of a large outflow of exports from that country) then the overall effect would be that foreign banks would be buying larger quantities of francs and the price of the franc in terms of the respective importing countries' currency would increase. It would be possible, therefore, to say at this stage that the exchange rate would be a result of the combined effects of supply and demand for a particular currency unit. Of course, apart from trade causing movements in exchange rates, the combined effect of overseas investment, short-term capital movements and the payment of invisible imports and exports, i.e. shipping, insurance and banking, would all play their parts in shaping rates.

Underlying all these movements, foreign exchange specialists also recognize the concept of the 'Purchasing Power Parity' theory. Briefly stated, this theory holds that the ratio of one currency to another will approximate to the relative purchasing powers of those two currencies in their respective countries. If, for example, £1 sterling in London will buy a parcel of goods costing, say, 9 French francs to buy in Paris, then the exchange rate would be in the neighbourhood of £1 = 9 French fr. There are, of course, certain objections to this concept. It is not always easy to compare purchasing habits of different countries and consequently comparable parcels of goods cannot always be obtained. Nevertheless, in the long run, the value of currency compared with those of other countries must of necessity determine the ultimate exchange rate. The various monetary policies practised by different countries, and the UK attempts to combat inflation, are all examples of the practical significance of this theory.

Although mention has been made above of the price of a currency (exchange rate) in terms of another currency, and this likened to any other commodity which can be allowed to respond to the mechanics of supply and demand, there are very great difficulties when applied to foreign exchange. The aim of monetary authorities is usually to stabilize exchange rates to allow for a smooth flow of international payments and to avoid erratic fluctuations which can become a prey to speculation, thus playing havoc with internal economies. Only a very few countries are in a position to isolate themselves from the effect of international currency. The more involved in international trade a country is, the more exchange rates will affect its internal economy and vice versa. The UK is, of course, an example of a country which is heavily involved in the international currency market.

One of the classic mechanisms which in the past has been used and advocated as a stabilizing factor is the gold standard. Without going into the intricacies of the various types of gold standard, it can be summed up as a system which relates a particular series of currencies to a gold value. If a currency tends to fall in exchange rate compared with other currencies, there will come a point when gold will begin to flow out of that currency's country; conversely, it will flow in if the currency in question appreciates in relation to others. In both cases, the assumption is that the movement of gold will affect the monetary policy and operations of the particular country involved. A drain of gold, for example, should lead to a tight and dear monetary policy, restricting the economy and causing a fall in the price level. This should be followed by a discouragement of imports and a stimulation of exports. Logically this should lead to an improvement of the exchange rate in relation to its gold value and a subsequent flowing back of gold into the country which can then bring about an expansion in industrial activity.

The years between 1919 and 1925 had been a period of instability and fluctuation of exchange rates accompanied in some cases by severe inflation. In 1925 there was a return to the gold standard but in 1931 this collapsed due to certain basic distortions in exchange rates and accumulations of gold in the hands of some countries, notably the USA and France. After the abandonment of the gold standard, a number of countries still maintained their currency link with the UK, notably, of course in the Commonwealth system. Despite this, however, the period up to 1939 was one of chronic instability with wide variations in exchange rates and great confusion in the field of international trade.

It is fully appreciated that some of the above and following comments are very largely purely historical. However, it is to some degree necessary to discuss the evolution of various types of international mechanism in order to appreciate and understand current operations and to follow future developments.

The International Monetary Fund

The end of the Second World War brought in its wake a determination by most of the leading nations to do all in their power to create a stable international economy. The International Monetary Fund was conceived at the famous Bretton Woods Conference in 1944 and established in 1946. The IMF, amongst other things, sought stabilized exchange rates and international trade by:

1 Accumulating a pool of gold and foreign currency,
2 the fixing of exchange rates, and
3 the creation of institutions such as the International Bank for Reconstruction and Development.

Briefly, IMF member states made contributions of gold and currency which could be drawn upon by members in time of need to

Rates at end of 1980 (100) US $2.34   DM 4.62   FF 10.70

Figure 9.6   Depreciation of sterling, 1980–1984

overcome some temporary imbalance in the exchange reserves. An essential component part of this system was the discipline of maintaining individual rates of exchange within a very narrow band of variation at time ± 1 per cent. This meant that individual countries had to control their economies with regard to inflation, etc., practising appropriate monetary policies.

Since June 1972, however, most currencies became free to float and respond to supply and demand, although in the UK, for example, the Bank of England often intervened to support sterling when under pressure.

The initial inflationary effect of the downward-floating pound was considerable and Figure 9.6 shows the effect upon sterling.

Recently, of course, there has been something of a return to more managed currencies which can be seen best perhaps by considering the attitude of the European Union and single market concept. We have seen the aim of the European Monetary System (EMS) as one of creating a Central Bank, and a uniform currency, the ECU. The mechanism leading to this was the Exchange Rate Mechanism (ERM) designed to oblige members to take appropriate policies on public expenditure and inflation and to maintain their exchange rates within a band of plus or minus 2.25%. Exceptions for example were the Spanish Peseta and UK Pound Sterling where the margin was + 6 per cent. The UK joined in 1990, but had to suspend membership after a drastic run on sterling and interest rates having to rise to an unacceptable level.

Obviously the future of the system is far from clear but if countries are really serious about a single market, then some form of common currency, banking system and monetary policy would seem inevitable. All these factors impinge upon the exporter and importer in the form of varying degrees of uncertainty as to how rates of exchange will move and how this will affect their international payments and receipts.

How the quotation will be expressed

A trader may of course quote overseas customers in sterling. In this case, the exchange variation risk is in effect passed to them because when the time for settlement of the debt arrives, they will have to pay in their own currency to produce sufficient sterling to meet the invoiced value. However, in a growing number of cases, UK exporters are being called upon to quote in the currency of their overseas buyers. This enables the prospective customer to ascertain the value of the transaction at a glance. In addition, they will know just what sum of money they will be called upon to pay when the time for settlement of the debt arrives. Generally speaking, therefore, a competent exporter will quote in foreign currency thereby being faced with a possibility of an exchange variation.

We will cite the case of a manufacturer who is going to sell £10000 worth of machine tools to a buyer in Paris.

Rate of exchange prevailing at time of transaction 9 fr = £1

Therefore quotation for 90000 fr, payment within three months.

Exporter will therefore receive that number of francs.

Now supposing, when the debt is settled in three months, the rate of exchange has moved to 9.5 fr (i.e. the franc has weakened) then:

$$\frac{90\,000}{9.5} = £9474 \text{ instead of the calculated } £10\,000 \text{ price}$$

and the exporter has lost a little in the transaction. On the other hand, if the rate has moved to 8.5 (i.e. the franc has strengthened) then:

$$\frac{90\,000}{8.5} = £10\,588$$

In this case, the exporter has gained.

The example variations have been magnified just to make it easier to compare the calculations.

Naturally, if large sums of money are involved in the transactions the gains and losses involved might be considerable and the exporter will have to consider what steps must be taken. These might be as follows:

1 No action at all if the sums of money are small; experience may show that over the year there are gains and losses which tend to cancel themselves out.
2 To incorporate an exchange clause in the contract such as 'the price quoted is based on an exchange rate of 9 fr = £1 and that any variation is for buyer's account'. This type of clause might be necessary, especially in long-term contracts, but it does leave the customer in a state of uncertainty which in some areas of trade might not be acceptable.
3 To cover the risk by using the forward exchange market.

Forward exchange cover

It must be remembered that when an exporter concludes an overseas contract there will usually be a period of time before payment. If business is being transacted in a foreign currency unit the floating up or down that might take place in exchange rates will, to some extent, have a bearing upon the amount of sterling received with the currency when payment actually takes place. The act of covering forward exchange, therefore, is one of attempting to remove uncertainty and to know exactly what proceeds will be received when the transaction is completed. Depending upon the nature and degree of forward movements it might also be possible to gain a little from the transaction. It should be borne in mind, however, that the exporter rarely wishes to get involved in exchange speculations and is concerned mainly with stabilizing the trading position.

In the foreign exchange market there are two basic component parts: (1) the spot market, and (2) the forward market. Spot rates are those quoted for immediate sale or purchase of foreign currency. Forward rates are those which dealers or banks quote for (a) purchase of a foreign currency at some point in the future, or (b) sale of foreign currency at some future date. Usually the popular periods of time are three, six and nine months forward. A simplified example might be represented as follows:

Spot Rate Italian Lire	2493.00 = £1
1 month forward	8 Lr premium
3 months forward	10 Lr premium

The above are rather simplified figures but they are useful to illustrate the principles involved. It will be seen that the word 'premium' is used in this case. This means that the forward Lire is stronger in relation to the sterling equivalent and to arrive at the actual forward rate we must always *deduct* the premium figure. Therefore, in the above case the one month forward rate would be 2493 less 8 = 2485L, and, for three months, 2493 less 10 = 2483L. It will be seen in both cases that *less* Lire will be given in exchange for pounds.

Conversely, we might find that the forward market quotes for a currency at a *discount*:

Spot Rate Italian Lire	2493.00 = £1
1 month forward	10 Lr discount
3 months forward	20 Lr discount

In this case, the forward Lire is weaker in relation to sterling and this time the figure is added to the spot rate. Thus, the result would be 2493 plus 10 = 2503, and 2493 plus 20 = 2513 Lr.

The exporter will then have to make a decision as to the forward sale of the foreign currency. This decision is based upon a desire for certainty and the prevailing discount or premium which, in many respects, will in turn be based upon prevailing interest rates, plus supply and demand, existing in the money market. It should also be remembered that if the forward currency is strong, the exporter will stand to gain from the exchange rate. For example, if a spot rate is $1.48 = £1 and the forward rate is $1.47, there will be a 0.01 advantage. Also, it should be borne in mind that a UK importer could be *buying* forward foreign currency to meet overseas debts and an exporter will be *selling* forward the proceeds of an anticipated sale.

In practice, in the foreign exchange market, two rates are usually encountered, namely the buying and selling rates. For example:

US Dollar
1.6332–1.6342

The left-hand figure is the rate of which a bank or foreign exchange dealer will *sell* dollars and the right-hand figure is the one at which they will be *bought*.

We might in this case, therefore, envisage an importer arranging to buy dollars at the rate of 1.6332 = £1 to meet overseas debts and an exporter arranging to sell forward the dollars expected from an overseas transaction at the rate of 1.6342 = £1. The difference between the two is the profit margin of the dealer, and there will also be a commission charged.

The above dollar rates can now be developed further and shown as follows:

Spot dollar	1.6332	1.6342
Forward 1 month	.07 premium	.06 premium
1 month rate	1.6325	1.6336

Taking the above figures as an example, if an exporter has sold to a customer in Boston on the basis of one month's credit, and had quoted in dollars, then on receipt of the currency it could be sold at 1.6336.

The undermentioned represent a typical series of rates taken from a financial newspaper which indicates the premiums and discounts encountered in several series of exchange rates for different currencies:

Forward rates	*One month*	*Three months*
Austria	15–13 gr.pm.	40–37 gr.pm.
Belgium	30–24 c.pm.	79–70 c.pm.
Canada	0.52–0.46 c.pm.	1.31–1.23 c.pm.
Denmark	$3\frac{1}{4}$–2 ore pm.	$9\frac{1}{8}$–$7\frac{7}{8}$ ore pm.
France	$2\frac{1}{2}$–$1\frac{5}{8}$ c.pm.	$5\frac{1}{4}$–4 c.pm.
Germany (W)	$2\frac{1}{2}$–$2\frac{1}{4}$ pfg.pm.	$6\frac{7}{8}$–$6\frac{1}{2}$ pfg.pm.
Holland	$2\frac{1}{4}$–2 c.pm.	$6\frac{3}{8}$–6 c.pm.
Italy	par–3 lr.disc.	5–10 lr.disc.
Norway	$\frac{1}{4}$ pm. – $\frac{5}{8}$ ore or.disc.	$\frac{5}{8}$–$1\frac{1}{4}$ or.disc.
Sweden	$3\frac{1}{2}$–$4\frac{3}{8}$ or.disc.	$11\frac{1}{4}$–12 ore disc.
Switzerland	$2\frac{1}{4}$–2 c.pm.	6–$5\frac{5}{8}$ c.pm.
United States	0.57–0.54 c.pm.	1.52–1.47 c.pm.

Depending upon the relationship between exporter and banker, it may sometimes be necessary for a deposit of money to be lodged with the bank when a forward contract is arranged. A typical set of conditions related to a forward exchange contract is set out as follows:

FORWARD EXCHANGE

Terms on which INTERNATIONAL BANK LIMITED
enters into contracts with ....
for the purchase or sale of foreign currency for forward delivery:

1 On the making of each contract the customer will deposit with the Bank by way of cover either cash or approved security equal to . . .% of the sterling value of the currency calculated at contract price and maintain such cover until the completion of the contract.

2 At any time between the making of each contract and its completion the customer, if so requested by the Bank, will lodge and maintain with the Bank, in addition to the deposit referred to above, further cash or approved security sufficient to keep the Bank fully covered against depreciation (in the event of a sale by the Bank) or the appreciation (in the event of a purchase by the Bank) in the market value of the currency.

3 If the customer fails in any respect to fulfil the terms of the contract (including the provision above) the Bank is authorized (but not compelled) to close the contract without notice at the market price of the currency at the time of such default, notwithstanding that the maturity of the contract may not have been reached, and to debit or credit the customer with any resulting difference.

4 Any cover lodged with the Bank in accordance with the above provisions may be applied by the Bank in or towards satisfaction of any resulting difference.

To INTERNATIONAL BANK LIMITED .... Branch

I/We AGREE that the terms set out above shall be deemed to be incorporated in all contracts which from time to time I/We may conclude with you for the purchase or sale of foreign currency for forward delivery.

Date .... Signature ....

Option contracts

In cases where it might be uncertain as to the exact time of receipt of proceeds an 'option' contract could be utilized; for example, *3/4 months option* enabling the exporter to transact the exchange contract at any time between those two periods.

Credit institutions and sources of finance

Both exporters and importers need to be familiar with the various types of financial and credit institutions which will often play both a part in underpinning the credit risk and cash flow aspect, or actually provide sources of funds available for international trade. These institutions both large and small will range from private and public sector and also increasingly international and multi-national organizations. They can be broadly categorized as follows:

International lending agencies

One such is the World Bank Group which consists of the International Bank for Reconstruction and Development (IBRD), International Development Association (IDA) and the International Finance Corporation (IFC). Within the broader international framework can be found a considerable number of more specialized agencies such as the European Development Fund (EDF), Inter-American Development Bank (IDB), the Arab Fund for Economic and Social Development (AFESD) and of course, many United Nations' organizations such as the United Nations Industrial Development Organization (UNIDO). Naturally, most of these organizations will place considerable stress upon the infrastructures of developing countries.

Export houses

It has already been seen how confirming houses have traditionally acted on behalf of overseas buyers, and nowadays their services extend well into the financial field. Such confirming houses would provide finance to cover the gap between the goods leaving the factory and being purchased by the end user. Credit is provided for periods of 30 to 180 days and is available for all types of goods. Exports of capital goods can often be covered for periods of up to five years. The charges made usually take the form of a commission based on period of credit, average invoice value, volume of business and the amount of other services provided. Also, interest is charged on an annual basis for the period of the credit granted. Usually, when acting on behalf of the buyers, all charges are borne by them, although they are credited with any cash discounts.

Factors

Another type of institution which enables the exporter sometimes to simplify their trading position is the factor.

In a sense, a factor is an organization which will buy from a trader their outstanding book debts. In practice, the exporter will send all invoices at specified intervals and will receive a cheque for an agreed initial percentage of the total invoice value usually in the area of 80–85%. In fact, the invoices are assigned to the factor who mails them to the individual purchaser. As payments are made the balance of sums due are credited to the exporter. The cost of most factoring services depending on volume and turnover lies between 1 and 2 per cent of sales figures. In addition, interest charges are made in the region of 1.5–3 per cent above basic bank lending rates. Factoring of this type originated very largely in the USA but its use is growing in the UK, where there has been considerable growth in the amount of exports operated using a factoring system.

Some of the major advantages stemming from the use of factors are that they

1 remove the burden from senior management of credit control and debt collection,
2 reduce funds tied up in outstanding debts, and
3 simplify accounting and administration involved in sales ledger work.

Important in the field of factoring would be such companies as Alex Lawrie Factors and International Factors. These organizations have widespread international interests, and quite apart from the cash flow advantage to the exporter, is the wide range of services in the fields of collection proceeds, credit control and foreign exchange which would be carried out on their behalf.

Many of the major operators are associated with the larger banks and in the UK for example belong to the Association of British Factors. An example of some of the members is as follows:

Barclays Commercial Services
Century Factors
Griffin Factors
H & H Factors
International Factors
Alex Lawrie Factors
Lombard NatWest Commercial Services
RoyScot Factors
Security Pacific Business Factors
UDT Commercial Finance

The above forms of financing can usually be made available upon either 'with recourse' or 'non-recourse' or 'limited recourse'. As was mentioned earlier in this chapter, when discussing the discounting of bills of exchange, this would mean, in effect, the creditor being covered in case of say, the insolvency of the buyer in the case of non-recourse financing whereas recourse financing would still leave the possibility of the seller covering any credit loss. Many factors would operate in relationship with some form of credit insurance policy as well. It will be seen later in this chapter that this concept also has important application in 'forfaiting' finance.

Banks

Moving away from the specific international institutions which operate over the wider field of overseas trade, importers and exporters will be utilizing their own banking facilities. The UK exporter, for example, is fortunate in having a wide range of experienced financial institutions which may at times help in financing exports. First of all, there are the clearing banks such as Barclays, Midland, Lloyds and National Westminster. For many exporters, these are the banks which will provide short- or medium-term credit by means of loans and overdrafts, as well as a considerable amount of short-term credit financing by means of advances against bills or actually discounting these bills of exchange. As has been seen in an earlier chapter, they can also provide considerable assistance and advice. They will also act as the main channel through which the various methods of payment, e.g. letters of credit and documentary bills, are transacted.

In international trade, the fraternity of merchant bankers can play an active part in financing exports on a long- and medium-term basis, particularly to the developing countries. They also undertake 'acceptance business', which means that they undertake to accept bills of exchange drawn on them by exporters, thus giving rise to 'bank bills'. These bills can then be discounted by merchant banks who specialize in the field of bill discounting. The bulk of the money used by these bill-brokers is obtained from the clearing banks on call and at short notice at fairly low rates of interest.

Credit insurance institutions

So far, the institutions considered have been those concerned with actually providing finance for the exporter, or smoothing the path by extending credit to the buyer, or speeding up cash flow, as, for example, by factoring. In addition, however, there are different types of 'credit insurance' institutions from which an exporter can obtain an insurance policy providing cover against various risks that may be encountered internationally which might prevent or delay the payment for orders from overseas. These might be private or government organizations, or indeed, combinations of both, such bodies as COFACE in France, HERMES in Germany or Export Credits Guarantee Department (ECGD) in the UK, the Dutch NCM Group and Trade Indemnity. In addition to giving actual credit risk cover, such organizations may extend various financial guarantees to buyer or seller, thus making lines of credit more easily available from banking or other financial institutions. An example of the evolution of such institutions can be seen in the acquisition of the Insurance Services Organisation of ECGD by NCM. The Government organization now tends to concentrate usually in association with the banking system in underpinning lines of credit and buyer finance.

A typical pattern of an export credit insurance cover can best be illustrated by the following extract from an NCM brochure:

NCM will insure you against both buyer risks, and, if appropriate, country risks in the same policy. NCM can meet the needs of any company – from the smaller business requiring full and overall protection, to the more sophisticated, usually larger company, looking for a specific form of insurance tailor-made to cover particular aspects of its operations.

Buyer Risks Covered
- The insolvency of the buyer.
- The buyer's failure to pay within six months of due date for goods accepted.
- The buyer's failure, or refusal, to accept goods despatched which comply with the contract.

Country Risks Covered
- Delays in transferring money from the buyer's country.
- Any action of the government of a foreign country which wholly or partly prevents performance of the contract.
- Political events or economic, legislative or administrative measures occurring outside the UK which prevent or delay transfer of payment.
- War, civil war and the like, outside the UK (other than war

between the five major powers) preventing performance of the contract.

- Cancellation or non renewal of an export licence or the imposition of new restrictions on exports, after date of contract.
- When NCM agrees that the public buyer cause of loss applies – the failure or refusal to fulfil any of the terms of contract.

You are normally covered for 90 per cent of loss in cases of buyer default or insolvency and 95 per cent for the country risks. When the buyer's failure to accept or take up the goods is applicable, a first loss of 20% applies and NCM bears 90 per cent of the balance.

At another level the services of the Export Finance Co. Ltd. (EXFINCO) could be utilized by companies selling on terms of up to 180 days usually holding comprehensive, short-term insurance cover. This could mean the exporter receiving 100 per cent of the credit insured value of the sales in sterling at the time of shipment. The balance, less any deductions resulting from credit notes or other adjustments, is paid on the average due date of the exporter's sales. Regular cash flow is thus fully assured. This facility is priced competitively and has the particular advantage that as the exporter's sales expand so does the facility without continual re-negotiation.

Another example of inter-bank mechanisms of financing exports is that of 'forfaiting'. This, in essence, is a specialized form of bill or promissory note discounting mentioned earlier. It provides an appropriate method of medium-term export finance without recourse and involves the purchase by banks of the trade debts. The mechanics of this method can be seen from the following example:

1 The Hungarian International Bank is approached by a UK industrial goods manufacturer negotiating a contract for the supply of heavy industrial equipment to a state buyer in Turkey. The buyer desires repayment by four semi-annual instalments, i.e. over a two-year deferred payment term. Payments to be guaranteed by Turkiye Is Bankasi.
2 The relevant forfaiting rates are quoted to the UK company for financing deals in sterling, US dollars and Deutschmarks. The Turkish buyer opts for DM and the credit price and repayment values are calculated.
3 The sales contract is negotiated upon the basis of four bills of exchange drawn by the UK exporter in advance of contractual

performance. These are accepted by the Turkish importer and given an aval or guarantee by the above-named Turkish bank. The bills are then held by the Hungarian International Bank in the UK to be released to the exporter against presentation of the shipping documents in accordance with the contract.

4 Once the bills are released against documentary presentation, they are discounted by the Hungarian Bank at a committed discount rate and the exporter receives cash payment for the full contract value on a *non-recourse* basis.

5 The exporter, therefore, essentially deals on a cash contract basis whilst the buyer operates on deferred-payment terms. The costs involved are borne by the importer, apart from a commitment fee of 1 per mille per month, charged on the value of the financing arrangement from time of commitment to when the bills are discounted. These costs could be taken into account at time of contract arrangement and included by the exporter in the contractual price.

The above represents an illustrative example only, but is based upon a typical operation.

The expression is derived from the fact that the forfaiter (bank) agrees to waive or forfeit the right of recourse against the creditor (exporter) should the latter fail to receive payment from the buyer.

Countertrade

Although somewhat specialized, it would not be proper to conclude this chapter without a reference to counter trading or bartering. Essentially, this represents a number of possible permutations whereby the sales of goods to an overseas market may be linked contractually to an obligation to buy goods or services from that country. A recent study suggests that no less than eighty-three countries have at times been involved in countertrade. Figure 9.7 illustrates a straightforward Full Compensations Deal and a Triangular Compensation Operation.

The average exporter will need to rely heavily upon banks and specialized people such as commodity brokers, etc., to assist in matching up the disposal and sales of bartered goods in order to receive satisfactorily the resultant proceeds in cash terms. Barclays Bank plc, from whom the information was helpfully provided, operate a special countertrade advisory unit.

It will be seen from this chapter, therefore, that exporters and

TRIANGULAR COMPENSATION
(with Hard Currency Goods)

FULL COMPENSATION
(Value in Money)

1. Triangular compensation involves the movement of goods between three countries.
2. This arrangement is appropriate when the hard goods offered in compensation by Country B are readily saleable, but not necessarily in Country A.
3. The goods are sold in Country C who then settle in foreign exchange with Country A.

1. One hundred per cent two-way transfer of goods, by means of a single contract.
2. The goods are valued in monetary units.
3. Settlement is often achieved by setting off the sale proceeds of the compensation goods against the amount due from the importer in Country B.
4. The compensation obligation may be transferred to a third party, against payment to that party of a subsidy, called a disagio.

Figure 9.7   Illustration of countertrading

importers need to keep constantly abreast of the fast-moving developments in this vital area of financial institutions, their operations and cross-linking systems. This will be necessary both to cushion the various types of credit risks that could arise with an export sale and to be able to identify various sources of finance and ways of improving cash flow. Obviously, there is no one simple method since much will depend upon the nature of the product, type of market, length of credit period, etc. The skill required will be to identify appropriate sources suitable for a specific type of contract situation.

10 *Cargo insurance*

Insurance is a basic element both in our personal lives and in commerce. Privately, we insure our cars, our homes and possessions; in business, we insure our goods, our factories and transport. When we extend the practice of insurance to international commerce, it understandably takes upon itself a more complex pattern due to the wide variety of goods, countries and methods of transportation which are encountered in the exporting of goods and services. To the practising exporter, the class of insurance of interest is cargo insurance, particularly that falling under the headings of marine and air insurance policies. Marine insurance is not limited to transport by sea exclusively as it will, in practice, often cover any portion of a journey which is made over land. Similarly, insurance for exports by air is handled mainly through the marine insurance brokers, and a specialized market at Lloyd's deals with this type of cover. Air insurance still draws heavily upon the accumulated experience and principles or marine insurance.

No part of export is more interesting, or of greater antiquity, than marine insurance; plenty of evidence exists to show that forms of insurance for international trading were being practised in the Mediterranean before the Christian era. The very language and terminology used in insurance practice and documentation is rich and eloquent, still using Elizabethan and eighteenth-century phrases and expressions. In 1601, an Elizabethan Act set up machinery to define insurance and marine insurance policies and to prescribe rules and regulations for their settlement. The definition itself is couched in beautiful language and expresses its meaning clearly, as is shown by the following extract:

... by means of which policies of assurance it cometh to pass that upon the loss or perishing of any ship there followeth not the undoing of any man, but the loss lighteth rather easily upon many than heavily upon few, and rather upon them that adventure not than those that do adventure, whereby all merchants, especially the younger sort, are allured to venture more willingly and more freely.

Even today, it would be very difficult to describe the whole philosophy of marine insurance, and its principles more clearly than this, as it sums up the whole basis of insurance, namely the spreading of the risk element amongst many. If traders should lose whole cargoes without insurance cover, they might well be ruined. On the other hand, if a number of individuals undertake to cover a portion of the risk spread over many shipments and cargoes, then the risk becomes more acceptable. The term 'adventure' is still employed in insurance terminology to this day and refers to the actual consignment shipment covered. The last part of the quotation also shows how the tool of marine insurance can shield the trader from the hazards and losses, thus enabling the exporter to enter international trade more willingly. A government department today would give its warmest approval to this Elizabethan incentive.

The experienced exporter, then, must be able to handle insurance as one of the many technical processes encountered in the profession in order to transact business and make the necessary decisions. They must know how to apply the appropriate insurance elements to transactions. This will mean having a working knowledge of the following:

1 The extent of the exporter's liability for the insurance risk and the point at which risk passes from the seller to buyer. This will, of course, hinge upon the nature of the particular export contract, i.e. whether it is on an FOB, CIF, or other basis.
2 A background knowledge of the Marine Insurance Act of 1906 which originally encompassed the standard Lloyd's policy which, in turn, has been developed into the more simplified Marine All Risks (MAR) policy incorporating various Institute of London Underwriters (ILU) clauses.
3 The various parties and institutions involved in the marine insurance scene, for example, Lloyd's underwriters, insurance companies and brokers.
4 The procedures involved in arranging insurance and the

relevant documents employed such as policies, certificates and open cover.

5 Payment of premiums, calculations and procedures generally involved in the making and settlement of claims.

Even a brief expansion of these headings will show that a considerable amount of complex subject matter is involved in the entire process. It will be impossible for the average exporter to master completely such a specialized field, and indeed, there is no real need. They can utilize the skill and experience of brokers or insurance companies who will advise on the best type of cover and the cost of the premium. In practice, some shippers will instruct their forwarding agents to take complete responsibility for the insurance of their exports. Nevertheless, professionals will feel that it is incumbent upon them to gain a knowledge of the basic principles of marine insurance so that they can relate them to particular orders and understand the background of the different types of risk and hazard, the appropriate type of cover available and how this will affect the premium to be paid. It will be necessary to achieve the correct balance between adequate cover and yet at the same time obtain as favourable a rate of premium as possible. Obviously, it would be a great mistake to ship goods which are not adequately covered against the types of hazard appropriate to the nature of the goods. Equally, it would be unsatisfactory to over-insure and pay high premiums covering types of risk which may not be particularly relevant to the category of goods involved. Only a clear understanding of the various insurance risk clauses will enable the exporter to select the type of cover relevant to the transaction.

There must be sufficient understanding of the requirements specified by the customer. For example, an order may arrive calling for a specific type of cover which perhaps is not included in the exporter's normal policy. Action would have to be taken to make adjustments to the insurance cover and, if appropriate, to advise the customer of any extra premium payments which may be involved.

The two primary elements which will determine the exporter's course of action and condition the approach to insuring a transaction are:

1 terms of sale and type of contract, and
2 insurable interest.

When we considered export sales clauses (Chapter 2), it was seen that cost and performance obligations arose between buyer and seller and that they would also impinge upon the transferring of the property in the goods and risk transference. With an FOB contract, for example, the seller will need to arrange insurance cover and be responsible for its cost until the goods are actually loaded on board the designated vessel. We can say, therefore, that the risk passes to the buyer at that point, who will have to arrange the insurance. It should be stressed that, in the case of a pure FOB contract, the seller must advise the customer that the goods have reached this position, thus enabling the buyer to make all the necessary arrangements. After this point, they buyer will need to pay for them even if they are lost or arrive in a damaged condition.

With regard to the CIF contract, the duty of the seller is clear: to arrange for appropriate insurance cover for sufficient value and to provide a correct form of insurance document. The CFR contract will call for the buyer to arrange insurance from the same point as FOB but, as we shall see a little later, there can be complications because of a continuing interest, retained to some extent, by the seller.

Passing of risk in relation to passing of property

So far, then, the passing of risk has been considered. Export consignments are often complicated by the relationship of risk to the actual passing of the property. The FOB contract of a seller might, for instance, make provision for the passing of the property to take place upon satisfactory payment of a pro forma invoice. It may be, however, that property only passes after goods have been received and paid for. A CIF transaction would normally bring about the passing of the property by transferring shipping documents against some form of agreed payment such as documentary bill of exchange drawn at sight or on an acceptance basis, or perhaps against a letter of credit.

In the case of a CIF contract, for example, the position is usually clear cut, as the property passing stage is synchronized with the handing over of the relevant documents such as bill of lading, invoice and insurance policy. Supposing that damage has occurred to the consignment, and that the customer, for one reason or another does not take up the documents; the effect of this is that the property does not pass as per contract. Now the risk, which technically passed to the buyer at port of departure, could revert to the seller who has retained a continuing interest in the transaction. This would not be very pleasing to exporters but at least they would (1) possess the title to the goods in the form of the bill of lading, and (2) hold the appropriate insurance policy enabling claims for the loss sustained. In short, we have identified the possibility of risk passing from, and reverting to, the seller.

The position under an FOB sale might be less clear cut and could expose the exporter to rather more risk. Again, we start from the point of risk passing to the buyer, but in this case assuming damage to the consignment takes place as before, the buyer refuses to take up the goods, perhaps claiming that the advice of shipment indicated that the goods were not as specified in the contract. In this instance then, the risk might revert to the seller, but this time the seller might not be covered by any insurance and might not, therefore, be in a position either to obtain payment for the goods or to claim for the loss under an insurance policy.

A similar position would arise if the contract was a CFR one, with the added complication that exporter's interest had been extended by the existence of contracts of affreightment between ship owners. In this case, of course, they would have been responsible for booking shipping space and obtaining the bill of lading. Naturally the above concepts have to be applied in varying degrees to the whole range of quotation sales clauses from ex-works up to delivered, but it is felt that the FOB, CFR and CIF clauses are the most widely used and involve the greatest possibility of risk reversion problems.

The essential factor is that the exporter must be satisfied as to precisely when property passes and how the risk interest in the transaction is related to insurance cover. For FOB and CFR transactions, it is possible to allow for problems of this nature by both parties agreeing that the buyer's insurance policy could be used to cover the seller's interests if necessary. This would necessitate having the consent of the buyer's insurance company. Often this is a simple process, particularly when the insurer has offices in both the countries concerned. This type of arrangement is quite common in business transacted through the various types of export houses such as merchants and confirming organizations.

Another insurance practice is the use of special 'contingency insurance' or seller's risk. An exporter might elect to cover that portion of business transacted on an FOB or CFR by the insertion of a contingency clause in the normal insurance policy. This means that in the event of risk reversion, the insurance can be attached retrospectively to the beginning of the journey, and loss or damage by insured perils is recoverable. A premium would be necessary for this component part of the cover, of course, but it represents a very sound form of operation for an exporter who deals with overseas business on the basis of several different sales clauses.

The points so far can be summed up as follows:

1 nature of sales clause, FOB, CFR, CIF, etc.,
2 where risk passes,
3 passing of property,
4 possibility of risk reversion, and
5 methods of overcoming risk:
   (a) extension of buyer's policy to cover seller's interest,
   (b) arrangement by insuring company with branch office to hold exporter covered, and
   (c) contingency arrangements through exporter's own policy.

The law relating to the passing of property and risk is very complex and varies considerably from country to country. This point should be clarified wherever possible in the conditions of sale and embodied in the contract.

Marine Insurance Act of 1906/MAR policy

The legal framework for marine insurance is provided by the Marine Insurance Act of 1906, which represents the codification of law relating to this subject. Amongst other things, the Act defines:

Marine insurance,
insurable interest,
insurable value,
disclosure and representation,
the evidencing of the contract of insurance by the policy,
the voyage,
premium, and
types of loss.

For example, it makes quite clear that a 'contract of marine insurance may, by its express terms, or by usage of trade, be extended so as to protect the assured against losses on inland waters or on any land risk which may be incidental to any sea voyage'.

Insurable interest

Subject to the provisions of this Act, every person has an insurable interest who is interested in a marine adventure.

In particular a person is interested in a marine adventure where assured he stands in any legal or equitable relation to the adventure or to any insurable property at risk therein, in consequence of which he may benefit by the safety or due arrival of insurable property, or may be prejudiced by its loss, or by damage thereto, or by the detention thereof, or may incur liability in respect thereof.

Note that with regard to insurable interest, the marine insurance policy covers not so much the actual goods but a relationship to those goods.

Disclosure and representation

A contract of marine insurance is a contract based upon the utmost good faith, and, if the utmost good faith be not observed by either party, the contract may be avoided by the other party. This principle is frequently referred to in Latin as *uberrimae fidei*.

The policy also makes it clear that the assured (exporter) must disclose to the insurer every relevant material circumstance which is known to the assured. It is therefore of utmost importance that all facts, such as those relating to packing of goods and nature of voyage, etc., are set out clearly when insurance is being arranged.

Insurable value

In insurance on goods or merchandise, the insurable value is the prime cost of the property insured, plus the expenses of and incidental to shipping and the charges upon the whole.

It is customary to insure for an agreed value which is in the region of 10 to 15 per cent above the CIF value in order to cover incidental losses and out-of-pocket expenses should a loss occur. This is on the assumption that no other specific instructions have been received from the buyer. On occasions, the insured value might well be much higher than the CIF plus the 10 to 15 per cent figure. This is because there may be possibilities of duty payments being made and then loss or damage being sustained on long inland journeys after the discharge of the goods and clearance at the destination port.

It has been seen earlier that the original basic policy covered by the Marine Insurance Act 1906 was the Lloyd's Policy. This policy made provision for a number of different clauses covering particular degrees of risk to be inserted in the basic policy in order to tailor the cover to meet the varying needs of shippers. There were also basic rules for the construction and interpretation of these various clauses. For example, the use of the word 'average' appeared, and employed as a technical term as it meant 'partial loss' of the insured subject matter. For many years, therefore, exporters would have been familiar with such clauses as FPA (Free of Particular Average) not covering partial loss, and WA (With Particular Average) covering partial loss, now known as Institute Cargo Clauses (C) and (B). Other clauses such as 'all risks' were also employed; this became what is known as Clause (A).

Over a period of time naturally these different types of terminology have become very complex and the whole subject was studied by UNCTAD (United Nations Conference on Trade and Development). The result of these deliberations was the introduction of the Marine All Risks Policy with a series of restructured risk clauses.

The use of the MAR policy has been obligatory from 1 April 1983, following UNCTAD's *Report on Marine Insurance*, which was considered by the Institute of London Underwriters, after much detailed study of technicalities and various clauses by a special committee of ILU. The underlying purpose is to bring marine/cargo insurance cover into line with the movement of goods by a variety of transport modes coming into common usage during the past few years, the main one being containerization, and to make sure the international trading community world-wide works to fully-accepted standards and conduct in insurance.

The new policy is dissimilar to its predecessors in that it is simply a document taking in ILU clauses which constitute the cover terms and conditions. All that is recorded on a MAR policy is: full name of assured, the place whence the insurance commences or attaches, the overseas vessel or conveyance, ports or places of loading, ports or places of unloading, final destination, insured value, currency of cover, details of what is insured and its packing. There are spaces for ILU clauses incorporated in that particular policy, and instructions about procedures in the event of loss or damage, for which the underwriter has become liable.

There are five basic sets of ILU cargo clauses: Institute Cargo Clauses (A), (B) and (C), Institute War Clauses (Cargo) and Institute Strike Clauses (Cargo):

ILU Clause (A): covers 'all risks of loss of or damage to the subject matter insured', subject to a general exclusions clause, exclusion of damage due to unseaworthiness of the vessel and to war risks and strikes. The duration is warehouse-to-warehouse and is defined specifically. Other sections deal with claims, the age-old duty of the assured to minimize losses and to avoid delay. The insurance is subject to English Law and practice. The point to remember here is that each member country of the EEC is bringing its statutes more and more into balance and tune with Community legislation, so insurance will doubtless be one of the first commercial activities to 'cross' or 'parallel' its legal obligations and liabilities, as insurance is so fundamental to any transactions, big or small.

ILU Clause (B): covers 'loss of or damage to the subject matter insured reasonably attributed to fire or explosion, vessel or craft being stranded, grounded, sunk or capsized, overturning or derailment of land conveyance, collision or contact of vessel, craft or conveyance with any external object other than water, discharge of cargo at a port of distress, earthquake, volcanic eruption by general average sacrifice, jettison or washing overboard, entry of sea, lake or river water into vessel, craft, hold conveyance, container, lift van, or place of storage, and total loss of any package lost overboard or dropped whilst loading on to, or unloading from, vessel or craft'. As with ILU Clause (A), there are exclusions and the other duties and paramount law.

ILU Clause (C): cover provides basic standard protection against major casualties, but is not as comprehensive as ILU Clause (B) and not as full as ILU Clause (A). (A useful way of rule of thumb when arranging insurance, is that cover decreases in power or force as we go through the alphabet.) Clause (C) says loss or damage to subject matter reasonably attributed to fire and explosion, vessel or craft being stranded, grounded, sunk or capsized, overturning or derailment of land conveyance, collision or contact of vessel, craft or conveyance with any external object other than water, discharge of cargo at a port of distress, loss of or damage to the subject matter insured caused by general average sacrifice or jettison. As with Clauses (A) and (B), there are exclusions, and the other duties and paramount law.

A very important fact to notice is that delay, inherent vice, or nature of the subject matter losses are excluded from clauses and need careful attention to avoid unpleasant results from wrong assumptions or ignorance.

ILU Clauses War Risks (Cargo) and Strike Risks (Cargo): losses by risks of war and strikes are incorporated in the MAR policy by adoption of the appropriate ILU clauses. War risk cover exists only whilst goods are on board and ceases upon discharge (or can be earlier in certain circumstances – underwriter and insured must be quite clear about start and finish of war cover, say, in the Middle East today).

MAR has been tailored to take in many of the older trade clauses appertaining to special interests, and once all have been accommodated satisfactorily the Lloyd's policy would become superfluous.

Because exporters and importers may, for a time, still come across a mixture of old and new terminology, as a guide we could bear in mind the approximate (not exact) equivalents:

Free of Particular Average   now Institute Cargo Clause (C)
  (FPA)
With Average (WA)   now Institute Cargo Clause (B)
All Risks (AR)   now Institute Cargo Clause (A)

Care should be taken when, for example, handling letters of credit, that there is no confusion between the old and new terminologies.

Air cargo

Air cargo is covered by ILU Air Cargo Clauses (All Risks).

The speed and ease of handling air freight makes an insurance risk attractive to the underwriter/insurer, characteristics which are reflected in the lower rates charged generally. Whilst an air disaster is spectacular and concentrates the public attention exceptionally, it is true that air traffic is one of the safest methods of travel/ moving goods and has been over many years. Statistically, it is far removed in the safety factor league from street/pedestrian/road accident which is notoriously high!

By the nature of air movements, very short transit times, lighter packing required, quick clearance at destination points and, in most places, stricter theft-pilferage control, a significant number of export dispatches are sent by air these days, and no longer is it only a service for smaller items, lighter weight and valuables. A typical aircraft manifest, or loading list, shows a wide variety of goods carried.

Though it is possible to arrange lesser cover, it is recommended that the all-risk ILU clauses be used since these give such good protection. Total loss, theft, pilferage and non-delivery are the main worries to be eliminated, if we are prudent.

In Chapter 5, the carriage of dangerous or hazardous goods is mentioned and we refer again to this activity; for obvious reasons, 'restricted articles' regulations bulk large in air freight handling and it is emphasized strongly that the description of what is offered to the airline must be precise. If it is found later, perhaps in less than total 'casualty', that this was not done, the insurers will declare that cover is null and void and cancelled. It is never worthwhile being less than completely frank and honest about your goods – you are not only endangering the passage of inanimate objects, you are endangering lives.

General average

The use of the term 'average' must be quite clearly distinguished from that so far considered. It is quite separate and distinct inasmuch as it envisages the sharing of a loss between shippers and ship-owners. First of all, 'general average' is based upon a relationship between the ship-owner and *all* the shippers who have cargo aboard the same vessel on a particular voyage. All these parties are said to be bound together in the 'adventure'. If, in order to save the ship and some of the cargo, a particular shipper's goods have to be sacrificed, then an act of general average is declared and the ship-owners and the other shippers, whose cargoes have arrived safely, are called upon to contribute towards the loss of the shipper whose cargo has been sacrificed. An example might be of a ship with a full load which takes fire in No. 5 Hold. Action is taken by hose and by throwing overboard burning cargo. The danger is averted and the ship makes port safely with the rest of the cargo intact. All the cargo in No. 5 Hold, however, has been sacrificed. In such a case a general average would be declared and the ship-owner and the owners of the remainder of the cargo would contribute towards the lost cargo in proportion to the value of the ship and freight.

The rule of maritime law in general average is extremely ancient. It can be found in the *Digest* of Justinian and has, throughout the centuries, become a part of the Common Law of England. There are in existence the York–Antwerp Rules which relate to general average. These rules, first formulated in 1877, have been revised several times, the present set dating from 1950 and 1974. They consist of a series of lettered and numbered rules, the following being two specimens:

Rule A There is a general average act when, and only when, any extraordinary sacrifice or expenditure is intentionally and reasonably made or incurred for the common safety for the purpose of preserving from peril the property involved in a common maritime adventure.

Rule 2 No jettison of cargo shall be made good as general average, unless such cargo is carried in accordance with the recognized custom of the trade.

The rules are not a complete code of law but provide a framework and basis of reference and interpretation which can be modified or supplemented by different legislation and practices of individual ship-owners. The Carriage of Goods by Sea Act 1924, 1971 allows for the insertion in a bill of lading of clauses covering any lawful provision regarding general average. The exporter would find such clauses printed amongst the terms and conditions on the back of the bill of lading which might contain the following type of wording:

> General Average, if required, according to York–Antwerp Rules 1950, 1974. Adjustment shall be prepared at such port as shall be selected by the Ship-owners. Such deposits as the Ship-owners or their Agents may deem sufficient to cover the estimated General Average contribution and any salvage and special charges to be made by the Shipper, Consignee, Owner of the goods and/or Holder of this Bill of Lading before delivery.

A general average loss, therefore, takes the form of a deliberate sacrifice of property or the incurring of expense. The following basic elements must be in existence before such a general average can be declared:

1 The purpose of the act must be to preserve the whole maritime adventure. Any such expenditure or sacrifice of property merely to help preserve a part of the adventure would not constitute a general average loss.
2 The particular act must be voluntary and deliberate. General average is a system of making good intentional losses, not those which happen by accident.
3 The loss must be extraordinary.
4 The loss must be reasonably and prudently incurred bearing in mind all the prevailing circumstances. Any hasty or panic action would not result in general average.
5 The particular loss must be a direct result of the general average act. Indirect losses such as alternative opportunity costs, etc., would not be admitted.
6 The exporter or shipper must study the appropriate clause on the back of the bill of lading which will show in detail the particular implications that arise with the ship-owner, should general average arise.

When a ship arrives 'under average' the ship-owner will appoint an 'average adjuster' whose task it is to arrive at an impartial assessment of the values involved, and ensure an equitable apportionment of the sums of money due. This is a highly complex and exacting profession calling for a deep knowledge of maritime law and marine insurance. Basically, the contribution will be levied on the net values of the various interests at the point of destination, as follows:

Ship Value at place where voyage ends. If the ship is damaged the cost of repairs is deducted from the estimated sound value.
Freight Any freight earnings which accrue to the ship-owner which might not have done so if the ship had not made port. This might apply to consignments shipped on a freight forward basis.
Cargo Market value of the cargo on arrival at destination.

Even a simple case of general average will often take a long time to assess completely. It may be necessary to examine and analyse many different cargoes in order to trace damage which is allowed in general average and that which is not. This, for example, could be a very complex affair if damage was by fire.

Owners of cargo will be called upon to produce declarations of value and to substantiate these with appropriate documentation. They will then be expected to sign an 'average bond' which represents an undertaking to pay any amounts which may become due. Sometimes deposits may be called for and these will be based on a rough estimate of the respective values involved. The ship-owner has a lien on the goods until such deposits, if called for, are paid by the cargo owner.

The insured cargo owner will of course, be covered for such general average amounts as may become due, and the following clause would be found in the cover:

GA Clause: General Average and Salvage Charges payable according to Foreign Statement or to York–Antwerp Rules if in accordance with the contract of affreightment.

If a GA Guarantee is called for by the ship-owner, this would be signed by the insurers of the cargo.

Again, it should be emphasized that the provisions in the bill of lading and the type of contract affreightment will often specify the particular code which is going to condition the average adjustment. When no such code is specified, then the adjustment will usually be according to the law and practice in the port where the voyage ended.

Insurance procedures

Having considered the background of legal aspects of marine insurance affecting the policy, and the various types of risk cover available, we can now consider how the exporter will enter into the contract of insurance, obtain cover and the relevant types of policy. In practice it is more usual for a Certificate of Insurance to be issued for documentary purposes. An outline type of certificate is illustrated in Figure 10.1.

Insurance will be arranged by the exporter approaching an insurance company having a department specializing in cargo insurance. There are at least 100 such companies, many of them maintaining offices in the principal commercial cities, especially London and Liverpool which are the two main insurance centres.

The services of brokers may be utilized. The job is to 'shop around' for the right type of cover and, wherever possible, obtain competitive premium rates. Insurance brokers are highly skilled

---

MARITIME INSURANCE CORPORATION

Ref: ....   Dated: ....

CERTIFICATE OF INSURANCE

We hereby Certify that the undermentioned interest has been effected for account of

Sum insured ....

on ....

Marked ....

from ....   ☐ All Risks (Clause A)

to ....   ☐ WA (Clause B)

per ....   ☐ FPA (Clause C)

                         for and on behalf of
                         MARITIME INSURANCE CORPORATION

                         ....
                         Duly authorized to sign on behalf of the Company

UNDERWRITERS – LLOYD'S
Subject to all conditions of the Policy

Figure 10.1   Certificate of insurance

technicians and tend to specialize individually in specific forms of transport, commodity groups or market areas. Consequently, their assistance can be of enormous benefit. Their success will depend on their obtaining sound and reliable cover consistent with favourable premiums. It is of little use going for lowest premium rate if, in the event of a claim, the insuring company is slow, reluctant and unhelpful.

It is possibly true to say that the hub of insurance, certainly in the UK, and having an immense reputation throughout the world, is the Corporation of Lloyd's. This is in effect a market place for insurance where millions of pounds worth of premium income p.a. is transacted, over half from abroad. There are 'named' members of Lloyd's and insurance can only be placed with them through some approved brokers. Marine, motor and aviation business is conducted in various parts of a very futuristic-looking building. Members have to deposit a substantial amount of money to act as security for their business; the standards which result are very high. The members operate in groups known as 'syndicates'. The whole principle of insurance can be seen to operate through the underwriting system as each syndicate, when presented with a 'slip' which sets out the details of the risk to be covered, can elect to accept a portion of the risk, which it does by 'writing a line'. The task of the broker, both at Lloyd's and with other insurance companies, is to obtain a series of 'names' so that all the risk is covered. This is done at the best premium rate which is consistent with good cover and security. It should be stressed that the various syndicates are in competition with each other so that the Lloyd's brokers are not restricted and can approach other insurance companies for competitive conditions.

The broker acts as an agent of the assured, and yet is remunerated by the insurer in the form of a commission which, while varying somewhat, in London is around 5 per cent. Usually, a 10 per cent discount is allowed originally as an incentive for the assured to pay the premiums promptly. When cargo insurance has been affected, the broker is liable for the payment of premium but can exercise a lien on the policy for unpaid premiums. They may take care of the collection of claims, but only if specifically requested to do so, and would normally be entitled to charge collection commission. It might be useful to trace the relationship of the various parties by means of Figure 10.2.

Some traders will ask their shipping and forwarding agent to take care of the insurance on their behalf. In this case, such agents would apply this against their own block policy cover.

Warranties

We have seen so far that the general terms of the insurance required are put forward by the broker on the 'slip'. At this stage it is necessary to remember that a fundamental principle of all insurance is utmost good faith, coupled with the disclosure of all relevant facts pertaining to nature of goods, destination, value and packing, etc. Sometimes it will be necessary for the cover to be based on the concept of a warranty which means in effect an undertaking that some particular condition will be observed. With delicate scientific equipment or aircraft parts, for example, it may be a condition of

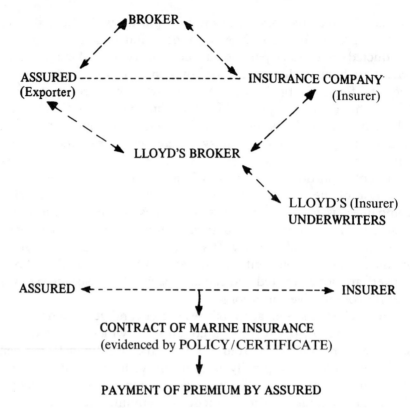

Figure 10.2   Relationship of parties in marine insurance

the terms of insurance that they should be 'warranted professionally packed'. Equally, the nature of the packing may require a warranty, such as '200 cartons of textiles warranted packed in internal polythene bags'.

A breach of such warranties could well discharge the insurer from liability. There may be a compromise made in the shape of a warranty such as 'packed in steel drums or held covered'. In this case, should the consignment be going forward not, in fact, packed in steel drums, then the insurer will require immediate notification in order to arrive at an additional premium although the consignment would in fact be covered for risks.

Type of insurance policy

The basic instrument in a marine insurance contract is the *policy*, essential features of which are:

1 name of assured (or agent who effects insurance),
2 *bearer* policies, although used in some countries, are not normally effective in the UK,
3 subject matter designated with reasonable certainty and clarity,
4 destination,
5 name of vessel and/or steamer or conveyance,
6 types of risk covered,
7 where claims are payable,
8 sum insured, and
9 dated and signed.

Against Item 5, when showing the name of the vessel, or other methods of transport, it is usual to indicate it in a general manner such as:

mv HEINRICH and/or Steamers as per Institute Classification Clause attached and/or Conveyances.

The reference above to the 'classification clause' might be encountered when the insurance cover requires the employment of a vessel of a particular standard, such as Lloyd's Register 100A1. When the policy has been prepared and received by the exporter usually (for example in a CIF transaction) 'assigns' the policy to the buyer by endorsing it on the back with the name of the company, together with a signature by an appropriate official of that company. There may be a degree of similarity with a bill of lading sometimes inasmuch that a policy or certificate could be made out either in the name of the consignee or alternatively the shipper, and suitably endorsed.

Open cover and the floating policy

From the standpoint of a busy exporter, it is not practicable to arrange individual insurance cover and obtain policies of insurance for each shipment of goods. We find, therefore, two basic types of mechanism which are designed to overcome this problem. They are 'open cover' and the 'floating policy'.

Open cover

These contracts may be run for a fixed period with automatic renewal, or may continue indefinitely until cancelled. They are represented by a written undertaking on behalf of the insurer that certificates will be issued within the terms of a generally agreed form of insurance cover.

Floating cover

This type of policy describes the insurance in general terms, leaving the detailed particulars to be defined by subsequent declarations. An average premium is paid at the beginning of the period and if subsequent shipments are made with varying premium rates, there is a periodical adjustment.

Floating policies operate in a manner very similar to open cover, except that an actual policy is in existence. Each shipment is declared, written off the policy until the total coverage has been exhausted and then, in most cases, a new policy is issued. These policies are tending to decline since they are somewhat cumbersome to administer and premiums have usually to be paid in advance.

With both open cover and floating policies, the assured is required to make a series of declarations covering the individual shipments as they take place. Usually these are done by filling in a particular type of declaration form similar to the following:

Please insure the following under the open policy in the name of
Messrs
Vessel
From   To   Via
Marks   Description of goods   *CFR value Insured value
Please send cover notes to *us   messrs
*Please delete as applicable

Another method which is now more usual among exporters is for them to complete an actual certificate of insurance which they are empowered to sign. This acts as a declaration of the details and value of the consignment for the insurer, and other copies can go to the customer as documentary proof that insurance has been effected. Although strictly speaking, a CIF contract, for example, requires a *policy* of insurance, commercial practice has established internationally the tradition of providing certificates of insurance. Indeed, most letters of credit allow for the production of this type of document.

Because of the somewhat vague terms which operate under open cover, and to a slightly lesser extent floating policies, a number of clauses have been developed to enable the insurers to maintain a degree of control over the various aspects of the risk cover. These can be outlined in the following manner:

1 *Basis of Valuation Clause* indicates how the consignment is to be valued, e.g. CIF plus 10 per cent.
2 *Declaration Clause* states the manner and the periods of time involved in declaring shipments to the underwriters.
3 *Classification Clause* (example as above) relates to the requirements of vessels being up to a satisfactory standard and age.
4 *Location Clause* specifies amount of insured risk at any single place on land such as a warehouse or shed at the dock.
5 *Cancellation Clause* provides for an agreed period of notice required for the cancellation of a cover.
6 *Limit per Consignment Clause* means that an individual shipment may operate only up to a specified value.
7 *Advice Clause:* provisional advice may only be required if the shipment value exceeds an agreed level.

The Marine Insurance Act makes provisions for 'valued' and 'unvalued' policies. The former is self-explanatory in the light of earlier comments on insurable value. The unvalued policy does not specify the value of the subject matter insured. This might be applicable to products and commodities whose market value fluctuates markedly. In such a case as this, the basis of valuation clause may operate.

Premiums

So far it has emerged that there is a wide variety of risks for marine insurance cover and a number of ways in which they can be covered by the insertion of the appropriate set of clauses. Naturally, the premium to be paid will be relative to the risk, and the skill of the underwriter will be directed towards all the various factors that together will give rise to the cost of the insurance of a commodity or a market. Any attempt to be very precise would be misleading as there are enormous variations in premium rates. These are often set for each policy on an individual basis. In many cases, large international trading organizations would receive preferential rates because the large volume of business enables the underwriter to spread the risk element. Again, rates must vary widely with different product categories and market areas.

Many other factors will enter into an underwriter's calculations and it might be of value to consider an exhaustive list of such factors which has been prepared by the Insurance Company of North America. They list fourteen specific factors which will be considered when the underwriter calculates a rate of premium for a policy. These are:

1 Type of coverage (risk, etc.)
2 Commodity characteristics.
3 Origin, destination and voyage.
4 Carriers used.
5 Any warehousing or transhipment during voyage.
6 Possible effect of shrinkage, loss of weight, etc.
7 Seasonal character of shipments.
8 Type of packing.
9 Relationship of value to packing, susceptibility to pilferage.
10 The experience of the assured as an exporter.
11 Normal shipping and handling practices appropriate to the particular trade involved.
12 Relationship of assured to consignee and their outlook towards claims.
13 Efficiency and attitude towards third party claims and recoveries.
14 Possible salvages applicable to the type of product and market.

It will be seen from the above that prudent exporters, acting in an efficient manner, can in some respects conduct business in a way which will enable them to obtain good premium rates. If the record is good with regard to action against third parties, packing, steps taken to prevent pilferage and efficient handling of insurance business, this will naturally place them in a beneficial position.

Premiums are, of course, based on value for insurance declared by the exporter.

It has already been stated that the assured will normally declare values of at least CIF plus 10 per cent and often much higher, owing to inland journey cover and possible loss of duty. There are two points to be borne in mind with regard to these possible 'uplifts'. First, if in doubt, the assured should always give details of large uplift figures to the insurer who may desire to check the position in order to ascertain if there is, in effect, valid insurable interest. Secondly, where high duty figures are involved, they should be shown separately as often the premium on the actual duty component can be lowered if assessed separately rather than simply lumped together in a total CIF value.

The following is an example of a typical breakdown figure which might be found on an insurance certificate.

£2200.00 + £500.00 Stg. to cover Duties from time of arrival in New York, USA. We hereby declare for Insurance under the said Cover Two thousand seven hundred Pounds Sterling on interest as specified hereon so valued per TRIAS TRADER at and from Works UK via London to Works New York, USA, subject to the terms of the Standard Form of Lloyd's Marine Policy and the special conditions stated below and on back hereof.

Franchise and excess

A 'franchise' refers to a percentage of the loss or damage which it is agreed will not be covered by the underwriter. An ILU Clause (B) for example, may incorporate a franchise of say, 5 per cent. Let us assume this applies to a cargo of cartons of books. Assuming the cartons arrive and on return it is found that 2 per cent of the value of the books were damaged; in this case no claim would be payable. If the value lost was above the 5 per cent figure, then a claim would be payable.

An 'excess' is where the exporter would undertake to be responsible for a certain percentage of any loss sustained.

Claims

When considering a CIF contract, one would expect the exporter to arrange insurance, procure the appropriate policy or certificate and send it to the customer with other relevant documents such as bill of lading and the invoice. The policy or certificate would be *assigned* accordingly to the customer, who, in the event of loss, would normally be responsible for actually carrying out the claim procedure. However, in many cases it will be necessary in the interest of good customer relations to assist the buyer in claiming. It is interesting at this point to remember the 'ex-ship' type of contract which, as distinct from CIF, is an obligation actually to effect physical delivery of the goods. In a case such as this, the obligations would probably rest upon the exporter's shoulders to lodge a claim for any loss.

As has been seen when analysing the structure of the marine insurance policy, it is incumbent upon the assured to take all appropriate steps to minimize damage, and the *Sue and Labour Clause* may, in certain circumstances, entitle them to payment for any expenses involved in carrying out such operations, although they would be wise to check with the insurer's agent and representative first.

A typical declaration of the action that the assured is required to take is represented by the following instructions that might well be attached to a policy:

Important notice to assured concerning liability of carriers, bailees or other third parties.

It is the duty of the Assured and their Agents, in all cases, to take such measures as may be reasonable for the purpose of avoiding or minimizing a loss and to ensure that all rights against Carriers, Bailees or other third parties are properly preserved and exercised. In particular, the Assured or their Agents are required:

1 To claim immediately on the Carriers and on the Port Authorities for any missing packages.
2 To apply immediately for survey in the docks by Carriers' representative if any loss or damage be apparent and claim on the Carriers for any actual loss or damage found at such survey.
3 In no circumstances except under written protest, to give clean receipts where goods are in doubtful condition.
4 To give notice in writing to the Carriers' representative within three days of delivery if the loss or damage was not apparent at the time of taking delivery.

Note: The consignees or their Agents are recommended to make themselves familiar with the Regulations of the Port Authorities at the port of discharge.

The assured, as soon becoming aware of loss or damage, should send written notice to the insurance company or their agent in order to arrange a survey and obtain the necessary survey report. The Corporation of Lloyd's, for instance, has some 1500 agents throughout the world and it is often the practice for policies to state that, in the event of loss or damage, settlement of claims will be facilitated if Lloyd's agents are called in to hold survey.

It is customary for the maritime insurance company groups to issue handbooks covering the marine claims settling agencies which they utilize throughout the world. It should be also noted that sometimes the appropriate agents might only arrange surveys while another centre would have to be used for making claims.

The exporter will be concerned with claiming for the loss under one of three basic headings, namely, 'partial loss', 'total loss', or 'constructive total loss'. The first two are self-explanatory. Constructive total loss applies, for example, when the consignment may not be 100 per cent damaged, but is in such a state that it would cost more money to put it back in its original form and it might therefore have to be sold for scrap.

For total unit loss of part of the cargo, the claim calculation would be simple, following the lines of the following example:

10 cartons of Automobile Spare Parts which should have a gross arrived value of	£20 000
Actual consignment arriving has a value of (owing to loss of one carton)	£18 000
Amount of loss	£ 2 000

Loss = £2000 or 10 per cent
Therefore claim based upon 10 per cent of insured value, say 10 per cent of £22 000 = £2200

An example of partial loss, if, say, one carton was not lost but was only damaged, might be as follows:

Gross arrival value should be	£20 000
Less damaged carton	£ 2 000
Actual arrival value, 9 cartons sound	£18 000
Damaged carton realizes	£ 1 000
	£19 000

Amount of loss = £1000 or 5 per cent of gross arrived value.

The claim should be filed with the insurance company as soon as possible. The assured should check the policy or certificate to see if any express instructions pertaining to claims are contained therein, but would normally expect to send the following documents:

1 Insurance policy or certificate suitably endorsed.
2 Survey report.
3 Possibly an Outturn Report.
4 Carrier's or Master's Protest – usually a formal statement commenting on the conditions and causes relating to the loss.
5 Bill of lading or appropriate transport document.
6 Invoice.
7 Accounts sales if there are proceeds of sales.
8 Any correspondence with ship-owner or other third parties.
9 Letter of Subrogation which transfers any rights of claimant against carriers to the insurer (see Appendix B).

It should be borne in mind that the question of carrier's liability may arise and that it is always possible that an insurer may want to proceed accordingly. As has been seen in earlier chapters, liabilities under, say, IATA, Hague–Visby Rules, or CMR may become relevant.

The number and type of documents will, to some extent, depend upon the type of loss. In the case of total loss, a set of transport documents would normally be expected. For partial losses, additional weight notes or packing lists would have to be produced.

Care should be taken with regard to the actual place where the claims are payable. This should normally be covered in the original contract, when we would expect to find, perhaps, 'Claims Payable Abroad' (CPA) inserted in the policy. At all times it must be ensured that any settlement of claims at destination does not conflict with existing laws or financial regulations.

The simplification of documentation

Most exporters, be they new to the field or experienced practitioners, are to some extent bound to be frustrated by the various documentary processes to which they have to conform. Even if they have mastered all the technical details and have become experts in preparing and processing documents with complete success, there is still the feeling that much of the work is really fruitless and that if one country can accept goods without a lot of complicated documentation why cannot other countries? The very wide variations themselves also contribute to the great difficulty in training new personnel: there seems at first glance to be little uniformity.

Our preceding consideration of export practice will have made us realize that there are so many functions in an export transaction that there will be a stream of documents from different sources. Equally, we must be realistic and accept the fact that a large number of these will almost always be essential. If we insist on a letter of credit in order to enjoy a great degree of security, then this will impose certain documentary demands. If we ship goods, we shall in many cases want a receipt and title to ownership; this will mean a bill of lading, etc. In order to ensure risk cover, combinations of insurance policy or certificates will have to be arranged.

Equally, we must see the whole process as a dynamic one and be prepared for a constant state of flux. Trading agreements may arise between countries which allow for some documentary relaxation but, at the same time, new sovereign nations are emerging which may call for new documentary systems and obligations. The conclusion of some preferential tariff arrangement between countries will be enthusiastically welcomed by international traders, but will, at the same time, inevitably lead to the necessity of some type of documentation to substantiate the origin of the goods in order that they should qualify; examples of EUR 1 forms and other similar types of certificates of origin illustrate this point. Similarly, even if the actual forms themselves could be eliminated, there would still be the necessity to provide some form of input data for statistical and other purposes.

These remarks are not intended to be a form of apology for documentation but simply to remind ourselves that when we look at the international order and its various stages, we are bound to accept the fact that there must always be a fair measure of documentary procedure involved. Our task at this stage is to examine the efforts that have been made to improve the position and the very substantial improvements that have, in fact, already been achieved.

The process of simplification

It might be fruitful at this stage to consider the concept of simplification under three main headings:

1 *The technical production process*. Under this heading, we consider the actual production and typing of the individual documents themselves. How can the forms be so designed that a number of different documents can be produced at one typing? How can devices such as photocopying processes and computerized systems or word processing be brought to bear upon the problem?

2 *The simplification of the actual export transaction itself*, which automatically brings about a reduction of documentary requirements. An example of this is the growth of the container system which means that a number of individual organizations previously handling the transaction can be concentrated into one organization and can issue one document covering a series of hitherto separate functions. The CTO is a practical example.

3 *An examination by different governments of possibilities of reducing their actual demand for certain documents*. It might be possible, shall we say, for consular invoice requirements to be relaxed or customs entry procedures to call for less, or at least simpler, documentary procedures.

It is possibly fair to say that up to now the greatest progress has been made in category 1, the streamlining of document production. The first move in this field must of necessity be an attempt to achieve some form of international understanding with regard to the shape, size and layout of the documents themselves. The concept is, of course, not new. As far back as 1874, the Universal Postal Union introduced standardized forms for international postal traffic. The Berne Convention (CIM) similarly achieved the standardization of forms for international rail carriage. In 1953, the French delegation to the Customs Co-operation proposed that a technical committee should examine the possibility of reducing the number of documents used in international trade and to see if the remaining indispensable documents could be standardized in design and format. As a basis of study, the documents required by the customs officials of member countries were collected and examined. This revealed the fact that there would be considerable difficulty involved in the standardization of all these documents because of the variety of legislative requirements of the countries concerned.

The credit must go to Sweden as the country which, starting in 1955, was the first to achieve a standard layout of international trade documents with particular reference to seaborne trade. Later, Denmark, Finland and Norway adopted an aligned series of commercial and official documents. It was soon apparent that extremely worthwhile savings could be achieved. Scandinavian companies were reporting cost savings on documentation of up to 70 per cent, and cuts of up to 20 per cent were being made in some export administration departments.

Work in this field was extended internationally when Sweden brought the matter before the United Nations Economic Commission for Europe (ECE) and in 1960 a working party was set up to investigate systematically the various possibilities of standardizing and simplifying export documentation. Meeting in 1961, the working party invited each country to set up its own national committee. Governments and international organizations, particularly the International Chamber of Shipping and the International Chamber of Commerce, aimed at an agreed standard size and layout which could become the basis of a simplified system for all the main export documents. The result came to be known as the 'ECE layout key' now known as 'UN layout key', and was based upon a standard bill of lading Model B which was on international A4 size paper (297 × 210 mm), a size which was already finding favour on an international level.

One of the results of the working party was the formation in the

UK of the Joint Liaison Committee on Documents used in the International Carriage of Goods (JLCD). This committee was formed in 1962 and later developed into the very important body known as the Simplification of International Procedures Board (SITPRO). This body, formed in 1970, is an independent organization set up by the Department of Trade. Its board and specialist working groups draw on a wide range of interests, including exporters, carriers of all modes, freight forwarders, bankers and government departments. SITPRO staff are recruited by the Board itself with an eye to practical experience of international trade and information systems. Work is carried out in the closest possible consultation with British interests likely to be affected by, and benefit from, the results. About 200 people from business and relevant government departments help directly in the practical work. In this way any product, solution or service marketed by SITPRO is moulded to the needs of British international trade.

SITPRO master systems

The terms of reference are to survey the whole range of existing documents needed for the international carriage of goods with reference to simplification methods. It was also essential that any investigations should consider the problems of all parties concerned including exporters, shipping and forwarding agents, port authorities, insurance companies, ship-owners and government departments.

It soon became apparent that, as has already been implied, the greatest obstacle to streamlining was the variety of sizes, shapes and designs of the relevant documents currently in use in export transactions. Their standardization and layout were, therefore, the first step towards an all-round improvement. As a large proportion of international trade is still seaborne, most governments, including the UK SITPRO, tended to concentrate first of all quite naturally on maritime documentation, although it was always envisaged that ultimate application would be extended to other forms of transportation. This was illustrated by the emergence, in 1982, of the new UN-aligned air waybill.

Although the very term 'export documentation' can be applied to all documents associated with the export transaction from the stage at which the order is received and acknowledged right through to the delivery of the goods to the dock and ultimate loading on board ship and then extended to the ultimate receipt of payment, it was felt initially that certain of these stages could not be effectively covered. The many invoice-based forms and financial documents had obviously been designed to meet the special commercial requirements of individual exporters and indeed, many of them were designed to meet the statutory requirements of overseas governments such as consular invoice forms, preferential certificates of value and origin and straight certificates of origin. Consequently, committees like SITPRO have concentrated on the 'consignment-based forms' which are controlled and issued by the ship-owners, chambers of commerce and government departments. However, over the past few years great strides have been made in extending the master layout schemes to a wider range of documents such as invoices, etc., as will be seen later. Incidentally, it is of interest to note that, quite apart from any other consideration, the move towards a standardization of shape, size and layout by itself makes it easier for an exporter to look at the various forms and understand them and to complete them with the relevant data. One has only to look back over time to remember the many shapes and sizes of bills of lading and how difficult it was to remember where particular details had to be inserted. To anybody but an experienced practitioner, it was difficult to believe that the many types of bill of lading from different shipping companies were in fact the same basic document and fulfilled the same purpose.

Consequently, the first stages of simplification usually take the shape of a basic standardized key layout which can then be used with a number of prime documents which have in turn to be modified in shape and size to enable them to be used with the master key. Usually, the first phases concentrate on the 'consignment-based forms', over which government committees can, in fact, exert some control or influence. Following upon this it has become increasingly feasible for the individual exporters to modify many of their own office-produced documentation.

It is evident, therefore, that the design of the UN key layout has to be very precise, with its objective nothing less than a concentration of all the essential information required for various trade documents in an export transaction. This information includes:

- name and address of buyer and/or consignee or order
- notify address
- name and address of exporter or shipper
- name and address of forwarding agent (if applicable)

- country of origin
- country of destination
- trading country
- method of transport
- marks and numbers of packages
- gross and net weight
- quantity and specification
- value of goods
- appropriate statistical numbers
- date and place of issue of documents
- appropriate reference numbers
- insurance value
- terms of sale
- method and terms of payment
- currency involved
- appropriate signature

Some degree of flexibility must always be allowed for by designing a blank space within the layout key which can be utilized for unusual or infrequent requirements.

From the concept of the 'master copy' certain principles emerge which apply to the design and co-ordination of a documentary system.

The standardization is aimed at questions of size and layout only. The object should be to provide standard positioning of the data which is actually included on the form.

Very careful initial measurement is required for the spacings used in order to correspond with a wide variety of office machine in use, dimensions of vertical columns, etc.

There should, wherever possible, be a natural sequence to the various groups of information.

Spaces reserved for addresses should be standardized and placed in positions suitable for use with window envelopes.

The system is intended to assist many different categories of exporter, operating under diverse circumstances, and utilizing a wide variety of office equipment. Any new system must be flexible enough to be a practicable proposition in small offices on simple equipment as well as in the offices of large organizations complete with elaborate reproduction equipment and technical expertise to operate them.

So far we have arrived at the concept of a master copy on which all possible information is placed, plus the fact that all the main documents have been brought into line as far as shape, size and layout are concerned. It should be possible to complete the master and then, by various reproduction methods, using an appropriate masking system, to produce at one run a set of shipping documents. This is known as the aligned 'one-run' system. During the design stages of this system, SITPRO surveyed thousands of consignments shipped to all parts of the world and came to the conclusion that this master/aligned series method should prove capable of accommodating the details of a large proportion of the consignments examined (Figure 11.1).

Range of documentary simplification

This method of completing a set of shipping documents has the obvious advantage that only one document actually needs typing and, equally important, that once it has been checked, the accuracy of all the other forms is assured. Once the concept has been accepted, it is really most gratifying how many individual documents can be brought into line with the aligned series system. An example of some of the documents conforming to the SITPRO aligned systems include:

1 Bill of lading/waybills/consignments notes
2 Standard shipping note/DGN
3 Invoices/certificates of value and origin
4 Certificates of insurance
5 Application forms for special stowage (hazardous goods, etc.)
6 Movement certificates
7 Bank instruction forms
8 Export cargo shipping instructions

This range is already quite extensive; a surprising number of functions which form part of the overall transaction are covered. We can expect the range to be extended considerably in the none-too-distant future. There must, of course, be some limiting factors on the amount of information which can be contained on a master key. Companies exporting very complicated items such as machinery or prefabricated buildings are often called upon to provide on their transport documents and invoices, etc., very long and detailed specifications which, in many cases, could not be incorporated in a master copy system.

© SITPRO 1992

MASTER DOCUMENT

Exporter	VAT reg. no.	Invoice no.		Customs reference/status	
		Invoice date	Carrier's bkg. no.	Exporter's reference	U
		Buyer's reference		Forwarder's reference	N
					I
					C

Consignee	VAT reg. no.	Buyer	VAT reg. no.

Freight forwarder	VAT reg. no.	Country of despatch	Carrier	Country of destination code
		Country of origin		Country of final destination

Other UK transport details		Terms of delivery and payment

Vessel/flight no. and date	Port/airport of loading		
Port/airport of discharge	Place of delivery	Insured value	EUR 1 or C. of O. remarks

* DANGEROUS GOODS: Refer to IMDG, ADR, IATA, CIM and UK regulations as appropriate and specify: proper shipping name; hazard class; UN no.; flashpoint °C

Shipping marks; container number	Number and kind of packages; description of goods*	Item no.	Commodity code		
			Quantity 2	Gross weight (kg)	Cube (m³)
			Procedure	Net weight (kg)	Value (£)
			Summary declaration/ previous document		

LIMIT OF SAD ▷ BOX 31

	Commodity code		
	Quantity 2	Gross weight (kg)	Cube (m³)
	Procedure	Net weight (kg)	Value (£)
	Summary declaration/ previous document		

	Commodity code		
	Quantity 2	Gross weight (kg)	Cube (m³)
	Procedure	Net weight (kg)	Value (£)
	Summary declaration/ previous document		

Identification of warehouse	FREE DISPOSAL	Invoice total (state currency)	
		Total gross wt (kg)	Total cube (m³)

Freight payable at	Signatory's company and telephone number
Number of bills of lading Original Copy	Name of signatory
	Place and date
	Signature

J468/001

Form No. 810

Published and sold by FORMECON SERVICES Ltd., Gateway, Crewe CW1 1YN Tel. 0270 500800 Fax. 0270 500505

SITPRO Approved Licensee No. 21

Figure 11.1   SITPRO master document

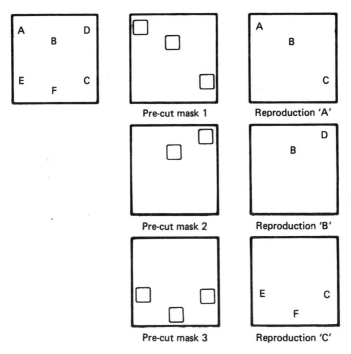

Figure 11.2 Masking a master key layout to obtain different combinations of details by superimposition upon a master document.

There are, of course, problems in the sense that if we look at the types of form which can be used with the aligned series system, a number of these, such as the customs entry form and standard shipping note, together with bills of lading, might very well be handled by the exporter's shipping and forwarding agent or loading broker. Nevertheless, all exporters should consider carefully the use to some extent of the master key/aligned series system (Figure 11.2). There is no reason why internal paperwork systems should not be adapted so as to dovetail with the streamlined system. For example, quotation layouts, stock letters, acknowledgements of orders, dispatch notes, pro forma invoices and other domestic documents are in many ways capable of modification. Nor should it be overlooked, where space limitations restrict the amount of data which can be contained on a master copy, that considerable savings can still be achieved if only a portion of the data is reproduced, as the time needed in a separate operation to complete the required details might still be less and therefore bring about staff economies. Considerable work is being done in this field by specialists in organization and methods, office managers and manufacturers of reproducing equipment. In short, the whole area is capable of much development.

Many exporters are inhibited from attempting to develop such systems because they feel that they are appropriate only to the large, heavily mechanized organization handling a very large volume of export orders. This is a pity, because although there are limiting factors to all systems, it is very often worthwhile to use the aligned system even if the documents are being produced manually.

Types of copying process

Photocopier systems

This method is probably at present the most popular, since it employs equipment which is often already installed in the office ·and could be applied to many different areas of a company's business operations. It fits in ideally with the master/overlay system and a wide range of overlays is available from SITPRO. For companies processing a large volume of export orders the manipulation of individual overlays on small photocopiers might prove a little cumbersome, and in this case more sophisticated systems employing a 'web' or 'reel' system (such as produced by Rank Xerox) can be pre-set and operated, say, under microprocessor control.

Computers

The use of these is continually growing and many applications are now possible. For example, they can be made to link up to the company's internal operations, via, say, photocopiers and word processors.

The computer could be used to produce a pro forma invoice for the customer to obtain an import licence, and a word processor to write the letter giving details of the potential order.

The letter of credit arrives. The system is set to produce banking documentation requirements, having processed the factory instructions and dispatch instructions to vessel, perhaps through a freight forwarder. An interesting fact is the possibility of direct connection between customs and private entities for computer import entries, and this is likely to become commonplace for both imports and exports. This is known as DTI (Direct Trade Input).

This direct connection is used extensively by freight agents, and the trend will be to encourage links between customs and private authorized dispatch points, or through inland container facilities, for example. For speeding paperwork and to save costs by simplification of method, computerization of the physical distribution side of exports – say, assembly of goods, handling, packing and exit overseas of an order – shows significant benefits, which will grow.

In the UK, the Customs Authorities in close co-operations both with industry and carriers, have worked hard on completing CHIEF (Customs Handling of Import and Export Freight) which is now being phased into operation. It represents a considerable extension to the DTI already mentioned, and would envisage to application of EDI (Electronic Data Interchange) and thus lead to a marked increase in paperless import and export processing. Whatever system is being used, of crucial choice is of course the appropriate software. This must be researched carefully in the light of the individual exporter's requirements. Lack of planning and research in this area can lead to disappointment and represent a very costly mistake. There are today many specialist consultancy companies who can help to advise and select a suitable hardware/software system consistent with the exporter's needs and resources.

One of the most world-wide in operation is the SITPRO Spex, a leader in the field of micro-computer packages. This system can store large amounts of data drawn from the company's mainframe computer and prepare a wide range of documents for many overseas markets and also produce the appropriate calculations.

The above is intended to give only an outline of some of the methods available and a sample of the appropriate terminology. It will, however, be realized that ranging from the smallest exporting organization to a sophisticated office system, there will be available some form of process which can be adapted to meet specific requirements.

The other move towards documentary streamlining and simplification will obviously proceed hand-in-hand with improved systems of transportation. It has long been accepted that large segments of the overseas transaction are much simpler when air transport is used. A substantial proportion of air-carriers actually handle clearing and customs facilities, etc., and, as they concentrate a number of activities into their hands, there is a diminution of documentary requirement. By tradition, the air waybill is not employed so often as a transferable document of title and therefore the documents go forward by air to the consignee. The fact that airlines, by their very nature, have built up more closely-woven international organizations, also enables them to incorporate many functions in the overseas country.

We now see changing sea and land transportation methods play their part in simplifying documentation. We may consider, for example, a container transaction where the shipping company will often arrange to collect from an inland factory or clearing depot and issue a 'received for shipment' bill of lading, thus removing many of the intermediary stages. Some shipping lines can now issue 'non-negotiable' sea waybills which, if suitable for the exporter's financial arrangement, can often streamline documentary operations and assist in avoiding demurrage charges. This type of waybill has, in effect, brought sea transport operations into line with air transport from the point of view of paperwork. In some instances, container companies have block insurance cover enabling them to issue combined bills of lading and certificates of insurance. It is true that there are many genuine difficulties associated with traditional insurance cover and risk-spreading, but these are all pointers to the future and indicate the areas where we can look for improvements.

It was seen earlier that a segment of documentation falls under what we have chosen to call the 'regulations' heading and this has always proved something of a stumbling block to documentary simplification efforts. The International Chamber of Commerce has pointed out that there are still major difficulties arising out of consular requirements and formalities and customs requirements. Although much progress has been made towards reducing the demand by various countries for consular invoices/consular legalization or chamber of commerce certification, there are still some countries, particularly in Latin America, which require these types of documentary process. Sometimes these requirements are also linked with unreasonable demands regarding documentation, with unnecessary rules with which it is often almost impossible to comply, and with the ultimate outcome of heavy fines.

The number of customs requirements calling for special invoices and valuation amount to what is often a very severe trade barrier. In many cases, countries are being asked to look at their requirements to see if irrelevant data can be omitted and if certain declarations can be combined on one document such as value and origin. The widespread adoption of uniform customs description in the shape of the tariff/trade classifications such as the Harmonized System has also been a step forward. It is a salutary thought, and one on which the exporter might dwell when considering all the various organizations, many of which we have mentioned above, who are constantly working in an untiring effort to smooth the path of the international trader.

Happily, many of the above requirements are actually phasing themselves out with the growing coalescence of countries into trading groups, FTA, PTA and, for example, the European single market where whole areas of documents and procedures have been swept away. Paul Cecchini's research has indicated that savings in trans-border related costs of customs and other associated expenses could be as high as 2 per cent of the value of the average consignment at both its import and export phases. Another of his researches estimates a saving of around 25 per cent of profits in many sectors.

Appendix A:
Typical freight calculations

Consignment specification 25 cases total weight 10 000 kg
total meas. 15 m³
(note ratio 10 weight tonnes 15 meas.)

Total EXW value £50 000

Contract based upon a DDU-ICD duties/taxes/ins. excl.)

Freight quotations obtained:

Carriage charges from works to port of departure including clearance, port and loading charges £350.00

Ocean freight from departure to arrival port of destination £175.00 per ton weight/measurement

Unloading charges at destination/port £275.00

Carriage to ICD destination including customs clearance £500.00

Result will be:

	Seller, £
EXW	50 000
FOB Port of departure	350
Freight 15 × £175.00	2 625
CFR Port of destination	52 975
Unloading charges	275
CFR Landed	53 250
Carriage to inland clearance depot including customs clearance charges	500
	53 750
DDU Customs cleared (excluding duties/taxes and insurance) =	£53 750

Appendix B:
Letter of subrogation

Vessel ....

Voyage ....

Sum Insured..

In consideration of your paying us for a total loss on the under-mentioned goods insured with you (in virtue of which payment you will become subrogated to all our property, rights and interests in the said goods and in any monies payable or recoverable in respect thereof on account of general average, salvage, or otherwise howsoever) we hereby authorize you to make use of our name for the purpose of any proceedings or measures, legal or otherwise, which you may think fit to take in respect of the said goods, and we declare that we were the owners thereof at the time of the loss, and we undertake to furnish you with all the papers and correspondence in our possession or control relating thereto, and to make any affidavits and to give any oral evidence which we can properly make or give, and generally to render to you any such assistance as you may from time to time reasonably require, in connection with any such proceedings or measure, you indemnifying us against all liability costs charges and expenses incurred in connection therewith and with the use of our name therein.

Dated .... day of 19

Description of Goods ....

Appendix C:
Self-assessment questions

1. Discuss some of the attributes essential for international sales personnel.

2. Itemize the main overseas channels of distribution and marketing.

3. Draw a diagram of a typical export office organization.

4. Outline the four major component parts of an export order.

5. Detail the provisions encountered in four of the major clauses encountered in Incoterms looked at from both the points of view of seller and buyer.

6. Give two reasons for the use of the Commodity Code Tariff Classification Systems.

7. Explain the Total Distribution Cost Concept.

8. Air-freight rates may appear relatively high but indicate some possible compensating savings.

9. Enumerate the advantages of free ports/zones.

10. Describe some of the services of a shipping and forwarding agent.

11. Compare the negotiable characteristics of a ship's bill of lading with those of an air waybill. Outline as many types of these two documents as possible.

12. State the main reasons for the vital importance of the exporter's invoice in international trade and describe how the EU single

market VAT requirements have influenced this document.

13. Compare a free trade area with that of a customs union.

14. Enumerate four main methods of payment encountered in international trade.

15. Contrast a documentary bill collection with a documentary letter of credit and explain the terms 'irrevocable' and 'confirmed'.

16. State briefly the fuction of a forward foreign exchange contract.

17. Construct a checklist for a letter of credit.

18. Write brief notes on:
    (a) general average
    (b) floating policies
    (c) insurance certificates
    (d) sellers' risk
    (e) subrogation.

19. What are the possible problems associated with the passing of risk with a DDP contract?

20. Show how the development of the SITPRO master document has assisted the development of simplified documentary systems and procedures.

Appendix D:
Outline letter of credit

XYZ GLOBAL BANK
LONDON UK.
(known as the advising/paying/negotiating bank)

BENEFICIARY   IRREVOCABLE DOCUMENTARY CREDIT NO . . .
Name and address   DATE.
of exporter.   DATE OF EXPIRY OF CREDIT
                               AMOUNT OF VALUE IN APROPRIATE CURRENCY.

OPENING BANK   APPLICANT
Normally in   Normally name and address of buyer/
importer's   importer.
country.   DATE OF CREDIT.

THIS LETTER OF CREDIT IS AVAILABLE WITH XYZ GLOBAL BANK BY
NEGOTIATION AGAINST PRESENTATION OF THE DOCUMENTS DETAILED
HEREIN AND OF YOUR (Beneficiary) DRAFTS AT SIGHT DRAWN ON
(For example Opening Bank) for 100 PERCENT OF INVOICE VALUE.

DOCUMENTS REQUIRED: - (A typical example)

1 – SIGNED COMMERCIAL INVOICE IN SIX COPIES.

2 – BENEFICIARY'S CERTIFICATE CONFIRMING THAT ONE SET OF NON
NEGOTIABLE SHIPPING DOCUMENTS HAVE BEEN SENT DIRECT TO
APPLICANT WITHIN 7 DAYS OF SHIPMENT.

3 – SHIPMENT SHOULD BE MADE ON VESSEL CLASSIFIED A1 AT LLOYD'S
AND A CERTIFICATE TO THIS EFFECT IS REQUIRED.

4 – REQUIRED SHIPPER'S FAX ADVICE TO APPLICANT RE
PARTICULARS OF SHIPMENT, I.E. B/L NO. AND DATE, VESSEL'S
NAME, FAX TO BE DATED LATEST 7 DAYS AFTER B/L DATE QUOTING
L/C NO.

5 – 3/3 ORIGINAL CLEAN ON BOARD OCEAN BILL OF LADING AND
THREE NON NEGOTIABLE COPIES. ISSUED TO ORDER OF OPENING
BANK AND MARKED FREIGHT COLLECT. NOTIFY ADDRESS:

APPLICANT. B/L SHOULD MENTION SHIPPING AGENT'S NAME AND
SHOW IMPORT LICENCE NO . . .
COVERING THE FOLLOWING GOODS: - (A typical example)
1 - CONTAINER OF AUTO SPARE PARTS REF NOS. 15, 16, 17 AS PER
    PROFORMA INVOICE NO . . . .
     DATED . . . . . .   HS NO. 8708 10 COUNTRY OF ORIGIN UK
FREE ON BOARD UK PORT   PARTIAL SHIPMENT NOT ALLOWED
TRANSHIPMENTS NOT ALLOWED.
SHIPMENT FROM UK PORT NOT LATER THAN . . . .

THIS LETTER IS SOLELY AN ADVICE OF A LETTER OF CREDIT ISSUED
BY THE ABOVE MENTIONED <u>OPENING BANK</u> AND CONVEYS NO
ENGAGEMENT ON OUR BEHALF.
(This would be a typical wording for an <u>unconfirmed credit</u>)
OR
WE ARE REQUESTED TO ADD OUR CONFIRMATION TO THIS CREDIT AND
WE HEREBY UNDERTAKE TO HONOUR ALL DRAFTS WITHIN ITS TERMS
ETC. (Confirmed Credit)

THIS CREDIT IS SUBJECT TO THE UNIFORM CUSTOMS AND PRACTICE
FOR DOCUMENTARY CREDITS (1993 REVISION), ICC PUBLICATION
NUMBER 500.

Bibliography

Barnes, Colin, *Metric Conversion Manual*, Croner Publications, Kingston-upon-Thames, Surrey, 1974

Benson, Don and Whitehead, G., *Transportation and Distribution Made Simple*, W. H. Allen, London

British International Freight Association, *Exporter & Forwarder 1990 – The Professional Guide*, BIFA, 1990

Brodie, P. R., *Dictionary of Shipping Terms*, Lloyd's of London Press, 1985

Brown, Largent, *Customs 88 – A Briefing for Freight Management*, Kogan Page, London, 1988

Cecchini, Paolo, *The European Challenge*, Gower International, 1992

Commission of the European Communities, *The Maastricht Agreement – Background Report*, Brussels, 1991

Coopers & Lybrand, *The 1993 EC VAT System*, CCH Editions International

Davies, Gary, *Managing Export Distribution*, Heinemann/Seabourne Express, 1984

Day, D. M., *The Law of International Trade*, Butterworths, London, 1981

Dow, Frank W., *Understanding Documentary Bills and Credits*, Croner Publications, 1990

Formecon Services Ltd, *Documents for Export* (catalogue, 1994), Formecon Services Ltd, Crewe

Hardy Ivamy, E.R., *Casebook on Carriage by Sea*, Lloyd's of London Press, 1979

Hill, D. J. and Messent, A. D., *CMR: Contracts for the International Carriage of Goods by Road*, Lloyd's of London Press, 1984

ICC, *Case Studies on Documentary Credits*, ICC, Paris, 1989

Ishani, Manzoor G.K., *The European Community*, Fourmat Publishing, London 1992

Lowe, David, *Dictionary of Transport Terms and Abbreviations*, Headlight, 1984

McLoughlin, J., *Introduction to Negotiable Instruments*, Butterworths, London, 1975

Major, W.T., *Law of Contract*, Longmans, 1988

Mitchell, Alan, *Bills of Lading – Law and Practice*, Chapman & Hall, London 1982

Owen, Richard and Dyne, Michael, *The Times Guide to Europe Without Frontiers*, Times Books, 1992

Roll, Eric, *Where Did We Go Wrong? From Gold Standard to Europe*, Faber & Faber, 1995

Schmitthoff, Clive M., *The Export Trade – a Manual of Law and Practice*, Stevens, London, 1986

Sherlock, Jim, *Principles of International Distribution*, Blackwell Business, 1994

Sinclair, G. and Wheble, B., *Documentary Letters of Credit – a Comparative Index*, 1993

SITPRO, *Instant Export Payments – Exporter's Guide to UK Short-term Finance*, SITPRO, London, 1990

SITPRO, *Letters of Credit Management and Control*, SITPRO, London, 1990

Spencer, Julia, *Principles of International Marketing*, Blackwell Business, 1994

Swift, Eric, *Managing Your Export Office*, Business Books Communica-Europa, 1977

Symes, Tony, *The Easy Guide to Import/Export Procedures*, Export Link

Thomas, Michael J., *International Marketing Management*, Houghton Mifflin, New York

Ventris, F.M., *Bankers' Documentary Credits*, Lloyd's of London Press, 1983

Wainwright, Ken, *Principles of Marketing*, Blackwell Business, 1994

Winkler, John, *Pricing for Results*, Butterworth-Heinemann, 1986

Regular publications and reference sources

Barclays Bank plc, London, International Trade Services: A wide range of publications such as *Forfaiting* and *Contract Guarantee and Bonds* bulletins

British Overseas Trade Board, London and branches: provides a range of services, publications and guides for industry and functions in conjunction with the DTI

Croner Publications, New Malden, Surrey: Reference books for exporters, air transportation and conference lines, etc. Very valuable documentation reference

Formecon Services Ltd: A wide range of publications, handbooks and export /import forms and documents

HM Customs and Excise, London and branches: Publishes through the HMSO London the three volumes of the Integrated Tariff of the United Kingdom which amongst other items contain the various chapter headings and classifications. Also publishes the *Intrastat Classification Nomenclature* of the EU. In addition produces a wide range of Customs Notices covering various requirements and procedures as well as a regular issue of *Business News*

Institute of Export: Annual Education Handbook

Institute of Export Journal, London: A wide range of data and articles

International Air Transport Association (IATA), Geneva: A wide range of air traffic publications, in particular the *Air Waybill Handbook* and *Dangerous Goods Regulations*

International Chamber of Commerce, Paris, London and other centres throughout the world: A wide range of essential brochures and publications. Of particular relevance: Incoterms and Brochure 500 etc.

International Civil Aviation Organisation (ICAO): Publishes in London *The Technical Instructions for the Safe Transport of Dangerous Goods by Air*

International Maritime Organisation (IMO): Provides amongst other data and information the *IMDG Dangerous Goods Code* which in practice has replaced the Blue Book

Kompass Guides, Reed Information Services, West Sussex: A regular series of directories

Lloyd's of London publishes the weekly Loading List together with such supplements as air cargo contacts and sailing schedules. Classifies categories of ship and publishes *Lloyd's Maritime Atlas*

National Westminster Bank, London and branches: Monthly *Exporters' Bulletin* and a range of export/finance publications

Office for Official Publications of the European Union, Luxembourg

The Simpler Trade Procedures (SITPRO) London: A wide range of publications, systems and research data

United Nations Geneva, New York: Operates through many worldwide agencies such as UNCTAD, UNDP and WTO to produce a wide range of reports and publications

Index